Romanticism, Realism and the Lines of Mimesis

Romanticism, Realism and the Lines of Mimesis

Polly Dickson

EDINBURGH
University Press

Edinburgh University Press is one of the leading university presses in the UK. We publish academic books and journals in our selected subject areas across the humanities and social sciences, combining cutting-edge scholarship with high editorial and production values to produce academic works of lasting importance. For more information visit our website: edinburghuniversitypress.com

Edinburgh University Press Ltd
13 Infirmary Street
Edinburgh, EH1 1LT

First published in hardback by Edinburgh University Press 2024

Typeset in 11/13pt Sabon LT Pro
by Cheshire Typesetting Ltd, Cuddington, Cheshire

A CIP record for this book is available from the British Library

ISBN 978 1 3995 0650 2 (hardback)
ISBN 978 1 3995 0651 9 (paperback)
ISBN 978 1 3995 0652 6 (webready PDF)
ISBN 978 1 3995 0653 3 (epub)

Contents

Figures

Acknowledgements

This book has the slightly uneasy status of being the first published version of (at least) three doctoral dissertations on Hoffmann and Balzac to have been completed over the last fifty years or so. My first debt of thanks must go, therefore, to Tim Lewis and to the late George Edgar Slusser. Not only have their insights been illuminating and challenging, but it is reassuring to have felt in good company, even in the strange state of solitude demanded by the task of writing a book.

The initial doctoral research on which this book is based was supported by the Wolfson Foundation. Postdoctoral fellowships funded by the Alfred Töpfer Stiftung and the Modern Humanities Research Association gave me the time and space to write it up and to seek out new projects. I returned to the book during an Early Career Fellowship funded by the Leverhulme Trust at Durham University, where I am fortunate enough to have found a home.

I am very grateful to the archivists and librarians who have helped me to source the images for this book and given me permission to reproduce them here: at the Staatsbibliothek Bamberg, the ETH-Bibliothek Zürich, the British Library and the Met Museum.

For their wisdom, kindness and patience, I must thank my PhD supervisors, Andrew J. Webber and Nick White. Andrew saw me through both my undergraduate and postgraduate degrees, and my writing here and elsewhere is immeasurably indebted to his supervision. More recently, I must thank Claudia Nitschke for her generous and inspiring mentorship, but most importantly for her friendship and for the many sustaining cups of coffee. Sincere thanks also to Michael Minden and Steven Connor, who helped to shape the project at an early stage; to my doctoral examiners Lucia Ruprecht and Diana Knight; and to my two anonymous readers at Edinburgh University Press. All of them showed me – with kindness and enthusiasm – how this book could be something better. Thank you to Friedrich Ulfers for a conversation about the chiasm, which changed the course of my thinking. And heartfelt thanks to the many other colleagues and friends with whom I have discussed this work over the years, at Cambridge and Durham but also at the other institutions to which this book, in its different forms, has taken me: the Freie Universität Berlin, the Humboldt Universität Berlin and New York University.

For their encouragement, support, and for continual inspiration, I thank my family: my parents, Kerry and Rodger, and my siblings, Katie and William. To Chris, who has been there from the early days of this book and has helped orient me through its many drafts, amongst everything else; to Ellen, whose unbounded energy has motivated me to bring it to a close; and to the nameless one whose appearance we await, now that it is done – you all make this make sense.

This book is dedicated to the memory of Annie Dickson, a keen reader and storyteller.

Parts of Chapters 2 and 3 have been previously published in the articles below and I am indebted to those journals for permitting me to reproduce some of that work here:

Polly Dickson, 'Tracing Squiggles: Laurence Sterne, E. T. A. Hoffmann, and Honoré de Balzac', *Comparative Literature* 72.1, 53–67. Copyright 2020, University of Oregon. All rights reserved. Republished by permission of the publisher. www.dukeupress.edu

Polly Dickson, 'Figures of Feeling in Honoré de Balzac's *La Peau de chagrin*', *Nineteenth-Century French Studies* 45.3/4, 149–62. Copyright 2017, University of Nebraska Press.

Note on Abbreviations and Translations

B   Balzac, Honoré de, *La Comédie humaine*, ed. by Pierre-Georges Castex and others, 12 vols (Paris: Gallimard, 1976–81)

H   Hoffmann, E. T. A., *Sämtliche Werke*, ed. by Hartmut Steinecke and others, 6 vols (Frankfurt am Main: Deutscher Klassiker Verlag, 1985–2004)

All citations of French and German texts have been translated into English in the body of the text. I have indicated all consulted translations under the author's name in the Bibliography. I have often modified consulted translations to bring them closer to the original. Where no translated edition was available, I undertook the translation myself – with invaluable help from Richard Riddick. Any mistakes, however, are my own.

Introduction: Balzac and Hoffman

Die Freunde waren darin einig, daß nichts so toll und wunderlich zu ersinnen, als was sich von selbst im Leben darbiete.

(The friends were united in their conviction that nothing was so strange and surprising as life itself.)
—E. T. A. Hoffmann, *Die Serapionsbrüder* (H IV 894)

Mimetic fiction has, since Plato, referred to a portion of the world recognised in an artwork, as though reflected in a mirror or projected by a trick of the light. As a literary commonplace, mimesis is characterised by this inherent strangeness: that what might seem a flat reflection is in fact a shimmering mirage, liable to shatter at the slightest touch or shift in perspective. Another strange dimension of mimesis is that, despite its essentialisation into a commonplace of literary discourse, it has suffered a near-constant, though shifting, series of assaults that have aimed to dislodge it entirely: from Plato himself, who characterised the mimetic artwork as a bad copy, being distanced from the truth, to poststructuralist writers who accuse mimesis of postulating a naive relationship to a reality that it cannot properly understand. All that mimesis does, such thinkers have argued, is offer reflections of an endless chain of prior representations which are themselves unacknowledged as such.

This book advances a defensive account of mimesis that pays close attention to the role played by the senses in representation. It does so through an investigation of the works of two writers – E. T. A. Hoffmann and Honoré de Balzac – who are paradigmatic of two literary modes that have been considered to hold antagonistic attitudes towards the question of representation: Romanticism and realism. By returning to, and readjusting, such assumptions concerning mimesis and its place in early nineteenth-century literary culture, and thereby making a case for a particular realignment of Romanticism and realism, I also aim to redeem mimesis as a relevant concept for both: one that has less to do with the stabilising reproduction of natural forms than with the interference and confusion between art and what lies beyond it.

The readings put forward in this book emphasise those creative and complicating aspects of literary mimesis that have been ignored in certain standard accounts by countering a narrative that arose in the 1950s in the works of M. H. Abrams and René Wellek, which understands Romanticism to have rejected mimetic thought altogether. Despite its typically being understood to refer to a mirror-like copying, this book, drawing from recent developments loosely stemming from what is sometimes called the 'material turn', approaches mimesis in a more productive and expansive manner: as an embodied act of mimicry, an impulse to become like, and not just to make a likeness. In this sense, mimesis is understood not as an imperative to reduplicate objects in the world but as a discursive negotiation of the subject's sensory entwinement with those objects. This renewed understanding of mimesis can, in turn, help us understand how texts reflect upon their own relationship to the world, and can shed light on the entanglements between Romanticism and realism as literary modes.

The investigations of this book begin and end with the figure of the line as self-reflexive graphic gesture and as trace of that sensory entwinement. It is a figure that emerges repeatedly – in both textual and pictorial forms – across the works with which I am concerned. At once suggestive of the traces and marks made in writing or drawing, and, in a more symbolic register, of narrative's logic and form, the figure of the line is fundamentally bound up with mimetic thinking. As I will show in Chapter 2, the undulating narrative line performatively and playfully reverses the mimetic logic of textual narrative. If mimetic literature reproduces sensory material as text, the line unshackles itself from text to become something else again, something pre- or post-textual. That the pictorial line is almost always contained within the text itself, often in textual form, knots it over itself again, turning it into a self-reflexive bundle as the text reflects on itself, on its conditions for being, on its boundaries and porousness, on what might lie before or beyond it.

A baffling hallucinatory vision accosts the narrator of Honoré de Balzac's 'Théorie du conte' [Theory of the tale], in words that ring in a curiously un-Balzacian key:

Hier en rentrant chez moi, je vis un nombre incommensurable d'exemplaires de ma propre personne, tous pressés les uns contre les autres à l'instar des harengs au fond d'une tonne. Ils répercutaient dans un lointain magique ma propre figure, comme, lorsque deux glaces se répondent, la lueur d'une lampe posée au milieu d'un salon est répétée à l'infini dans l'espace sans bornes contenu entre la surface du verre et son tain.

Pour un bourgeois de la rue Saint-Denis, c'eût été un effrayant spectacle; pour moi, ce n'était rien. Il n'y avait rien d'extraordinaire à ce que le fantastique fût venu frapper à la porte d'un pauvre homme qui vit de fantaisie.[1]

Yesterday, on returning home, I saw an incommensurable number of copies of my own person, all of them pressed up one against another after the fashion of herrings at the bottom of a barrel. They echoed my own face in an enchanted faraway, just as, when two mirrors face one another, the glow of a lamp placed in the middle of a drawing room is repeated to infinity in the boundless space between the surface of the glass and its silvered backing.

For a bourgeois of the Rue Saint-Denis, it would have been a terrifying spectacle; for me, it was nothing. There was nothing extraordinary in the fantastic coming to knock at the door of a poor man who lives on fantasies.

Critics have recognised in this fragment the crisis of the *conteur* (writer of tales) reflecting on his cycle of tales *Les Cent Contes drolatiques* (Hundred Droll Tales) and responding to an urge to move on from short fiction as the French *folie du conte* (craze for the tale) of the early 1830s reached its peak: a Balzac 'avant Balzac', or perhaps a Balzac on the brink of Balzac.[2] The brief sequence might also be read as an explicit scene of reflection on the authorial process. The narrator's hallucinations are compared to the distorting effects cast by mirrors and a lamp – those two ubiquitous instruments of mimesis and poeisis – thus casting the finite, intimate place of his home as an infinite, otherworldly space. The effect is to highlight both the potency of the *conte* and its distortive effects, duplicating, and thereby fragmenting, his identity ad infinitum. Balzac's

---

[1] Honoré de Balzac, 'Théorie du conte', *Œuvres diverses*, ed. by Pierre-Georges Castex and others, 2 vols (Paris: Gallimard, 1990–6), I, pp. 517–18 (p. 517). Unpublished and undated, this piece was 'probably written in late 1831 or early 1832 as an introduction to the *Contes Drolatiques*', according to Tim Farrant in *Balzac's Shorter Fictions: Genesis and Genre* (Oxford: Oxford University Press, 2002), p. 120 n. 52.

[2] Farrant, *Balzac's Shorter Fictions*, p. 121. See also Claire Barel-Moisan and José Luis-Diaz (eds), *Balzac avant Balzac* (Paris: Christian Pirot, 2006).

narrator here is not yet the duplicitous manipulator of identities of *La Comédie humaine*. He is, instead, a visionary made subject to the multiple versions of himself he sees pitched against the wall. For the 'poor man' who 'lives on fantasies', moreover, such experiences are the stuff of his everyday. The fragmentary fantasy itself suggests the brief confession of a writer who reads: one who reads, in particular, the fantasy literature of Romanticism, cast in the familiar form of the specular encounter.

This book argues for an understanding of Balzac – who has been considered, since the latter half of the nineteenth century, the founder of French realism – as an enthusiastic reader of E. T. A. Hoffmann, famous for a particularly Gothic strain of late German Romanticism. It positions itself against Ernst Curtius's argument that Romanticism is a part of Balzac, but Balzac not a part of Romanticism; that Balzac's works reproduce Romantic motifs but represent, at most, a 'phenomenology' of Romanticism.[3] It argues, correspondingly, against other twentieth-century critics such as Maurice Bardèche, who dismisses the importance of Hoffman for Balzac's works as a mere feature of his taxonomising sweep across nineteenth-century French culture.[4] Such claims underestimate the important role played by Hoffmann's tales in the development of European realism. Balzac's early fiction, as this book will show, grapples with a set of problems relating to his representational attitude, and it does so in part by working through his readings of Hoffmann's tales, which repeatedly unfold such problems on their own terms. Indeed, as Erich Auerbach suggests, it is precisely from within its engagement with those problems of Romanticism that realism emerges as a category in its own right.

In equal measure, this book insists upon a reading of Hoffmann as a proto-realist: as a writer who pays acute attention to human sensory experience, particularly to vision and its perilous misfirings. A concept usually reserved for discussions of realism, literary and artistic mimesis is a topic of explicit obsession in Hoffmann's late-Romantic literature, which returns again and again to scenes concerned with writing, painting or theatre. In what way is life

---

[3] Ernst Robert Curtius, *Balzac* (Bern: A. Francke, 1951), pp. 304–5.
[4] Maurice Bardèche, *Balzac, Romancier* (Paris: Librairie Plon, 1940), pp. 207–8: 'L'hallucination hoffmannienne dans les contes de Balzac en 1830 et 1831 demeure toujours descriptive. [. . .] Il ne faut donc pas exagérer, croyons-nous, l'influence d'Hoffmann sur Balzac en 1830' (Hoffmannesque hallucination in Balzac's tales of 1830 and 1831 always remains in a descriptive mode. [. . .] We should therefore avoid exaggerating the influence of Hoffmann on Balzac in 1830).

compromised in the name of fiction, of the artwork? This question recurs compulsively in Hoffmann's tales, in repeated and near-repeated scenarios in which the everyday is pitted against a fantastic, ideal or delusional alternative. His persistent staging of 'real life' scenarios alongside a set of otherworldly alternatives has encouraged critics such as Georg Lukács, Hans Mayer and Gerhard Neumann to detect in his work the traces of a realist tendency before 'realism' itself had yet developed as a literary category.[5]

In the early works by Balzac I consider in this book – all of which, with the exception of later editions of *Le Chef-d'œuvre inconnu*, fall into the pre-1835 era, during the most lively French reception of Hoffmann – Balzac calls up images, tropes and details that relate to Hoffmann. One such image, not an explicit reference so much as an unwitting repetition, is the most crucial piece of evidence for my comparative work: it is an undulating line copied out by both authors from Laurence Sterne's *Tristram Shandy*, tracing a strange and unexpected synchronicity in thought. This particular crossover, overlooked by previous studies of Hoffmann and Balzac and examined here in detail in Chapter 2, accompanies a series of allusions and overlaps that stake out Hoffmann's spectral but insistent presence across *La Comédie humaine*.

Adapting its structure from that figure of the narrative line – the continuous line of plot that unfolds like thread from a spool – this book is motivated by the conviction that the relationship between Hoffmann and Balzac is most helpfully imagined not in terms of filiation or influence, but through a more tangled interplay of imitation, repression, resistance and prefigurement. As Peter Brooks, J. Hillis Miller and Tim Ingold have shown, the line, as story-line, is an archetypal shape for the movement of narrative.[6] In subsequent chapters, I explore sensuous and embodied representations of the act of writing and drawing across the works of Hoffmann and of Balzac by starting with the conventional motif of the narrative line – both as a figure for the movement of narrative and as an index of writing or drawing – and following it through various forms and

[5] Georg Lukács, *Skizze einer Geschichte der neueren deutschen Literatur* (Berlin: Aufbau Verlag, 1953), p. 57; Hans Mayer, 'Die Wirklichkeit E. T. A. Hoffmanns' in *Begriffsbestimmung des literarischen Realismus*, ed. by Richard Brinkmann (Darmstadt: Wissenschaftliche Buchgesellschaft, 1969), pp. 259–300.

[6] Peter Brooks, *Reading for the Plot: Design and Intention in Narrative* (Cambridge, MA: Harvard University Press, 1992); Tim Ingold, *Lines: A Brief History* (London: Routledge, 2007); J. Hillis Miller, *Ariadne's Thread: Story Lines* (New Haven, CT: Yale University Press, 1992) and *Reading Narrative* (Norman: University of Oklahoma Press, 1998).

complications: the arabesque, the scribble and the cross, scored across the body or the text.

Hoff-manie: Hoffmann in France

'Hoffmann est populaire en France, plus populaire qu'en Allemagne' (Hoffmann is popular in France, more popular than in Germany):[7] since this remark made by Théophile Gautier in 1836, it has been a truism in the critical literature that Hoffmann enjoyed a warmer reception in France than he did in his native Germany. In 1822, the year of E. T. A. Hoffmann's death, his friend David Koreff, one of the most famed authorities on animal magnetism, had moved from Berlin to Paris, where he lit the match of Hoffmann's posthumous literary career, which took off in 1829 with a series of translations and culminated in the blazing 'vogue d'Hoffmann' of the early 1830s. Koreff was by all accounts a curious figure, resembling something close to a literary invention himself. As a member of Hoffmann's literary circle the *Seraphinenbrüder* (later renamed the *Serapionsbrüder*), Koreff was immortalised as the character Vinzenz in *Die Serapionsbrüder* and as 'Dr. K.' in *Das öde Haus*. Koreff has therefore retained the status not just of witness to but of participant in Hoffmann's fictional world. He provided François-Adolphe Loève-Veimars, Hoffmann's translator and biographer, with information about Hoffmann's life gleaned from Hoffmann's friend, Julius Eduard Hitzig, and with the sketch of Hoffmann on which his biographical portrait was based – and he thus in a very real way delivered to Paris the image of Hoffmann on which his French admirers and imitators were to base their own works. The trail Koreff traces leaves us with the strange impression of a fictional character arriving in Paris to tell the story of his author.

From 1829 a stream of translations of Hoffmann's works was undertaken, primarily by Loève-Veimars, for the newly founded *Revue de Paris*. This prolonged publicity trail led to the first four-volume instalment of Loève-Veimars's *Œuvres complètes d'Hoffmann* (Complete Works of Hoffmann), published with

---

[7] Théophile Gautier, 'Les contes d'Hoffmann', in *Souvenirs de théâtre, d'art et de critique* (Paris: Charpentier 1883), pp. 43–50. Originally published in *Chronique de Paris*, 14 August 1836, pp. 133–5. This claim is echoed by several critics, including John Reddick, in 'E. T. A. Hoffmann's *Der goldne Topf* and its "durchgehaltene Ironie"', *Modern Language Review*, 71.3 (1976), 577–94 (p. 577) and Francesca Brittan, in *Music and Fantasy in the Age of Berlioz* (Cambridge: Cambridge University Press, 2017), p. 18.

Renduel in December 1829 (dated 1830). It was quickly shadowed by a rival edition translated by Théodore Toussenel, who even began his version with volumes numbered 5 to 8, as though his were the official continuation of Loève-Veimars's preliminary four. The two translations grew side by side as each translator raced to seize works as yet untouched by the other. As a result, Loève-Veimars's official version, even when it reached twenty volumes in 1833, was left incomplete.

In practical terms, the doubling of Hoffmann's oeuvre into two competing translations – they would be joined by a third in 1836, that of Henry Egmont – was a remarkable publicity stunt.[8] The frantic marketing of Hoffmann's works in this way was symptomatic of a newly profitable reading economy that Balzac himself participated in not just as author and commentator but as investor, purchasing a printing press himself in 1826. Loève-Veimars engaged a number of further strategies for his publicity campaign during these years. The most controversial and effective of these was to pit Hoffmann against Walter Scott by publishing a translation of Scott's damning critique of Hoffmann from the *Foreign Quarterly Review* in the first issue of *La Revue de Paris* and reprinting it as the preface to the first volume of the *Œuvres complètes d'Hoffmann*.[9] Scott's infamous essay aimed to distance his own method from the lack of discipline he associated with fantastic and Gothic works. Yet it descended into an acerbic critique of Hoffmann's works and of his moral, physical, and physiognomic decrepitude, focusing on his 'ill-regulated' imagination and 'hypochondriac and whimsical disposition, which carried him to extremes in all his undertakings'.[10] Despite admitting his appreciation of the rather more sober *Das Majorat* (The Entail), Scott argued that tales such as *Der Sandmann* (The Sandman) do not possess even the 'seeming authenticity' of a hallucination and can only be compared to 'the feverish dreams of a light-headed patient'.[11]

---

[8] Germán Gil-Curiel has described the 'literary-discursive framework' of Hoffmann's emergence in France in *A Comparative Approach: The Early European Supernatural Tale. Five Variations on a Theme* (Frankfurt am Main: Peter Lang, 2011), p. 29.

[9] Walter Scott, 'On the Supernatural in Fictitious Composition; and particularly on the Works of Ernest Theodore William Hoffmann', *Foreign Quarterly Review* 1 (1827), 60–98; 'Du Merveilleux dans le roman', trans. by Adolphe-François Loève-Veimars, *Revue de Paris*, 1 (1829), 25–33.

[10] Scott, 'On the Supernatural', pp. 81, 74. See Victor Sage's discussion of Scott's critique of Hoffmann, and of Hoffmann's critique of Scott, in 'Scott, Hoffmann, and the Persistence of the Gothic', in *Popular Revenants: The German Gothic and its International Reception, 1800–2000*, ed. Andrew Cusack and Barry Murnane (Rochester, NY: Camden House, 2012), pp. 76–86 (p. 78).

[11] Scott, 'On the Supernatural', p. 97.

It was thus in the terms of excitement and of pathology that Hoffmann and the genre Scott attributed to him – 'the FANTASTIC mode of writing', defined as the product of an unregulated imagination – entered French literary discussion.[12] If Hoffmann did not 'create' the genre, as Jules Janin claimed, then he gave it new credibility in French literary discourse.[13] Scott's attempt to undermine Hoffmann's works proved spectacularly unsuccessful, at least in France, where his readers responded with enthusiasm both to the label 'fantastic' and to the image of the sick writer.[14] In 1830, a critic for *Le Mercure de France* wrote, with a hint of glee, of the spreading *Hoff-manie*: 'C'est une fureur, c'est un engouement, mais il est contagieux' (It is a furore, it is an infatuation, but he is contagious).[15] The stream of imitations, translations and homages that had begun in 1829 fast became a deluge. They included, to name just a few significant examples, the short stories and essays of Théophile Gautier from 1831 ('La Cafétière' onwards); Jules Janin's short story 'Kressler', a continuation of the life of Johannes Kreisler, Hoffmann's musical alter ego, signed 'Hoffmann' and reprinted in Janin's *Contes fantastiques et contes littéraires* (1832); and Gérard de Nerval's publication of an extract of *Kreisleriana* in *Gastronome* (1830) and his translation of *Die Abenteuer der Silvester-Nacht* (1831). It is no exaggeration to say that in the early years of the 1830s in France, the name Hoffmann was synonymous with 'le fantastique', the genre to which he had given new life. Dictionaries such as the *Littré* of the 1870s continued to cite his name in its definition of 'le fantastique'.[16]

One major characteristic of the success Hoffmann enjoyed in France was that the entanglement between life and fiction that became synonymous with his name was transferred back onto his own character. Gautier's tale 'Onuphrius Wphly', initially published in 1832

---

[12] Ibid., p. 72.

[13] 'Hoffmann a fait le genre [du fantastique]' (Hoffmann created the genre [of the fantastic]), cited in Brittan, *Music and Fantasy*, p. 17.

[14] Sage, 'Scott, Hoffmann, and the Persistence of the Gothic', p. 84.

[15] An article in the *Gazette médicale*, 27 October 1832, titled 'De l'influence hygiénique du fantastique en littérature' (On the hygienic influence of the fantastic on literature) criticised the potential dangers of the fantastic genre – namely that it 'bouleverse les lois de l'hygiène' (overturns the laws of hygiene) and risks tempting its readers to suicide. Both are cited in Elizabeth Teichmann, *La fortune d'Hoffmann en France* (Geneva: Droz, 1961), pp. 84–5.

[16] 'Un genre de contes mis en vogue par l'Allemand Hoffmann' (a genre of tales made fashionable by the German Hoffmann), Émile Littré, *Dictionnaire de la langue française* (Paris: L. Hachette, 1873–4). Electronic version created by François Gannaz <https://www.littre.org/definition/fantastique> [accessed 1.06.23].

and republished a year later as 'Onuphrius ou les vexations fantastiques d'un admirateur d'Hoffmann', is perhaps the most explicit fictional response to the feverish Hoff-mania of the 1830s, assuming the form of a fictional case study. The protagonist Onuphrius, a painter, is a reader obsessed with Hoffmann's tales and sick with the delusions they inspire – delusions that ultimately kill him.[17] The tale strikes a neat parallel to Balzac's 'Théorie du conte', which was written at around the same time and which also features a narrator driven into madness by his readings of the fantastic. The *conte* was not only the medium *of* the fantastic, exploited by Hoffmann for its brittle narrative structure and potentially destabilising effects, but was also, in these years, a form in which to reflect back Hoffmann's fantastic mode and the pathology his French readers associated with it: the infection, and dysregulation, of 'real life' by fiction.

Hoffmann as Realist

From the earliest days of his European reception, Hoffmann's fantastic mode had been understood by some to contain, in what might at first appear a contradiction, the kernels of realism. Even a critic as unsympathetic as Walter Scott found praise for his capacity as 'a close observer of nature, [. . .] who, if this sickly and disturbed train of thought had not led him to confound the supernatural with the absurd, would have distinguished himself as a painter of human nature'.[18] But it was not until the efforts of Henry Egmont, his third major French translator, that a more sober image of Hoffmann took hold in France. In the preface to his four-volume translation of 1836, Egmont praises Hoffmann's 'mérite d'observation si précieux' (valuable observational powers), his 'profonde connaissance du cœur de l'homme' (deep understanding of man's heart).[19] He counters Scott's critique by pointing out that Hoffmann's narrators mobilise ironic and distancing effects precisely in order to show up the dangers of the unregulated imagination that so interested him. In a sense, the

---

[17] See Victoire Feuillebois, 'Théophile Gautier's "Onuphrius" (1833) and the Critique of the Etiology of Pathological Reading', *Literature and Medicine*, 34.2 (2016), 370–88.

[18] Scott, 'On the Supernatural', p. 82.

[19] Henry Egmont, 'Notice sur la vie et les ouvrages d'Hoffmann', in E. T. A. Hoffmann, *Œuvres complètes de E. T. A. Hoffmann. Contes Fantastiques de E. T. A. Hoffmann, traduction nouvelle, précédée d'une notice sur la vie et les ouvrages de l'auteur par Henry Egmont*, trans. by Henry Egmont, 4 vols (Paris: Camuzeaux [vol. I] and Béthune & Plon [vols II–IV], 1836), vol I, v–xxxi 'Préface' (p. xxix).

fantastic illness contained its own cure: for once the unhealthy fictions were understood to be aware of themselves *as* fictions, their pathological and splintered excesses emerged not as a defence of the irrational and the absurd, but rather as searching illuminations of real structures that might otherwise remain invisible: the dark corners of the human psyche and the errors and misjudgements of human perception.

Egmont's protégé Gautier would become an emphatic proponent of Hoffmann's realism, declaring him a 'réaliste violent' (fierce realist) in a text from the 1850s.[20] In an earlier review of Egmont's translations, he praises Hoffmann's ability to grasp the physiognomy of external forms:

> Son crayon est vif et chaud; il a l'esprit de la silhouette et découpe en se jouant mille profils mystérieux et singuliers dont il est impossible de ne pas se souvenir, et qu'il vous semble avoir connus quelque part.

> His pencil is warm and lively; he has a sense for silhouettes, and with the greatest of ease he cuts out a thousand mysterious and singular profiles which it is impossible to forget, profiles that you feel you have come across somewhere before.[21]

Foreshadowing Walter Benjamin, who was to dub him the 'Physiognomiker von Berlin' (physiognomist of Berlin), Gautier puts forward a reading of an uncanny realism in which resemblance is displaced by the feeling of déjà vu, or, as Hoffmann himself would put it in his praise of Jacques Callot, 'etwas fremdartig Bekanntes' (something strangely familiar) (H II.1 17).[22] This leads Gautier to conclude that Hoffmann's tales are 'plus réels et plus vraisemblables' (more real and more lifelike) than many works 'conçus et exécutés avec la plus froide sagesse' (conceived and executed with the coldest wisdom).[23]

Critics from Nodier to Freud, Todorov and Pierre-Georges Castex have argued that the Hoffmannesque fantastic distinguishes itself from the literary tradition of the supernatural ('das Wunderbare' or 'le merveilleux') by incorporating bizarre and inexplicable phenomena into everyday life, thus adapting that older genre for a

---

[20] Théophile Gautier, *Histoire de l'art dramatique en France depuis vingt-cinq ans* (Paris: Édition Hetzel, Librairie Magin, Blanchard et Compagnie, 1859), p. 230.

[21] Gautier, 'Les contes d'Hoffmann', p. 44.

[22] Walter Benjamin, 'Das dämonische Berlin', in *Gesammelte Schriften*, ed. by Theodor W. Adorno and Gershom Scholem with Rolf Tiedemann, 7 vols (Frankfurt am Main: Suhrkamp, 1972–99), VII.1, pp. 89–91 (p. 89).

[23] Gautier, 'Les contes d'Hoffmann', p. 47.

modern and urban context. Such a reading takes Hoffmann at his word when he writes, somewhat laconically, of his method in *Der goldne Topf* in a letter to Kunz in 1813: 'Feenhaft und wunderbar aber keck ins gewöhnliche alltägliche Leben tretend und sein[e] Gestalten ergreifend soll das Ganze werden' (The whole thing should become fairy-like and wonderful, but boldly stepping into normal everyday life and seizing its figures) (H I 301). Marxist readings of the 1950s and '60s point to Hoffmann's bitingly satirical portraits of authority figures and state officials; of the comfortable banality of middle-class concerns; and, most of all, of philistines.[24] For Hans Mayer, the intrusion of fantastic phenomena into concrete localities works not 'als Entschärfung der Wirklichkeitsdarstellung' (as a dilution of the representation of reality) but as a representation which, in dealing with its own age and contemporaries, 'keine Möglichkeit sieht, die tiefen Lebenskonflikte anders als durch Ausweichen in den mythischen Bereich lösen zu können' (sees no other possibility for resolving life's deep conflicts than by flight into a mythical realm). Hoffmann's works, that is, make use of magical figures *as part of* their representation of reality.[25]

Hoffmann's investment in a mimetic understanding of art cannot be uncoupled from his innovative fantastic and distortive strategies, nor from his deep concerns for the contingencies and interferences of his medium, which will also play a role in this book. Critics including Claudia Liebrand and Victor Sage have explicitly labelled Hoffmann as anti-mimetic in his approach, and little mention of him is made in works such as Frederick Burwick's *Mimesis and its Romantic Reflections*, which sets out a case for the role of mimesis in Romantic literature.[26] But in his contribution to the co-edited volume *Mimesis und Simulation*, Gerhard Neumann assembles a convincing account of Hoffmann's mimetic strategy, which he defines in the terms of anamorphosis: an experimental technique in visual artworks which works on the basis of a 'Wechselmuster von Entstellung und Wiedererrichtung des Wahrgenommenen, seiner Defiguration und anschließenden Refiguration' (a shifting pattern deforming and reconstituting the perceived material, its defiguration

---

[24] Lukács, *Skizze*, p. 57.
[25] Mayer, 'Die Wirklichkeit', p. 271.
[26] Claudia Liebrand, *Aporie des Kunstmythos: Die Texte E. T. A. Hoffmanns* (Freiburg: Rombach, 1996), p. 12; Sage, 'Scott, Hoffmann, and the Persistence of the Gothic', p. 79. Frederick Burwick, *Mimesis and its Romantic Reflections* (University Park, PA: Pennsylvania State University Press, 2001).

and subsequent refiguration).[27] Within Hoffmann's disfigurative manoeuvres, Neumann argues, lies an anamorphic attempt to expand 'das Blickfeld und die Penetranz der Wahrnehmung über das bislang Sichtbare' (the field of vision and the penetrative faculty of perception beyond the conventionally visible), to reveal 'verdeckte Strukturen des Realen' (hidden structures of the real) and thus 'damit zugleich eine neue Auffassung dessen zu begründen, was "literarischer Realismus" heißen kann' (to establish a new understanding of what 'literary realism' can mean).[28] By introducing new possibilities of how the world might be or appear, Hoffmann incorporates into his representations elements that remain otherwise invisible – the perceptive faculties of the artist and viewer, the contingencies of the medium itself – and thus expands mimesis's remit, whilst at the same time showing up (often in order to mock) rehearsed conventions and codes of representation, both of Romantic and of more classical orientations. For Hoffmann, disfiguration turns out to be a way of getting closer to reality – just as it does, for example, in the model of caricature, which produces, in the words of E. H. Gombrich and Ernst Kris, 'a likeness more true than mere imitation could be'.[29]

The intention here is not to argue that Hoffmann is a chronological misfit, a displaced realist, and thus to take sides in the tussle between those who discover forward-looking and remarkably modern elements in Hoffmann's works, and those who insist on rooting him in his proper (Romantic) context.[30] Instead I will show, across an account that is rooted in the context of Hoffmann's emergence in the French literary world, that Hoffmann's contributions to theories of representation were rich enough to enter into a

---

[27] Gerhard Neumann, 'Anamorphose. E. T. A. Hoffmanns Poetik der Defiguration', in *Mimesis und Simulation*, ed. by Andreas Kablitz and Gerhard Neumann (Freiburg im Breisgau: Rombach, 1998), pp. 377–417 (p. 399).

[28] Ibid., p. 404.

[29] E. H. Gombrich and Ernst Kris, 'The Principles of Caricature', *British Journal of Medical Psychology*, 17 (1938), 319–42 (p. 319).

[30] Ricarda Schmidt has been a particularly ardent critic of twentieth-century Hoffmann criticism that claimed Hoffmann as 'Vorläufer der poststrukutralistischen Theoreme von der Auflösung des Identitätsprinzips und des Sinns' (precursor of poststructuralist theorems of the dissolution of identity and meaning). Schmidt counters this tendency with readings of Hoffmann that aim to resituate him within Romantic discourses that he simultaneously transcends through critique and irony. Ricarda Schmidt, 'Narrative Strukturen romantischer Subjektivität in E. T. A. Hoffmanns *Die Elixiere des Teufels* und *Der Sandmann*', *Germanisch-Romanische Monatsschrift*, 49 (1999), 143–60 (p. 144). See also Ricarda Schmidt, *Wenn mehrere Künste im Spiel sind: Intermedialität bei E. T. A. Hoffmann* (Göttingen: Vandenhoeck & Ruprecht, 2006).

dialogue with the writer we have come to view as the arch-realist of the nineteenth century.

Balzac's Hoffmann

Balzac was a keen reader of the *Revue de Paris*, the primary stage for the new translations of Hoffmann, in which he published some of his own earliest works of fiction.[31] He corresponded with Loève-Veimars from at least as early as 1827, and in 1828 his own press printed one of Hoffmann's tales, *Der Baron von B.*, translated as *L'Archet du Baron de B*. It is thus reasonable to assume that Balzac was amongst the first major wave of Hoffmann's readers in France.[32] Given Hoffmann's relatively recent death, in 1822, the two authors were able to share a friend in Dr Koreff, and they also shared an illustrator in Tony Johannot, who completed illustrations for the Renduel translations of Hoffmann and for the major *Furne* edition of *La Comédie humaine* (1842–6).

Whilst this book is not in any straightforward way a study of influence or reception, Balzac's readings, reflections and imitations of Hoffmann are necessarily one of its predominant interests. Throughout the 1830s Balzac faced repeated comparison with Hoffmann, primarily by critics including Charles de Bernard and Amadée Faucheux in reviews of his *Romans et contes philosophiques*, which were published in 1831.[33] One of the major assumptions of this book is that Balzac's reflections of Hoffmann and the 'hoffmannien' open up moments of reflection on the

---

[31] The earliest of these are *L'Élixir de longue vie* and *Sarrasine* in 1830; *L'Auberge Rouge* and the second part of *La Femme de trente ans* in 1831; *Les Orphelins* and *La Femme abandonnée* in 1832. The dates of works by Balzac in this book follow those given in 'Balzac's Work: An Overview of "La Comédie Humaine"', in *The Cambridge Companion to Balzac*, ed. by Owen Heathcote and Andrew Watts (Cambridge: Cambridge University Press, 2017), pp. xviii–xxii, which are based on those given by S. Vachon in *Les Travaux et les jours d'Honoré de Balzac: chronologie de la création balzacienne* (Paris: Presses du CNR and Presses universitaires de Vincennes; Presses de l'Université de Montréal, 1992).

[32] Balzac had bought the collected translations of Loève-Veimars by the end of February 1834. See Teichmann, *La Fortune*, p. 105.

[33] Amadée Faucheux wrote to Balzac, in a letter of May 1831: 'vos articles de la *Revue de Paris* sont charmants, je les préfère beaucoup aux *Contes* d'Hoffmann avec lesquels ils ont quelques rapports' (your articles in the *Revue de Paris* are charming, I much prefer them to Hoffmann's *Tales*, to which they bear some similarity). Honoré de Balzac, *Correspondance*, ed. Roger Pierrot and H. Yon, 2 vols (Paris: Gallimard, 2006–), vol. 1, p. 348. See also Teichmann, *La Fortune*, pp. 75–9.

limits of artistic representation. Such questions are in particular evidence in the early years of the 1830s: a period in which Balzac was honing his method and experiencing his first real successes as a writer, and in which the very mention of Hoffmann's name could work as a legitimising force for his own capacity for literary invention.

To what extent, then, did Balzac express a desire to fashion himself as what Pierre Brunel has called 'un Hoffmann français'?[34] In correspondence and published essays Balzac made a number of comments about the apparent influence of Hoffmann on his literary works, comments that demonstrate a near-unparalleled sense of antagonism and frustration. They have been frequently referenced in the critical literature, although only patchily discussed, and it is therefore worth giving a sense of them here. The first, a public letter to Charles de Bernard on 25 August 1831, in reaction to de Bernard's reading of his *La Peau de chagrin* as an imitation of Hoffmann, is perhaps the most significant, and will be discussed in detail in Chapter 3. Balzac's response to de Bernard's suggestion is a somewhat tangled denial: 'Qui peut se flatter d'être inventeur? Je ne me suis vraiment pas inspiré d'Hoffmann, que je n'ai connu qu'après avoir *pensé* mon ouvrage' (Who can pride himself on being an inventor? I have truly taken no inspiration from Hoffmann, whom I came to know only after having *conceived* my work).[35] There is a peculiar rhetorical tension here, as Balzac first denies the possibility of literary 'invention', thus hinting at the inevitability of inspiration, imitation and intertextuality, only then to deny that he was inspired by Hoffmann's work. The tension is intensified by the fact that, in the same month, he makes his first literary references to Hoffmann in the short story *L'Auberge Rouge*.

The tension persists: in the 1831 preface to *La Peau de chagrin*, Balzac names Hoffmann as a man of genius alongside Petrarch, Byron and Voltaire (B X 47); but in a pseudonymous article in *La Caricature* a year later, he compares him to Ludwig Tieck, disparagingly calling them 'les deux brillans rivaux qui se partagèrent [. . .] la palme de la littérature légère' (two brilliant rivals who share the trophy of light reading).[36] Then, in a letter to his sister Laure Surville in October 1833, he boasts of having been told by some visiting

---

[34] Pierre Brunel, 'Notes', in Honoré de Balzac, *Sarrasine – Gambara – Massimilla Doni*, ed. by Pierre Brunel (Paris: Gallimard, 1995), pp. 8–32 (p. 18).

[35] Balzac, *Correspondance*, I, p. 571.

[36] Le comte Alex. De B—(Balzac), 'Œuvres complètes de Ludwig Tieck', *Caricature*, 5 July 1832, p. 698.

Germans that his literary achievements would soon lead him to replace 'Byron, Walter Scott, Goethe, Hoffmann' at the head of literary Europe.[37] But barely a month later, Hoffmann appears in a different light again, in a letter to Mme Hanska:

> J'ai lu Hoffmann en entier, il est au-dessous de sa réputation, il y a quelque chose, mais pas grand'chose; il parle bien musique; il n'entend rien à l'amour ni à la femme; il ne cause point de peurs, il est impossible d'en causer avec des choses physiques.[38]

> I have read Hoffmann cover to cover – he doesn't live up to his reputation, there is something there, but not a lot. He can talk music; he understands nothing of love, nor of women; he says nothing about fear; it is impossible to say anything about it with material things.

Critics have suggested that this excessively forceful dismissal of a writer whom Balzac claims to have read in full, and whom only a month ago he had listed in the same breath as the much admired Scott, scarcely conceals a simmering rivalry.[39] The one concession he makes – that Hoffmann 'parle bien musique' – forms the basis of a further set of ambiguities in a letter of May 1837 to Maurice Schlesinger, who had commissioned Balzac's explicitly Hoffmannesque novella *Gambara* for the *Revue et Gazette musicale de Paris*. Balzac describes the problems he faced in emulating Hoffmann's musical narratives:

> Lisez ce que votre cher Hoffmann le berlinois a écrit sur Gluck, Mozart, Haydn et Beethoven, et vous verrez par quelles lois secrètes la littérature, la musique et la peinture se tiennent! Il y a des pages empreintes de génie [. . .] Mais Hoffmann s'est contenté de parler sur cette alliance en thériaki, ses œuvres sont admiratives, il sentait trop vivement, il était trop musicien pour discuter: j'ai sur lui l'avantage d'être Français et très peu musicien, je puis donner la clef du palais où il s'enivrait![40]

> Read what your beloved Hoffmann the Berliner has written about Gluck, Mozart, Haydn and Beethoven, and you will see the secret

---

[37] Balzac, *Correspondance*, II, p. 392.

[38] Balzac, *Lettres à Madame Hanska*, ed. by Roger Pierrot, 4 vols (Paris: Laffront, 1990), vol. I, p. 84.

[39] John T. Hamilton, 'Mi manca la voca: How Balzac Talks Music – or How Music Takes Place – in Balzac's *Massimilla Doni*', in *Speaking of Music: Addressing the Sonorous*, ed. by Keith Chapin and Andrew H. Clark (New York: Fordham University Press, 2013), pp. 120–37 (pp. 120–1); Timothy W. Lewis, *The Influence of E. T. A. Hoffmann on Balzac* (unpublished doctoral thesis, University of London, 1991), p. 60.

[40] Balzac, *Correspondance*, II, p. 233.

laws by which literature, music and painting are connected! There are pages stamped with genius [. . .] But Hoffmann contented himself with speaking of this connection as an opium eater, his works are those of an enthusiast, he felt things too keenly, he was too much of a musician for the examination of them; I have the advantage over him of being a Frenchman and not much of a musician, I can provide the key to the palace of his intoxication!

Here is Balzac's clearest expression of appreciation for Hoffmann's *génie*, rooted in his inter-art sensibilities as visual artist, musician and writer, accompanied by the accusation, taken straight from Scott, that his works are the products of intoxication. What are we to make of these changing claims? Balzac himself reminds us of the artifice of opinion, and particularly of literary opinions, in Lucien's unnerving and sparkling journalistic performances of *Illusions perdues*. As a shifting intertextual coordinate for Balzac's works, Hoffmann will become a keyword for literary invention both unserious and otherworldly, one that works successively to position and pivot Balzac's narrative capacities, sometimes as antagonist and sometimes as forebear.

The situation is muddied further when we turn to Balzac's literary references to Hoffmann. The earliest and most complete of these is given in *L'Élixir de longue vie*, a short and grisly tale published in 1830, which is discussed at length in Chapter 5 of this book. Elsewhere across *La Comédie humaine*, Balzac writes of 'Hoffmann le berlinois' as the storyteller par excellence, the *fantaisiste* or 'chantre de l'impossible' (bard of the impossible) (B VII 956) whose practice is invoked in terms that seem initially to run contrary to that of the ostensible 'secretary' of French society. Hoffmann's narration is evoked as the narration of hallucinatory vision, of drunken reverie, of the eruption of fantasy or of blinding madness. One of Balzac's earliest and most bloodthirsty tales, *L'Auberge Rouge* (1831), is framed as 'une histoire allemande qui nous fasse bien peur' (a German story which causes us great fear) by 'une jeune personne [. . .] qui, sans doute, avait lu les contes d'Hoffmann' (a young person [. . .] who had, without doubt, read the tales of Hoffmann) (B XII 90). In *Le Cousin Pons* (1847), one of his last novels, the narrator speaks of 'ce besoin de prêter une significance aux riens de la création, qui produit [. . .] les griseries imprimées d'Hoffmann' (B VII 497) (this need to lend significance to the trivialities of creation, which gives rise [. . .] to Hoffmann's printed intoxications).

A cataloguing of explicit references to Hoffmann in Balzac's literary writings is not the primary interest of this book, for they have been fully documented elsewhere: Timothy Lewis's careful evaluation numbers them at twenty-seven.[41] But as Lewis reminds us, such catalogues convey only a small part of the picture, for Hoffmann's presence is also felt in murkier corners of *La Comédie humaine* – in Balzac's German characters and references to Germany and German literature; in his manipulation of fantastic perspectives and motifs; in references to nutcrackers, to doubles and to hallucinatory experiences. One recent account suggests that these references 'clearly connect to the contemporary cultural fad for the fantastic tale', demonstrating 'Balzac's knowledge of characteristic examples of this literary genre'.[42] For other critics, the inclusion of Hoffmann in his visionary catalogue of the nineteenth century is more than a concession to fashion: it is an explicit engagement with questions, motifs and obsessions specific to Hoffmann's works, not least 'mit dem bei Hoffmann thematisierten Verhältnis von Kunst und Natur' (with the relationship between art and nature thematised by Hoffmann) – that is, with the practices and theory of mimesis.[43]

Indeed, the small sample of direct allusions above already gives the sense that Balzac calls upon Hoffmann when referencing the inventive imaginary capacities of the author. This tendency will be underscored by the close readings offered in Chapters 3, 4 and 5 of this book. In emulating forms of representation such as the fantastic tale, the musical or artistic tale and the horror story, Hoffmann's name is frequently evoked both as shorthand and as guarantor of those forms. Such reflections, as I will show over the course of this book, are symptomatic of realism's tendency to turn back on itself and to reflect upon its own tacit conditions for being. The Hoffmannesque (and that perplexing '-esque' will form the main subject of my conclusion) in turn becomes the frustrated marker for the place of imaginative invention within realism's self-probing texture.

---

[41] See Marcel Breuillac, 'Hoffmann en France (Étude de littérature comparée)', *Revue d'histoire littéraire en France*, 3 (1906), 427–57, and 4 (1907), 74–105; Teichmann, *La Fortune*; Lewis, 'The Influence of E. T. A. Hoffmann', p. 57.

[42] David F. Bell, 'Fantasy and Reality in *La Peau de chagrin*', in *The Cambridge Companion to Balzac*, ed. by Heathcote and Watts, pp. 52–66 (p. 53).

[43] Andrea Hübener, *Kreisler in Frankreich: E. T. A. Hoffmann und die französischen Romantiker* (Heidelberg: Winter, 2004), p. 180.

Romantic Balzac

Though known as one of the founders of realism, Balzac lived, wrote and died before that term came to be used in literary discourse. It was applied to him retroactively, cemented primarily by two articles written by Henry James in the 1870s.[44] That the issue has come unstuck since then is demonstrated, for example, by the fact that Balzac is included, in a chapter alongside Alexandre Dumas *père* and Victor Hugo, in the *Oxford Handbook to European Romanticism* (2016).[45] Part of this narrative of unsettlement has to do with changing attitudes towards realism itself, as I will detail in Chapter 1. Balzac's narrative approach is far more complex, intrusive and urgent than is suggested by the old myths of realism as a method offering an 'easily negotiable access between the literary world and our own';[46] or by James's description of his project as a 'social botanizing, geologizing, palæontologizing', a scientific method that he compares favourably to more mystical endeavours such as alchemy and astrology.[47] Critics both before and since have unpicked a host of factors that emphasise a more strenuous, strange style than the obsessively documentary voice that James attributes to Balzac. We could point, instead, to the intricate workings of chance and coincidence in his extraordinary and often melodramatic plots; to his exaggerated heroes and villains and other caricatures; to a surprising degree of self-reflexivity in style that will be crucial for the readings in this book; and, equally crucially, to the eruption of elements of fantasy within his materialist universe. To find proof of some of this we need look no further than the first few pages of Balzac's *Avant-propos* to *La Comédie humaine*. Before he arrives at the famous image of the writer as secretary of history, Balzac describes his initial idea for the project not in the terms of field observation, anthropology or 'social botanizing', but as a vision – a dream: 'un rêve [. . .] un de ces projets impossibles que l'on caresse et qu'on laisse s'envoler; une chimère qui sourit, qui montre son visage de femme et qui déploie aussitôt ses

[44] Henry James, 'Honoré de Balzac', in *Literary Criticism: French Writers, Other European Writers, the Prefaces to the New York Edition*, ed. by Leon Edel and Mark Wilson (New York: Penguin, 1984), pp. 31–67.

[45] Bradley Stephens, 'The Novel and the (Il)legibility of History: Victor Hugo, Honoré de Balzac, and Alexandre Dumas', in *The Oxford Handbook to European Romanticism*, ed. by Paul Hamilton (Oxford: Oxford University Press, 2016), pp. 88–104.

[46] Audrey Jaffe, 'Introduction: Realism in Retrospect', *Journal of Narrative Theory* (2006), 36.3, 309–13.

[47] James, 'Honoré de Balzac', p. 37.

ailes en remontant dans un ciel fantastique' (B I 8) (a dream [. . .] one of these impossible projects that we caress and allow to fly away; a chimera that smiles, showing us its face of a woman, before spreading its wings to return to a heavenly realm of fantasy).

Balzac's earliest works, including the fragment *Falthurne* (1820), *La dernière Fée* (1822) and *Le Centenaire ou les deux Beringheld* (1824) among others, prove that his taste for the extraordinary aspects of imaginative life and for supernatural literary traditions extended far beyond the period in which he was explicitly preoccupied with Hoffmann. His ongoing interest in the transcendental mysticism of Swedenborg, Saint-Martin and Mesmer saturates *La Comédie humaine*, where it is expressed most clearly in the trilogy of *Le Livre mystique* – *Les Proscrits*, *Louis Lambert* and *Séraphîta*. The loose philosophy expressed across these volumes opens up a seductive mixture of materialism and spiritualism in which human will, 'volonté', is held up as a universal material substance governing human behaviour, and which forms the basic currency in human relationships of manipulation, charisma and control. Such elements appear as early on as in *Falthurne* and take centre stage in *Séraphîta*, but they can also be glimpsed in otherwise more everyday occurrences and details, as in the arch-criminal Vautrin's infamous 'regard magnétique' (magnetic gaze) (B III 217).

In a later essay, Henry James concedes that Balzac has a 'romantic side'.[48] In a much-cited evaluation by Baudelaire, Balzac is not just an observer, but a 'visionnaire passionné' (passionate visionary).[49] Pierre-Georges Castex goes so far as to claim that Balzac 'appartient au romantisme' (belongs to Romanticism).[50] Such arguments are rallied in part to salvage him from the claims of epistemological naivety and of ideological conservatism with which he, along with realism more generally, have consistently been charged. Alain Robbe-Grillet is perhaps most famous for accusing Balzac of thinking of language as an unproblematic vehicle of reality, and of reality itself as up for grabs: 'tout visait à imposer l'image d'un univers stable, cohérent, continu, univoque, entièrement déchiffrable' (everything aimed to impose the image of a stable, coherent, seamless,

---

[48] James, 'Honoré de Balzac, 1902', in *Literary Criticism*, ed. by Edel and Wilson, p. 112.
[49] Charles Baudelaire, 'Théophile Gautier [1]', *Œuvres complètes*, ed. by Claude Pichois, 2 vols (Paris: Gallimard, 1975–6), II, pp. 103–28 (p. 120).
[50] Pierre-Georges Castex, *Le Conte fantastique en France de Nodier à Maupassant* (Paris: José Corti, 1987), p. 169.

unequivocal, totally decipherable universe).[51] Such critiques do not address Balzac's evident unease with the flimsy and arbitrary signs that govern both literary and social meaning in the turbulent years of the early nineteenth century. The depth of this unease is embodied by a character like Lucien de Rubempré of *Illusions perdues*, an empty vessel of a protagonist who is forced to flaunt himself in a series of performances, changing his costume, name, political allegiance and journalistic voice, in order to succeed both as a middle-class *parvenu* and as a professional writer. Critics such as Auerbach and Lukács – and even, more recently, the economist Thomas Piketty[52] – have recognised in Balzac's works a deep and contradictory account of post-revolutionary, early capitalist society and the violent unmooring of those structures that once organised values, identities and meaning:

> If identity is no longer a given [. . .] but rather subordinated to an alienating structure, how does one go about making sense of one's place in the world, of giving meaning to one's existence? The categories taken to be 'natural' – family relationships, sexual identity, morality – are systematically shown in Balzac's work to be unnatural, relativized by the great upheaval wrought by the advent of market capitalism.[53]

Not far behind this recognition of the breakdown of stable referentiality is the Balzacian novel's ambivalence about its own epistemological presumptions; its tacit understanding that realism is no more than an illusionary strategy, dependent on our recognition of so many agreed-upon signs. Sandy Petrey's study of early realism in the 1830s shows realism's interest in how truths are created and essentialised following the disillusionments of 1830, when the Orléanist monarchy first harnessed and then denied the energies of the July Revolution: 'representation's power to make and unmake reality'.[54] Where Robert Alter sees the self-conscious tradition of the eighteenth century to be 'driven underground' in Balzac's novels,[55] a host of self-reflexive structures can be untangled: Balzac's own

[51] Cited in Andrew Watts, 'Introduction', in *The Cambridge Companion to Balzac*, ed. by Heathcote and Watts, pp. 1–10 (p. 6).

[52] Thomas Piketty, *Le Capital au XXIe siècle* (Paris: Seuil, 2013), pp. 184–7.

[53] Scott Lee, 'Balzac's Legacy', in *The Cambridge Companion to Balzac*, ed. by Heathcote and Watts, pp. 175–88 (pp. 186–7).

[54] Sandy Petrey, *In the Court of the Pear King: French Culture and the Rise of Realism* (Ithaca, NY: Cornell University Press, 2005), p. 35.

[55] Robert Alter, *Partial Magic: The Novel as a Self-Conscious Genre* (Berkeley, CA: University of California Press, 1975), p. 104.

teasing description of the novel as an 'auguste mensonge' (noble lie) in the *Avant-propos* (B I 15); the empty rhetoric and false appearances across such novels as *Illusions perdues* and *Le Père Goriot*; his playfulness with language; and the innumerable intertextual allusions to other products of art and literature across *La Comédie humaine*, all of which emphasise the identity of the novel as an artwork, urgent and imaginative rather than detached and reflective.

Such local acts of self-awareness are characteristic of a highly self-reflexive narrative attitude: one in which the presence of the narrative self and medium are as much a part of the reflected reality as are the lowly details of real life for which Balzac is noted – peeling old yellow wallpaper, the precise mechanical workings of a provincial printing press, a pair of old boots, a bowl of sugar. This book will show that attending to Balzac's Romantic impulses enables a more precise understanding of his realism: not as an inert structure but as a dynamic and self-questioning one, its relationship to reality no more straightforward or self-evident than that of Hoffmann's tales.

***

It is an odd fact that neither Hoffmann nor Balzac is known for being a great thinker or theorist of narrative. Despite Balzac's plentiful literary reviews, articles, prefaces, and of course the full *Avant-propos* to the *Comédie humaine*, nowhere did he formulate a rigorous definition of the style that would come to be known as realism which was, as I have noted above, applied to him only retroactively. A critic as prominent as Zola lamented Balzac's inability to implement a critical system, whilst modern criticism leading from early Marxist readings frequently seeks to read Balzac 'against himself', often as the unwitting conservative critic of capitalism. As for Hoffmann, theoretical literary pronouncements are scarce: the 'Serapiontic Principle' and the 'Callot Principle' emerge as guiding theoretical outlines but are far from formulations of a consistent approach (the former, indeed, is itself given in fictional form, as I discuss in Chapter 4). Yet both Hoffmann and Balzac were undoubtedly great practitioners. Their works, it need hardly be stated, have not only proven to be epoch-defining but continue to be canon- and syllabus-defining. If we accept that 'thinking' can happen on a plane other than a purely metadiscursive one, then their texts, as I will show, 'think' and theorise themselves in moments of self-reflexive challenge and complexity. As Kaltërina Latifi argues of Hoffmann: 'Hoffmanns Erzähltheorie bildet sich aus seinem Erzählen heraus'

(Hoffmann's narrative theory emerges from within his narrative).[56] Indeed, what has drawn numerous critics before me to bring together these two very different writers is to be found in their sustained attempts to 'express in fiction the problems of creating fiction', as Martin Kanes writes of Balzac.[57] It is for this reason that the figurehead of the fantastic mode and the father of realism can productively be read alongside one another for their insights into one of the most long-established and simultaneously most contested literary notions of all time: mimesis.

Lines of Mimesis is, as I have suggested, by no means the first attempt at a comparative set of readings of Hoffmann and Balzac. Not only a number of articles and book chapters, but at least two doctoral dissertations have taken on elements of this comparative work over the years.[58] In this book I hope as much to explore the richness of some of this previous work as to gesture beyond it in certain ways. Since Marcel Breuillac's two essays for *Revue d'histoire littéraire de la France* in 1906 and 1907, comparative scholarship on Hoffmann and Balzac has been overwhelmingly concerned with the difficult idea of influence, channelled through Balzac's approach to the fantastic as genre or style.[59] Influence was the focus of mid-twentieth-century criticism by Pierre Laubriet, Kurt Wais and Olivier Bonard; and of Elizabeth Teichmann's *La Fortune d'Hoffmann en France* (1961).[60] The 1970 edition of *L'Année Balzacienne*, 'Balzac à l'Étranger', yielded three further articles dealing exclusively with elements of Hoffmann's works found in Balzac.[61] Twenty-first-century

[56] Kaltërina Latifi, *Perspektivische Ambiguitäten: E. T. A. Hoffmann, poetologisch gelesen* (Baden-Baden: Rombach-Wissenschaft, 2021), p. 21.

[57] Martin Kanes, *Balzac's Comedy of Words* (Princeton, NJ: Princeton University Press, 1975), p. 261.

[58] Lewis, 'The Influence of E. T. A. Hoffmann'; George Edgar Slusser, 'Rameau's Nephew and his Progeny: The Artist as Performer in E. T. A. Hoffmann and Balzac' (unpublished doctoral thesis, Harvard University, 1974).

[59] Breuillac, 'Hoffmann en France'. See also Gerhard Pankalla, 'E. T. A. Hoffmann und Frankreich: Beiträge zum Hoffmann-Bild in der französischen Literatur des 19. Jahrhunderts', *Germanisch-Romanische Monatsschrift*, 28 (1939), 308–18 (p. 312).

[60] Pierre Laubriet, 'Influences chez Balzac: Swedenborg, Hoffmann', *Les Études balzaciennes*, 5 (1958), 160–80; Kurt Wais, 'Le roman d'artiste: E. T. A. Hoffmann et Balzac', in *La Littérature narrative d'imagination*, Colloque de Strasbourg (Paris: PUF, 1961), pp. 137–52; Olivier Bonard, *La Peinture dans la création balzacienne: Invention et vision picturale de* La Maison du Chat-qui-pelote *au* Père Goriot (Geneva: Droz, 1969).

[61] Lucie Wannufel, 'Balzac, lecteur des Élixirs du Diable', 57–67; Lucie Wannufel, 'Présence d'Hoffmann dans les œuvres de Balzac (1829–1835)', 45–56; Marie-France Janin, 'Quelques emprunts possibles de Balzac à Hoffmann', 69–75, all *L'Année balzacienne* (1970).

approaches have diversified considerably, with works appearing that deal more closely with, for example, Hoffmann's role in the development of the European Gothic and French Romanticism; with both writers' early contributions to the development of the detective story; and with Balzac's depiction of and relationship to Germany more broadly.[62]

José-Luis Diaz places considerable doubt on Balzac's enthusiasm for Hoffmann in an article of 2012 in which he describes Balzac's unique development of 'un fantastique social, qui tire le fantastique des entrailles même d'une société désorganisée, plutôt que de la fumée de la pipe d'un conteur allemand' (a social fantastic, which draws the fantastic from the very entrails of a disorganised society, rather than from the pipe fumes of a German storyteller). Whilst Diaz puts forward a convincing portrait of Balzac's 'fantastique réel' (real fantastic), I disagree with his dismissal of Hoffmann's place in this approach. The intertwining of fantastic elements with a kind of social realism is precisely what made Hoffmann's method successful in France, as this introduction has shown.[63] Whilst Balzac's explicit adoptions of 'le fantastique' came early in his career, disappearing after the furore for Hoffmann began to abate in around 1836, the notion that reality could appear in a shimmering, fantastic guise, as Diaz notes of Balzac's method, was thoroughly Hoffmannesque in tone. And Balzac's references to Hoffmann, as I will indicate in my conclusion, did not diminish after 1836, but persisted.

Despite their obvious usefulness, considerations of reception and influence have a limited role to play in the readings that unfold in this book. As Lewis's study makes clear, our knowledge about what concrete impact Hoffmann's writings actually had on Balzac will always be uncertain, given that we do not know for certain which works of Hoffmann he read or in what detail he read them – and given the significant alterations made to Hoffmann's works by his French translators, especially by Loève-Veimars. What I intend to do in this book, by contrast, is to allow my readings to be guided by moments of synchrony and crossover, coupling readings of Balzac's Hoffmannesque compulsions with attention to both

---

[62] Gil-Curiel, *A Comparative Approach*; Hübener, *Kreisler in Frankreich*; Robert Vilain, 'Bringing the Villains to Book: Balzac and Hoffmann as Antecedents of the Modern Detective Story', *Bulletin of the John Rylands Library*, 84.3 (2002), 105–23; *Balzac und Deutschland – Deutschland und Balzac*, ed. by Bernd Kortländer and Hans T. Siepe (Tübingen: Narr Verlag, 2012).

[63] José-Luis Diaz, 'Ce que Balzac fait au fantastique', *L'Année balzacienne* 13 (2012), 61–83 (pp. 79, 82, 83).

writers' representational attitudes. By taking on the ambitious topic of mimesis, my work builds on several shorter studies of the two authors' approaches to questions of art-making and moves beyond such works by engaging its close readings as a comparative case study for a new account of mimetic thought.[64] In this way, the book is also able to respond to a point made by Sotirios Paraschas in *The Realist Author and the Sympathetic Imagination* when he observes that 'Hoffmann's impact on realism' has yet to be investigated.[65]

Lines of Mimesis is divided into two major parts: in two theoretical chapters, Part 1 lays out the conceptual groundwork for the readings developed in the three chapters of Part 2. Chapter 1 develops an account of literary mimesis from Plato to Merleau-Ponty, showing that mimesis is most productively understood not as the inert reproduction of an object's appearance, but of a particular sensory experience of that object, an experience that involves all manner of projection and identification with the object. It does so by outlining accounts of mimesis that recognise the significance of its Greek etymology (its relationship to the words 'mime' and 'mimicry'), registering an embodied impulse to *become like*, and not just to make a likeness. Moving from Plato and Aristotle and their afterlives in eighteenth-century thought, to the German Romantics (who have been accused of rejecting mimetic thought entirely), the chapter finally draws from three significant twentieth-century thinkers – Erich Auerbach, Walter Benjamin and Maurice Merleau-Ponty – in order to develop a reading of mimesis which, like the Merleau-Pontian structure of the chiasm, describes a reciprocal subject–object intertwinement. This account is grounded in short readings of extracts from Balzac's *Illusions perdues* and from Hoffmann's *Die Abenteuer der Silvester-Nacht*.

Chapter 2 examines the motif of the line as a figure for comparison. It introduces the figure of an undulating line, printed

---

[64] Pierre Brunel, 'La Tentation hoffmannesque chez Balzac', in *E. T. A. Hoffmann et la musique*, ed. by Alain Montandon (Bern: Peter Lang, 1987), pp. 315–24; Marianne Kesting, 'Das imaginierte Kunstwerk: E. T. A. Hoffmann und Balzacs *Chef d'œuvre inconnu*, mit einem Ausblick auf die gegenwärtige Situation', *Romanische Forschungen*, 102.2/3 (1990), 163–85; Max Andréoli, 'Sublime et parodie dans les *Contes Artistes* de Balzac', *L'Année balzacienne* (1994), 7–38; Dominik Müller, 'Self-Portraits of the Poet as a Painter: Narratives on Artists and the Bounds between the Arts (Hoffmann-Balzac-Stifter)', in *Text into Image: Image into Text*, ed. by Jeff Morrison and Florian Krobb (Amsterdam: Rodopi, 1997), pp. 169–74; Sigbrit Swahn, 'Le Chef d'œuvre inconnu, récit hoffmannesque de Balzac', *Studia Neophilologica* 76.2 (2004), 206–14.

[65] Sotirios Paraschas, *The Realist Author and the Sympathetic Imagination* (Oxford: Legenda, 2013), p. 83.

initially in Laurence Sterne's *Tristram Shandy* and copied out both by Hoffmann, in a little-known piece of writing, 'Fragment eines humoristischen Aufsatzes' (Fragment of a Humorous Essay), and by Balzac, more famously, as the visual epigraph to *La Peau de chagrin*. Through attention to William Hogarth's line of beauty, Johann Caspar Lavater's physiognomic contour lines, and what Andrew Piper has called the 'Romantic line', the chapter considers the line as a symbol of narrative movement and as a figure for reading. As a 'reverse ekphrastic' figure – a visual depiction of the movement of text, in which modes of image-making and text-making are equally entangled – the line, for Sterne, Hoffmann and Balzac, represents a self-reflexive meditation on the act of writing as a form of gestural mark-making.

Part 2 of *Lines of Mimesis* puts forward comparative close readings of six texts. Each of the three chapters in this section addresses a pair of narratives via an enquiry into a particular linear motif. These chapters are arranged according to thematic concerns and to the closeness of the texts considered: they begin with a structural similarity in terms of genre in Chapter 3, move to one of Balzac's implicit citations of Hoffmann in Chapter 4, and end with Balzac's one explicit claim to having imitated Hoffmann, a claim that turns out to be erroneous, in Chapter 5. In this way the chapters track a path of intensifying interrelation and contradiction: from a pair of parallel lines to a progressive line of influence or inheritance, and finally into the line turned back against itself in the shape of a cross.

Chapter 3 considers the arabesque in Balzac's *La Peau de chagrin* and Hoffmann's *Der goldne Topf*. Both narratives are indebted to the tradition of the Oriental tale, a tradition that is preserved in the arabesque motif used as epigraph in *La Peau de chagrin* and which guides the interlacing narrative strands of *Der goldne Topf*. As the protagonist learns to write (in the case of Hoffmann's Anselmus) or to narrate (in the case of Balzac's Raphaël) the ornamental arabesque is engaged as a way of mediating between fantastic and realist modes, and as a way of thinking, self-consciously, about the framing of narratives. The arabesque thus intensifies an encounter with a self that is doubled through a mimetic projection – as narrative subject and as narrative object.

Chapter 4 studies ekphrasis and figuration in Balzac's and Hoffmann's artist stories through the motif of the facial feature or trait (*Zug*), focusing on Hoffmann's *Der Artushof* and Balzac's *Le Chef-d'œuvre inconnu*. In each case the delusory mimetic ambitions of the artist figure (Hoffmann's Berklinger, Balzac's Frenhofer) are channelled through the voice of a narrator who strains to equate the narrative act with the act of painting or drawing. In Balzac's tale, furthermore, the overweening mimetic ambition shared both by the artist figure and the narrative voice is drawn out through implicit citation of Hoffmann's works, for Frenhofer is painted – through specific facial traits and contortions – as a figure of explicit Hoffmannesque and indeed 'Serapiontic' heritage. In the attempt to create not lifelikeness but life itself, the representation erupts as fragment: as an incomplete and unsatisfactory image, whose representational worth lies in its communication of a disappointing or disillusioning aesthetic experience.

Chapter 5 examines Balzac's misleading claim, in the preface to *L'Élixir de longue vie*, that this tale was inspired by Hoffmann's *Die Elixiere des Teufels*. Scholarship has been quick to prove this claim erroneous. The chapter asks what motivates Balzac's claim of having used a Hoffmannesque text as its source, and what it might mean for the reader to take such a claim seriously. In doing so it develops a close reading of the texts that centres on the repeated figure of the cross: both as a Gothic motif, violently scored across the body, and as an emblem for the crossed or contradictory literary inheritance that relates the two texts.

It is important to acknowledge at this point that the story of mimesis is a story told by and about men. In Chapter 2, I draw out a bachelor's history that begins with Colonel Trim of *Tristram Shandy* waving his stick in celebration of a life unhampered by marriage, and thus triggers a narrative of male–male reproduction in the form of copying. It courses, via male *Doppelgänger* and other kinds of self-reflection, into the final chapter, which unlocks a more explicit set of fantasies of a male-only genealogy and an intensification of the role of fathers and sons in inheritance practices. In that sense, the narrative I put forward is not just of and about men, but is 'between' men, too, following Eve Kosofsky Sedgwick's famous paradigm – not least because the artwork itself is so often gendered as female.[66] The relationship that is transacted between Hoffmann and Balzac by various kinds of material, often itself unfolding complicated narratives of artworks between men, gives rise to a set of sometimes surprisingly queer moments. I identify a particular kind of camp excess in these encounters – following Susan Sontag's association of the camp

---

[66] Eve Kosofsky Sedgwick, *Between Men: English Literature and Male Homosocial Desire* (New York, NY: Columbia University Press, 1985).

with the 'curved line' and the 'extravagant gesture'.[67] This extravagant gestural sensibility takes the form of an '-esquing', in Balzac's canonisation of the 'Hoffmannesque' as style, in my conclusion.

By unfolding its lines of mimesis as extravagant, sensuous, self-reflexive figures pertaining, in each case, to the act of writing or drawing, this book seeks out new ways of thinking about the relationship between Hoffmann and Balzac, about the fraught status of mimesis across nineteenth-century Romanticism and realism, and about the practice of comparative reading.

[67] Susan Sontag, 'Notes on "Camp"', in *Camp: Queer Aesthetics and the Performing Subject: A Reader*, ed. by Fabio Cleto (Edinburgh: Edinburgh University Press, 1999), pp. 53–65 (p. 60).

Part I

Mimesis

Chapter 1

Mimesis and the Chiasm

The question, an ancient one, is still urgent: what business does fiction have with the world? Plato's suspicion of poetry in the *Republic* is not limited to what he sees as its ontological and epistemological impoverishment, standing at two removes from the truth. In Book III he also expresses a concern about its potential to seep into the minds of its audience, particularly of the young, where it might, as if by a process of contagion, skew their behaviour in detrimental ways. From nineteenth-century fears about the corrupting influence of novels on young women to the twenty-first-century panic that new forms of digital media might trigger aggressive or self-destructive impulses in young people (couched in the promise or threat known as 'going viral'), the concern is far from unfamiliar to the modern age. If the problem of mimesis is the problem of the business between life and representations of life, then it has never been a one-way street – a funnelling of life into art – so much as a set of entanglements between the two.

Since its introduction into literary discourse by Plato in the moment of its disenfranchisement – in the voice of Socrates, who recommends its expulsion from the ideal city state – mimesis has occupied a singularly important and singularly ambiguous position in our understanding of literature's relationship to the world. It is, indeed, just as much a commonplace to speak of mimesis's bad press across the history of literary theory, and of its conflictual and undefinable character, as it is to speak of its status as 'the most long-lasting, widely held and intellectually accommodating of all theories of art in the West'.[1] The task of the present chapter is not to

---

[1] Stephen Halliwell, *The Aesthetics of Mimesis: Ancient Texts and Modern Problems* (Princeton, NJ: Princeton University Press, 2002), pp. 5–6.

reproduce a history of mimesis, nor of these debates.[2] My account here will instead pay attention to a select series of thinkers with the aim of narrating an account of mimesis not as a structure that reifies subject–object relations by pinning down 'the world' or 'reality' like a rare butterfly for examination, but as a protean figure that complicates and interferes with the subject's relation to those other elements (or elements of otherness), and that in doing so encounters the otherness that is constitutive of the self. The chapter will move from some of the earliest accounts of mimesis by Plato and Aristotle to the engagement with these accounts in eighteenth-century neo-classical thought and the complex responses to them that arose in Romanticism, and finally to the emergence of mimetic thought in the works of three twentieth-century thinkers: Erich Auerbach, Walter Benjamin and Maurice Merleau-Ponty. The account of mimesis that I trace across the works of these thinkers underlines the significance of its Greek etymology, to look beyond its 'regrettably standard' translation as 'imitation' – a word which, as Stephen Halliwell has so convincingly shown, is unable to convey the full expansiveness of mimesis – and to rediscover within it the Greek sense of mimesis as registering an impulse to mime, to *become like*, and not just to make a likeness – pertaining thus not to the reduplication in literature of objects in the world, but to a negotiation of the subject's sensory entwinement with those objects.[3]

Only rarely has mimesis ever seriously been taken to mean a reflection of reality in any discussion of it at any length – beyond shorthand strawman formulae aiming to dismiss the notion – for the obvious reason that 'reflection' and 'reality' are preposterously protean concepts. For Plato, mimesis is actually defined by its tendency to distort truths; for Aristotle and others, it is an explicitly productive power, bound up more with what is possible than with what is real. Nonetheless, the most troublesome legacy of mimesis is its apparent presupposition of a singular, reproducible reality. For thinkers such as Roland Barthes and Jacques Derrida, for whom this is an unacceptable notion, the mimetic artwork is more accurately defined as reflecting an unending series of prior representations unacknowledged as such.[4] In *S/Z*, Barthes declares that realism 'consists

---

[2] A fuller historical perspective can be found, for instance, in Gunter Gebauer and Christoph Wulf, *Mimesis: Kultur, Kunst, Gesellschaft* (Reinbek bei Hamburg: Rowohlt Taschenbuch, 1992).

[3] Halliwell, *Aesthetics of Mimesis*, p. 13.

[4] See Eric Downing, *Double Exposures: Repetition and Realism in Nineteenth-Century German Fiction* (Stanford, CA: Stanford University Press, 2002), p. 6.

not in copying the real but in copying a (depicted) copy of the real'.[5] Mimetic art reproduces and legitimises the conventions of the dominant ideology, repressing any elements that do not fit them and seeking, in Christopher Prendergast's words, 'to mask the initial (and therefore potentially arbitrary) choices on which it is based'.[6] For Nidesh Lawtoo, who has recently called for a 're-turn' to mimesis as a human condition, mimesis is most productively understood not as a 'stabilizing' reflectionism, as in what he calls 'aesthetic realism', but as a set of 'immanent, affective, embodied, and relational' impulses of the self that disturb and trouble 'the boundaries of individuation'.[7] Mimesis governs intersubjectivity: it is what makes us participative, playful, performative, porous creatures. Lawtoo's work is informed as much by a return to the explicit recognition of mimetic affect by Plato and Aristotle, and by other theorists who build on those earliest debates, as by more pressing recent developments: advances in neuroscientific research into so-called 'mirror neurons'; new forms of crowd behaviour in a world of participative digital media; new manifestations of far-right populism; and renewed reflections on contagion across human and non-human worlds prompted by the Covid-19 pandemic.

Foreshadowing this renewed approach to mimesis is another return, one that is as lumbering as it is certain: the 'spectacular come-back' into critical favour of that literary mode most committed to a mimetic approach, realism.[8] If various twentieth-century movements, most of all poststructuralism, had cast realism in a sceptical light, if not openly denounced it, on account of its apparent complicity in essentialising bourgeois ideologies, defences of realism have resurged in several recent works of criticism. These works, often informed by New Materialist approaches, seek to counter claims of realism's conservatism and bad faith by revealing it to be an inherently complex, troubled – even resistant, subversive category.[9] Such defences point,

[5] Roland Barthes, *S/Z*, trans. R. Miller (New York, NY: Hill and Wange, 1974), p. 55.

[6] Christopher Prendergast, *The Order of Mimesis* (Cambridge: Cambridge University Press, 1986), p. 13.

[7] Nidesh Lawtoo, *The Phantom of the Ego: Modernism and the Mimetic Unconscious* (East Lansing, MI: Michigan State University Press, 2013), p. 2.

[8] Jens Elze, 'Introduction: Realism, Political Aesthetics and (New) Materialism)', in *Realism: Aesthetics, Experiments, Politics*, ed. by Jens Elze (London: Bloomsbury, 2022), pp. 1–26 (p. 4). See also Charlotte Jones, *Realism, Form, and Representation in the Edwardian Novel: Synthetic Realism* (Oxford: Oxford University Press, 2021), p. 1.

[9] See, in particular, Matthew Beaumont, 'Introduction: Reclaiming Realism', in *A Concise Companion to Realism*, ed. by Matthew Beaumont (Oxford: Wiley, 2010), pp. 2–10; Audrey Jaffe, 'Introduction: Realism in Retrospect'; *Worlding Realisms*

for example, to realism's often surprisingly self-aware rhetorical strategies: its frankness about its own constitutive tropes and commitment to the critique and renewal of those tropes. A further defence is made on the basis of realism's commitment to a new regime of signification: to registering apparently marginal, meaningless or previously disregarded aspects of human and non-human lives, and thus its reorganisation of the criteria by which things are counted as meaningful – its attention to 'the *in*credible and the *im*proper realms of reality that have been excluded from prior representation'.[10]

Bound up within the poststructuralist critique of realism's essentialising tendencies is the assumption that, in mimetic or realist logic, reality and self congeal, as a single perspective on the world is naturalised. But again, recent work has shown that this self can be recuperated or restored in productive ways. George Levine, insistent that realism always involves the effort to get beyond language, has argued for its paradoxical-seeming attachment to the legacies of both idealism and empiricism, in the sense that realism is committed to mediating reality, but also to 'the interiority that perceives and distorts or penetrates it'.[11] Body and mind are always in the way, because they too are part of reality, as well as being how we experience and understand that reality. This makes realist texts uniquely rich textures of the creative self – a self that finds itself hopelessly and helplessly caught up in the othering effects of its mimetic impulses and of its own repressions. All of these rehabilitative approaches to realism are prefigured in the specifically German brand of realism – what Otto Ludwig called 'poetic' realism – which is more upfront about its totalising impulses, makes more explicit its task of 'poeticising' reality, and underscores more openly its theoretical anchoring in Romanticism.

What is notable about realism's recent critical comeback is that in many of the above accounts, discussions of mimesis remain scarce; or where they appear, the term remains part of the old, naive understanding of realism, a conservative throwback that should be jettisoned. In Anna Kornbluh's remarkable *The Order of Forms*, she argues for a renewed approach to realism 'as model', one that

Now, ed. by Lauren M. E. Goodlad, (= *Novel: A Forum on Fiction*, 49.2 (2016)); Jens Elze (ed.), *Realism: Aesthetics, Experiments, Politics*; *Peripheral Realisms*, ed. by Joe Cleary, Jed Esty and Colleen Lye (= *MLQ*, 73.3 (2012)).

[10] Elze, 'Introduction', p. 4.

[11] George Levine, 'Literary Realism Reconsidered: "The world in its length and breadth"', in *A Concise Companion to Realism*, ed. by Beaumont, pp. 13–19 (p. 16).

'dispenses with the problematic of mimetic fidelity to the single world'.[12] The aim for such new accounts is to liberate realism *from* mimesis, as from some tendentious aspiration to copy reality, rather than to rethink both together. The point of this chapter, which takes much inspiration from these recent approaches, is to reintegrate mimesis into this narrative of renewal.

The mimetic claim to reality championed by the burgeoning realism of the 1830s, far from overturning Romantic approaches to representation, as dominant literary histories claim, overlaps with a Romantic renegotiation of mimesis. This renegotiation relates primarily to the mediating presence of the mind and body of the writing or narrating self within the artwork. Whilst indebted to their advances, I am less interested in New Materialist or object-oriented approaches to mimesis and their commitment to a speculative world 'out there' that should be listened to on its own terms – or in a vision of 'reality' as only unending textual play – than in a phenomeno-logical approach to mimesis as a structure of complex interaction between self and not-self, and one that plays out in complex and varying ways in the acts of painting, drawing or writing. I wish to show in this chapter that texts drawn from both Romantic and realist literary traditions are invested in theories of mimesis not just as a reflection of the object but as a renegotiation of the role played by body and mind in the experience of that object. Such reflective representations, as I will argue across the subsequent chapters of this book, form the core interest of the fictional works of Hoffmann and Balzac. And they occupy a place within a long tradition of think-ing that aims to account for the place of the mind and body in the artwork.

Plato, Aristotle and the 'mimetic turn'

It is a well-known curiosity of mimesis that its entry into literary dis-course comes in the moment of its prohibition, when Plato, speaking through the figure of Socrates in Book III of the *Republic*, bans the mimetic poet from the ideal city state.[13] Plato's critique of mimesis is notoriously difficult to follow because he switches between a

---

[12] Anna Kornbluh, *The Order of Forms: Realism, Formalism, and Social Space* (Chicago, IL: Chicago University Press, 2019), p. 16.

[13] In standard accounts, Plato is taken to be the first thinker to bring the question of mimesis into art, and the first to define art as mimetic. For a history of pre-Platonic mimetic thinkers, such as Aristophanes, see Halliwell, *Aesthetics of Mimesis*.

definition of mimesis as enactive narrative (direct speech, as opposed to third-person narrative) and of mimesis as representation. In Book III, his specific concern is direct speech and the education of the Republic's guardian class. 'We need to come to an agreement', he declares, 'about whether we'll allow poets to narrate through mimesis, and, if so, whether they are to represent some things but not others,' having already established that different genres of writing call for different intensities and quantities of mimetic (enactive) narrative.[14] Wary that our personalities can be shaped by the stories that we hear and enact, Socrates recommends the expulsion of mimetic narrative because the representation of wicked characters risks fostering similarly wicked behaviours in the pliable minds of their actors and audiences. 'They mustn't be clever at doing or imitating slavish or shameful actions,' he warns, 'lest from enjoying the imitation, they come to enjoy the reality.'[15] Here, significantly, are the first glimpses of a dynamic reading of mimesis in which actors, artists and audiences are re-formed and acted upon by objects of art.

The most well-known chapter in Plato's critique is given in Book X, when Socrates addresses the epistemological impoverishment of mimetic products. The visual or literary artwork, Socrates explains, is a version of experience placed at two removes from the truth. The hierarchy he establishes leads from ideal forms to phenomenal forms (appearances of the ideal forms), to mimetic forms (imitations of the appearances). To take his own example – a bed – the wooden structure we sleep on is the work of a craftsman, and is crafted in reference to an original pattern or 'idea'. A painted or a literary representation of a (particular) bed is a copy of the thing that is already a copy, and it is thus at one further remove from the idea. For this reason, mimesis constitutes a threat to knowledge and order: 'imitation is far removed from the truth, for it touches only a small part of each thing and a part that is itself only an image'.[16] A mimetic artist thus has no grasp on real knowledge. This means that the mimetic artist is a producer of illusions, having 'neither knowledge nor right opinion about whether the things he makes are fine or bad'.[17] The Platonic suspicion of mimesis is the fear of a world ruled by fragmentary appearances, of copies standing in for the real thing. The image he uses here is the mirror: 'With it you can quickly

---

[14] Plato, *Republic*, trans. G. M. A. Grube and C. D. C. Reeve (Indianapolis, IN: Hackett Publishing, 1992), 394d.
[15] Ibid., 395c.
[16] Ibid., 598b.
[17] Ibid., 602b.

make the sun, the things in the heavens, the earth, yourself, the other animals, manufactured items, plants, and everything else mentioned just now' – or rather, as Glaucon qualifies – 'I could make them appear, but I couldn't make the things themselves as they truly are.'[18]

In the final movement of Plato's critique, he turns to mimesis's threat to rationality. This is where Socrates speaks most severely, declaring that the mimetic poet 'arouses, nourishes, and strengthens [the irrational] part of the soul and so destroys the rational one'.[19] Mimesis, by virtue of its being a duplicative power, is also a duplicitous one, appealing to our most irrational selves and duping us into believing in false realities. Mimesis presents a taxonomical threat and an educational threat – a fundamental threat to systems of knowledge – for it can lead to unthinking imitation by weak or unformed minds. Most of all, then, it is a threat by virtue of its multifariousness and plasticity, of its claim that, like a mirror, it can take on anything, be anything; and of the worry, finally, that its audience might be convinced by its phantom reflections.

Whilst Aristotle, like Plato, designates all art as mimetic, he does away with its dependence on a hypothesised truth and instead makes a case for mimesis as a force innate to all humans, who grow and learn through imitating one another. Rather than being epistemologically damaged copies of imitations of truths, Aristotle argues, artworks deliver universal truths in particular forms. 'The poet is engaged in mimesis, just like a painter,' he writes, 'and the object of his mimesis must in every case be one of three things: either the kind of thing that was or is the case; or the kind of thing that is said or thought to be the case; or the kind of thing that ought to be the case.'[20] The significance of Aristotle's intervention is in his redefinition of mimesis as a dynamic interaction between the world, artist and artwork. Mimesis has more to do with making than with copying, being committed to the realisation of possibilities, of fictions: it is 'a positive, potent force, whose implications of productive control and purpose should dispel any lingering associations of the derivative or passive from the understanding of mimesis'.[21] Aristotelian mimesis is an ethical practice, one that through the successful arousal of 'pity' and 'fear' in its audience leads to the cathartic refinement or release of these emotions and helps to foster identification, self-reflection and empathy

---

[18] Ibid., 596d, 596e.
[19] Ibid., 605b.
[20] Aristotle, *Poetics*, trans. by Malcolm Heath (London: Penguin, 1996), p. 42.
[21] Stephen Halliwell, *Aristotle's Poetics* (Chicago, IL: University of Chicago Press, 1998), pp. 58–9.

in those beings upon whom it acts. Furthermore, his emphasis on a mimetic impulse or instinct innate to humans suggests that there is no point in banishing mimesis from the city state. It has long ago taken root and is already part of what we do and who we are.

Aristotle thus takes as given not only an understanding of mimesis as the making of representations but also as a faculty of human behaviour. Branches of mimetic thought have continued to address both of these kinds of mimesis and the potential crossover between them – from recent discoveries in the sciences about the 'mirror neurons' that govern our interpersonal behaviour, to René Girard's literary-anthropological concept of mimetic desire,[22] to Nidesh Lawtoo's claim that 'mimesis is first and foremost rooted in an immanent, embodied, and shared human condition on planet Earth that is constitutive of our post-literary, digitized and increasingly precarious lives'.[23] Certain human-oriented, behaviourist elements of mimesis, as attempts to account for the place of the self in the making of representations, are central to the writings of Walter Benjamin and Maurice Merleau-Ponty that will be discussed later in this chapter.

Romanticism and the Return to Nature

A persistent critical narrative, beginning in the 1950s, describes the emergence of Romanticism in Germany and England in the late eighteenth century as a fundamental 'turning point' in the history of literary representation, spelling the decline of mimesis and the emergence of 'the modernist insistence on the autopoietic nature of poetry'.[24] This leaves Romanticism as a clumsy and unconvincing break in the history of mimesis: a gap between the idealising 'imitatio' of neoclassicism and realism's commitment to reflecting the world 'as it is'. The most famous example of this narrative is given in M. H. Abrams's *The Mirror and the Lamp* (1953), which describes Romantic aesthetics in terms of a paradigm shift charted

[22] Colin Burrow, *Imitating Authors: Plato to Futurity* (Oxford: Oxford University Press, 2019), p. 39; René Girard, *Deceit, Desire, and the Novel: Self and Other in Literary Structure*, trans. by Yvonne Freccero (Baltimore, MD: Johns Hopkins University Press, 1965).

[23] Nidesh Lawtoo, 'The Mimetic Condition: Theories and Concepts', *Countertext*, 6.1 (2022), 1–22 (p. 5).

[24] Mattias Pirholt, *Metamimesis: Imitation in Goethe's* Wilhelm Meisters Lehrjahre *and Early German Romanticism* (Rochester, NY: Camden House, 2012), p. 3.

across a metaphorical field – from the passive, rationalist image of the artwork as reflective mirror to a set of new 'expressive' metaphors including the overflowing fountain and the glowing lamp. The shift from reflection to expression was indicative, Abrams argues, of a transformation in the relationship between mind and world, subject and object, leading from the philosophical revolutions of the late eighteenth century. In Romanticism, the mind projects itself into the universe, thus turning the world into the malleable property of the mind.[25] René Wellek writes correspondingly, in 1955, of the 'rise of an emotional concept of poetry [. . .] and the implied rejection of the imitation theory' in the Romantic period.[26] Lilian Furst claims that the Romantics 'vehemently rejected the whole idea of imitation in favor of the visionary powers of the imagination'; Lilian Furst claims that the Romantics 'vehemently rejected the whole idea of imitation in favor of the visionary powers of the imagination', and Romanticism plays no role in Gebauer and Wulf's *Mimesis* (1992).[27]

Romanticism, by all accounts, was a movement characterised by transformation and revolution. The Romantic circles in Germany, England and France wanted new things from their art and their criticism, including a rethinking of elements of neoclassical aesthetics that they saw as obsolete, and a renewed emphasis on artistic originality and the self-consciousness of the artwork. But correctives to the narrative of Romanticism's break with mimesis – offered notably by Stephen Halliwell, Matthias Pirholt and Frederick Burwick – show that a more ambiguous understanding of mimesis, dependent on a complicated relationship between the artist and a world perceived to be finite and contradictory, was at work within Romanticism's transformative projects. Mimesis has always been riddled with contradictions, and if the Romantics were hyper-aware of this, it did not lead them to reject it: on the contrary, they sought new ways to account for these contradictions. Romanticism did not jettison mimetic thought but refined it.

Even in the neoclassical period of the eighteenth century, when the doctrine of mimesis was more or less taken for granted, when placed under scrutiny the reality predicated by mimesis was a protean,

[25] M. H. Abrams, *The Mirror and the Lamp: Romantic Theory and the Critical Tradition* (Oxford: Oxford University Press, 1976), pp. 64–5.

[26] René Wellek, *A History of Modern Criticism: 1750–1950*, 8 vols (London: Jonathan Cape, 1955), II, p. 2.

[27] Lilian Furst, *All Is True: The Claims and Strategies of Realist Fiction* (Duke, NC: Duke University Press, 1995), p. 189; Gebauer and Wulf, *Mimesis*.

changeable thing.[28] As M. H. Abrams shows, the core doctrine of neoclassical poetics, wrested somewhat clumsily from Aristotle – the 'imitation of nature' – was so amorphous in practice that it came to mean a number of different things. The 'mirror' held up by the artwork to nature was variously a selective or improving mirror and nature was pruned, refined or embellished as necessary. Abrams cites two paradigmatic variations of the idea, the first given by Charles Batteux – who decreed that art should imitate the most beautiful elements of nature, 'la belle nature' – and the second by Winckelmann, who recommended the imitation of nature as glimpsed through the patterns of ancient classical works of art.[29] In both, 'nature' is less a transcendent reality, more a set of rhetorical patterns or schemata to inform the artist's approach.

Towards the end of the century, as, on almost every front, the old ways of doing things came under the strain of new dissenting approaches, the 'imitation of nature' doctrine was adapted in a way that would provide the material for new Romantic theories of poetic productivity. Karl Philipp Moritz argued in 'Über die bildende Nachahmung des Schönen' (On the Formative Imitation of the Beautiful, 1788) that beauty in art is to be understood as an autonomous and disinterested whole, analogous to beauty in nature. He writes that 'jedes schöne Ganze aus der Hand des bildenden Künstlers, ist daher im Kleinen ein Abdruck des höchsten Schönen im großen Ganzen der Natur' (every beautiful whole from the hand of the creative artist is therefore a print, in miniature, of the highest form of the beautiful in the great wholeness of Nature).[30] The artwork is not an imitation of natural forms; rather, the artist's creativity is to be understood in terms of the formative powers of nature. The relationship is not just one of analogy but of indexicality, in the sense that the artist's creative impulses are an 'Abdruck' (imprint) of natural creativity. Human beings, as parts in a natural system, are imbued with its formative potential, and that potential is realised in their artworks. Praising Moritz's insights, August Wilhelm Schlegel proclaimed in his Berlin lectures that art 'should' imitate nature, in this new sense of nature as creative process:

---

[28] Abrams writes: 'Through most of the eighteenth century, the tenet that art is an imitation seemed almost too obvious to need iteration or proof.' *The Mirror and the Lamp*, p. 11.

[29] See Abrams, *The Mirror and the Lamp*, pp. 35–9.

[30] Karl Philipp Moritz, 'Über die bildende Nachahmung des Schönen', *Werke*, 3 vols, ed. Horst Günther (Frankfurt am Main: Insel, 1981), II, pp. 549–64.

Wird nun Natur in dieser würdigsten Bedeutung genommen, nicht als eine Masse von Hervorbringungen, sondern als das Hervorbringende selbst; und der Ausdruck Nachahmung in dem edleren Sinne, wo es nicht heißt, die Äusserlichkeiten eines Menschen nachäffen, sondern sich die Weise seines Handelns zu eigen machen, so ist nichts mehr gegen den Grundsatz einzuwenden, noch zu ihm hinzuzufügen: *die Kunst soll die Natur nachahmen.* Das heißt nämlich, sie soll wie die Natur selbständig schaffend, organisiert und organisierend, lebendige Werke bilden, die nicht erst durch einen fremden Mechanismus, wie etwa eine Pendeluhr, sondern durch inwohnende Kraft, wie das Sonnensystem, beweglich sind, und vollendet in sich selbst zurückkehren.[31]

If nature is now taken in this most deserving sense, not as a mass of productions but as the productive process itself; and the word imitation in the more noble sense, where it does not mean to ape a person's appearance but rather to make his specific way of acting into one's own, then there is no more to protest at, or to append to, the law that art should imitate nature. It means, namely, that art should be, like nature, independently creative, organised and organising; should form living works which are operated not by a foreign mechanism, like a clock, but rather by an internal power, like the solar system, and should close in on themselves as fullness.

The artwork is a self-enclosed microcosm, Schlegel explains, containing its own possibilities for being. By revealing the formative powers of the artist, the artwork is analogous to a natural product. Whilst those powers are productive rather than reproductive, they are inherited from nature itself. When Schlegel does indeed dismiss certain kinds of imitative thought elsewhere in the lecture in the terms of 'Nachahmen, Kopiren, Widerholen' (imitating, copying, repeating), etc., he is disparaging a rhetorical mode whilst clearly preserving a strong mimetic understanding of art elsewhere.[32] Romantic mimesis is in this sense a re-turn to Nature, a redefinition of what Nature can mean for the artist. This renewed understanding of mimesis echoes Goethe's new understanding of the art–nature relationship in 'Einfache Nachahmung der Natur, Manier, Stil' (Simple Imitation of Nature, Manner, Style) (1789), in which he praises 'style' as the third and final stage of the artist's development leading from, first,

---

[31] August Wilhelm Schlegel, 'Ueber das Verhaeltniss der Schoenen Kunst zur Natur; Ueber Taeuschung und Wahrscheinlichkeit; Ueber Styl und Manier', in *August Wilhelm Schlegel. Kritische Ausgabe der Vorlesungen*, ed. by Ernst Behler and others, 4 vols (Paderborn: Brill/Schöningh, 1989–), vol. II.1, pp. 256–88 (p. 262).
[32] Ibid., p. 256.

the dutiful 'simple imitation' of natural objects and, second, the free-wheeling subjectivity of 'manner'. Style, for Goethe, arises from a penetrative understanding of nature, one that is able to do away with any superfluous elements in order to reveal the essence of things, unshackled by convention.[33]

As Frederick Burwick and others have so persuasively shown, the key contribution of Romanticism to mimetic theory was to doggedly pursue those interpretations by Goethe, Moritz and others of the 'imitation of nature' doctrine as pertaining to the imitation of natural creativity, rather than of natural products, such that the process of art-making becomes a process of revealing not only the object but also the 'shaping presence of the mind'.[34] Paradigmatic for Burwick's argument is the work of Samuel Taylor Coleridge, a keen reader of Schelling, and his differentiation between 'copy' as the replication of an object and the more expansive 'imitation, as an exposition of the mental process of apprehension'.[35]

In 1860, Victor Hugo remarked that 'Ce qu'on a appelé il y a trente ans la dispute des classiques et des romantiques n'était pas autre chose qu'un rappel à la nature. Traduire l'homme de l'homme même, et non de tel ou tel livre' (What was termed, thirty years ago, the quarrel between the classics and the romantics was nothing other than a return to nature. To translate man from man himself, and not from this or that book). As Maurice Z. Schroder points out, 'this is equivalent to saying that *romantique* means more or less what we mean by "realistic"'.[36] Realism, too, was oriented by what it saw as a return to nature, a return to the world as it is: to become aware of the conventions through which we see the world, and to think beyond them. Oscar Wilde, in the voice of Vivian, notes the frequency with which artistic movements begin with the familiar cry 'Let us return to Life and Nature.'[37] Thus Charles Rosen and Henri Zerner are able to claim that 'Realism is both a direct outgrowth of Romanticism and a reaction against it, a reaction that, as we have seen, is predicted and

---

[33] Johann Wolfgang von Goethe, 'Einfache Nachahmung, Manier, Stil', in *Goethes Werke*, 13 vols, ed. by Erich Trunz and others (Hamburg: Christian Wegner Verlag, 1948–), XII, pp. 30–4.

[34] Frederick Burwick, *Mimesis and its Romantic Reflections* (University Park, PA: Pennsylvania State University Press, 2001), p. 8.

[35] Ibid., p. 8.

[36] Maurice Z. Schroder, 'Roman – Romanesque – Romantique – Romantisme', in *'Romantic' and its Cognates: The European History of a Word*, ed. by Hans Eichner (Toronto: University of Toronto Press, 1972), pp. 263–92 (p. 282).

[37] Oscar Wilde, 'The Decay of Lying', in *The Complete Works of Oscar Wilde* (London: HarperCollins, 2003), pp. 1071–92 (p. 1078).

accommodated by Romantic theory.'[38] Romanticism and realism both set about to trouble received hierarchies of meaning; to sweep away the accumulation of conventional ways of understanding the world and get back to what the world *is*. It is from a study of these foundational connections between Romanticism and realism that Erich Auerbach derives much of his thinking on nineteenth-century mimesis.

Erich Auerbach

Erich Auerbach has been accused of ignoring the Romantics entirely.[39] But as the first modern writer to develop a full account of mimesis – though it is an elusive and implicit account, unfolding accumulatively through a series of close readings – Auerbach demonstrates that modern realism emerges from a set of Romantic impulses. *Mimesis: Dargestellte Wirklichkeit in der abendländischen Literatur* (Mimesis: The Representation of Reality in Western Literature, 1946) is the first full work dedicated to mimesis, and is probably the most well-known and acclaimed chapter of scholarship on it. Auerbach's reading of a passage from Balzac's *Le Père Goriot* in *Mimesis* has, in turn, become a canonical moment within Balzac scholarship.

Foundational to Auerbach's reading of Balzac is his principle of the mixing of styles or 'Stilmischung', and Balzac's realism is central to the formulation of that principle. Balzac does not appear until the eighteenth chapter of twenty, by which time Auerbach has moved us through readings of literary works from antiquity to the Enlightenment. But in two essays published in the decade prior to *Mimesis*, 'Romantik und Realismus' (Romanticism and Realism, 1933) and 'Über die ernste Nachahmung des Alltäglichen' (On the Serious Imitation of the Everyday, 1937), and in other appendages to the text such as the Epilogue and the Epilegomena, the importance of Balzac to the formulation of Auerbach's overarching ideas becomes apparent. In briefly outlining Auerbach's theory of 'Stiltrennung' (the separation of styles) and 'Stilmischung' (the mixing of styles), this chapter cannot attend to the fullness of the ideas expressed in *Mimesis*. I begin only to sketch out Balzac's place within them, and consequently to further develop the particular strain of mimetic

---

[38] Charles Rosen and Henri Zerner, *Romanticism and Realism: The Mythology of Nineteenth-Century Art* (New York, NY: Viking, 1984), p. 23.
[39] Burwick, *Mimesis*, p. 1.

thinking that is central to this chapter: one that locates the beginnings of modern realism in what Auerbach understands as a sensory experience that emerges from the literature and thought of Romanticism.

The readings in *Mimesis* are arranged around a set of contrasts between the principle of the separation of styles – the strict differentiation of elite from vernacular styles, of the sublime tragic from the lowly comic, which characterises the texts of antiquity and, again, of the neoclassical tradition – and the commingling of styles in Judaeo-Christian texts and, again, in modern realism. This principle is laid out in the well-known first chapter, in which Auerbach sets a passage from Homer's *Odyssey* – Odysseus's return to Ithaca – against the story of the sacrifice of Isaac from the Old Testament. Homer's text, Auerbach shows, deals with heroic figures in a style that befits their status. Every detail is given space in an overwhelming present; there is no tension, no background; nothing remains hidden or unexpressed or undetected. Narrative developments are set in a relationship of parataxis or appendage, rather than of subordination to one another.[40] In the piece taken from the Old Testament, on the other hand, we are given the externalisation of only what is necessary for the purpose of the narrative, such that it remains tense and mysterious, despite its direction towards a single goal. Where the Homeric poems are built upon the rigidity of the static hierarchy of Greek society, depicting only the life of the ruling class, the biblical passage shows the events and individuals of everyday domestic life to be resonant with the sublime. To track movements of historical significance through the actions of a humble individual represents the furthest literary remove from the separation of styles. Action taking place entirely amongst common people would, in antique terms, be mired in a low or intermediate style, betokening farce or comedy. But the Christian texts reveal 'das Sichentfalten geschichtlicher Kräfte' (the unfolding of historical forces) in the midst of everyday reality.[41]

In the afterword, one of the few parts of the book that offers something like a statement of methodology, Auerbach confirms that the story of Christ, with its 'rücksichtslosen Mischung von alltäglich Wirklichem und höchster, erhabener Tragik' (ruthless mixture of everyday reality and the highest, most sublime tragedy), had first conquered the classical principle of separated styles.[42] A second

---

[40] Erich Auerbach, *Mimesis: Dargestellte Wirklichkeit in der abendländischen Literatur* (Tübingen: Francke Verlag, 2010), p. 13. Translations consulted are listed in the bibliography: these have been modified at times to bring them closer to the original.

[41] Ibid., p. 47.

[42] Ibid., p. 516.

break in this literary history is effected by Dante's *Inferno*. Dante's is the closest that literature had ever come, Auerbach argues, to true realism, for never before had 'so viel Kunst und Ausdruckskraft' (so much art and so much expressive power) been used 'um die irdis-che Form der menschlichen Gestalt bis zu einer fast schmerzhaft eindringlichen Anschauung zu bringen' (to produce an almost pain-fully immediate impression of the earthly reality of human beings).[43] For the first time, humans are represented as concrete and physical, as well as sublime and tragic, beings. Stendhal and Balzac – whose human comedy tips its cap to the *Divina Commedia* – would be the next major figures in this narrative. In breaking with the highly regu-lated and conventionalised neoclassical literatures of the sixteenth and seventeenth centuries, Stendhal and Balzac present lowly indi-viduals from daily life as the subjects of 'ernster, problematischer, ja sogar tragischer Darstellung' (serious, problematic and even tragic representation).[44] The history Auerbach narrates, then, is a history of violations against stylistic regulation, in the place of which are offered alternative representational principles committed to the depiction of everyday life. No explicit definition of 'mimesis' is given in *Mimesis* – indeed, the text acts out the elusiveness of that term in its very refusal to define it. But realist literature, for Auerbach, is the product of intertwined aims: conveying lived experience in all its physical immediacy, and imbuing it with meaning.

Before returning to the eighteenth chapter of *Mimesis* and to its reading of a passage from Balzac's *Le Père Goriot,* one of Auerbach's earlier essays may help us more closely understand the developments in his thinking that led to this chapter and that help explain its importance in his wider narrative. As he recounts in the 'Epilegomena' to *Mimesis*, the motif of a stylistic break first became clear to Auerbach during his studies of Dante in the 1920s. It was later, during the time he spent teaching at Marburg before his exile to Istanbul, that he realised the principle of modern realism could be presented in the same way. This thinking was developed in the two essays of 1933 and 1937 to which I will now turn.[45] 'Romantik und Realismus', the first of these, opens with a characteristically lofty claim:

---

[43] Ibid., p. 191.
[44] Ibid., p. 515.
[45] Erich Auerbach, 'Epilegomena zu Mimesis', *Romanische Forschungen*, 65.1/2 (1953), 1–18 (p. 14).

Es wird wohl als die eigentümlichste literarische Leistung des 19. Jh. anerkannt werden müssen, daß es zuerst den Versuch gemacht hat, den Menschen in der ganzen Breite seiner alltäglichen Wirklichkeit darzustellen.[46]

It will be recognised as the literary achievement most characteristic of the nineteenth century that it made the attempt, for the first time, to represent humans in the whole breadth of their everyday reality.

To readers of *Mimesis*, this claim is familiar. So too is the argument that, in the texts of Stendhal and Balzac, serious tragedy is embedded in everyday reality, and that the condition for the emergence of tragic realism is a break with the classical principle of *Stiltrennung*.[47] Only in this way is everyday reality reconceived as a space in which serious events may take place: no longer as an 'Einbruch in das Tragische' (interruption of the tragic) but as the tragic's rightful home.[48]

The less familiar contribution of 'Romantik und Realismus' is its argument that Balzac's realism derives from his '*romantischer* Geist' (*romantic* spirit, my emphasis).[49] Readers will note that the adjective 'romantisch' appears as a descriptor for Balzac with remarkable frequency in chapter 18 of *Mimesis*. In the earlier essay, the rationale for this is made clear. It was not realism but Romanticism, with its commitment to interiority, subjectivity and 'die Sehnsucht nach der echten Wirklichkeit des strömenden Lebens' (the longing for authentic reality amidst life's turbulence), that first effected the breakthrough of reality in literature that would be necessary for the emergence of realism.[50] Realism was thus born *from within* Romanticism, occasioned by its departure from neoclassical doctrines and by its return to the immediate human subject. If the realists were not themselves aware of this, Balzac's Romantic tendencies can nonetheless be detected in 'seine Formlosigkeit, sein Gefühlsüberschwang, seine Neigung zu melodramatischer Erfindung und Kommentierung' (his formlessness, his abundance of feeling, his tendency to melodramatic invention and commentary) and in his imaginative prowess: 'Was Balzac gibt, ist nicht Bericht oder Kritik, es ist Leben. Und Leben verlangt, um ganz und unmittelbar erscheinend dargestellt zu werden,

---

[46] Erich Auerbach, 'Romantik und Realismus', in *Erich Auerbach: Geschichte und Aktualität eines europäischen Philologen*, ed. by Karlheinz Barck and Martin Treml (Berlin: Kadmos, 2007), pp. 426–38 (p. 426).
[47] Ibid., p. 428.
[48] Ibid., p. 429.
[49] Ibid., p. 432.
[50] Ibid,. p. 431.

Phantasie' (what Balzac gives is not reportage or criticism, it is life. And the full and immediate representation of life demands fantasy).[51]

This link between the representational attitudes of Romanticism and realism is expressed in an elusive formulation that denotes a sensory experience: 'Leib der Zeit', or the 'body of the age'. The inner connection between Romanticism and the first works of realism is to be found in their giving body to historical conditions, in their enactment of mixing styles: 'um den Geist nicht allein, sondern um einen *Leib der Zeit*' (not only for the spirit but for the *body of the age*, my emphasis).[52] Romanticism and realism are bound together by a common project of giving body to time, history, meaning: transforming them into characters, places, plots. By prioritising the place of bodily and sensory experience in Romantic and realist methods, which he sees not as antagonistic but as twinned aesthetic impulses, Auerbach elegantly refutes any history that sees Romanticism to have ignored, overturned or turned away from mimesis. On the contrary, Romanticism is understood as the material bedrock of the realist approach.

We are now in a position to turn to Auerbach's close reading of *Le Père Goriot* in chapter 18 of *Mimesis* and to its focus on what Auerbach terms a 'harmony' between the character Mme Vauquer and her 'Milieu'.[53] Choosing a passage of *Le Père Goriot* that is as rich in description as it is lacking in action – the introductory description of Mme Vauquer's boarding house – Auerbach identifies as specific to Balzac's method an osmotic, organic relationship between person and place. Madame Vauquer is a being who 'explique' (explicates) her environment, which reciprocally 'implique' (implicates) her character. Place is replete with character, character pregnant with place. The relationship is an explicitly reciprocal or chiasmic one. Neither can be understood without the other; each is the condition of the other's being. This 'harmony thesis' is a response to Balzac's enthusiasm for organic and animal metaphors. Balzac's character types are bound by necessity to their environment and are typified like animals under zoological scrutiny. Hayden White identifies Auerbach's reading as an example of a figural reading, wherein 'the literary text appears as a synecdoche of its context, which is to say it is a particular kind of a fulfilment of the figure of the context [. . .] or a fulfilment of the figure of the author's experience of his/her

---

milieu'.[54] Despite no explicit citation of 'Romantik und Realismus', chapter 18's reading is dependent on that earlier essay and on the crucial insight Auerbach makes within it: that sensory experience underlies the mimetic project, and that representation is a project of turning spirit into body.

The next stage in Auerbach's argument is to draw out elements in the passage that he characterises as 'dämonisch' (demonic) – mostly pertaining to Mme Vauquer's vaguely articulated witchiness – in order, implicitly, to tease out the Romantic streak that forms a crucial part of Balzac's realism: 'die Gegenstände und Personen, welche ein Milieu bilden, [gewinnen] fur ihn oft eine Art zweite, von ihrer rational erfaßbaren verschiedene, aber weit wesentlichere Bedeutung: eine Bedeutung, die man am besten mit dem Adjektiv "dämonisch" bezeichnet' (the objects and persons that form a *milieu* [earn] for him often a kind of second significance, far removed from their rationally comprehensible one but far more fundamental: a significance best characterised by the adjective 'demonic').[55] We find a clue to this reading in Auerbach's earlier essay 'Über die ernste Nachahmung des Alltäglichen', an essay often twinned with 'Romantik und Realismus', in which he describes Balzac as 'so sehr Kind seiner Zeit, dass er Wirtschaft, Gesellschaft, Politik, menschlich-innergeschichtliches Schicksal nicht mehr rein vernünftig und moralistisch zu zergliedern vermag, sondern geheime und magische Kräfte in ihnen spürt' (so much a child of his time that he is not merely able, judiciously and with moral acuity, to unpick the economy, society, politics and the intimate histories of human destiny, but rather feels secret and magical forces within them), such that Balzac may be said to 'demonise' the modern social life of humans.[56] This, too, is part of a fantastic, figural reading: Balzac is able to indicate social, economic and political forces and conditions through elements of the fantastic. The portrait of Mme Vauquer as a witch-like, greasy church rat is, as Auerbach points out, prefigurative of her character as it unfolds in the plot, which is expressive of the self-serving greed of the lower classes in the emerging economy

---

[54] Hayden White, 'Auerbach's Literary History: Figural Causation and Modernist Historicism', in *Literary History and the Challenge of Philology. The Legacy of Erich Auerbach*, ed. by Seth Lerer (Stanford, CA: Stanford University Press, 1996), pp. 124–39 (pp. 129–30).

[55] Auerbach, *Mimesis*, p. 439.

[56] Erich Auerbach, 'Über die ernste Nachahmung des Alltäglichen', in *Erich Auerbach: Geschichte und Aktualität eines europäischen Philologen*, ed. by Barck and Treml, pp. 439–65 (p. 461).

of the July Monarchy: 'zu jeder gemeinen Niedrigkeit fähig, um das eigene Los ein wenig zu verbessern' (capable of any baseness in order to improve her own situation a little).[57]

Auerbach has effectively established a framework through which the presence of E. T. A. Hoffmann – known for his dark, 'demonic' version of Romanticism – may be examined across *La Comédie humaine*. First, Balzac's interest in depicting the tragedy and melodrama of the everyday is dependent on the insights of Romanticism, a project that unpicks the conventions and hierarchical distinctions of neoclassicism and understands representation as a process concerned with the 'making bodily' of history and spirit. The notion of mimesis as a sensory experience will shortly be explored in the writings of Walter Benjamin, one of Auerbach's contemporaries. Second, the 'demonic' elements in Balzacian description are remnants of his particular attraction to the supernatural when alluding to irrational, impersonal forces – biology and history – that underlie Balzac's 'atmospheric realism' and zoological tropes. Romanticism, in its dark forms – as personified by Hoffmann – both energises and haunts Balzac's mimetic project.

Walter Benjamin

Walter Benjamin, a friend and contemporary of Erich Auerbach, was, like Auerbach, in political exile from Germany at the time during which he developed his own theory of mimesis. Benjamin's writings on mimesis take the form of two short essays. The first, 'Lehre vom Ähnlichen' (Doctrine of the Similar), was written in the unstable political atmosphere of Berlin in early 1933, the same year in which Auerbach published 'Romantik und Realismus'. At the end of February of that year, Benjamin wrote to Gershom Scholem of the problems he saw before him in the next few months: 'von denen ich weder weiß, wie ich sie in noch außerhalb Deutschlands überstehen kann' (which I do not know how I will survive, in or outside of Germany).[58] Benjamin returned to the mimesis essay in the summer of that year, which he spent in Ibiza, separated, like Auerbach, from his books and manuscripts. At that time, Benjamin was forced to write to Scholem to ask for a copy of an earlier essay

---

[57] Ibid., p. 440.
[58] Cited in Walter Benjamin, *Gesammelte Schriften*, vol. II.3, pp. 950–1. Hereafter references to Benjamin's *Gesammelte Schriften* will be abbreviated in the footnotes as *GS*.

on language theory, 'Über Sprache überhaupt und über die Sprache des Menschen' (On Language as Such and on the Language of Man, 1916), in order to complete the new piece on his return to Paris in the autumn, in a version now called 'Über das mimetische Vermögen' (On the Mimetic Faculty).

For Auerbach, taking mimesis as a serious question means to turn to the conditions of historical reality as they are disclosed through texts. For the two German Jewish scholars forced into emigration from National-Socialist Germany, literary mimesis emerges explicitly as a topic in the state of exile: a state of forced reflection on a Western tradition from which prevailing historical forces have excluded them.[59] A sparse correspondence persisted between the two during the years they spent abroad in the mid-1930s, beginning with Auerbach's response to the earliest published passages of Benjamin's *Berliner Kindheit um 1900* (Berlin Childhood around 1900). For Auerbach, who, like Benjamin, was born and grew up in Berlin-Charlottenburg, Benjamin's writings ring with nostalgia. In a letter from Rome dated 23 September 1935, he writes of Benjamin's 'verschollen-heimatliche Töne' (forgotten homely tones); and in a subsequent letter from Florence dated 6 October 1935, he describes the *Berliner Kindheit* as 'Ihr Kindheitsbuch, das ja auch das unsere ist' (your childhood book, which is also ours).[60] Two years later and settled in Istanbul, in a letter of 3 January 1937, he writes more explicitly of the political situation facing them both:

> Immer deutlicher wird mir, dass die gegenwärtige Weltlage nichts ist als eine List der Vorsehung, um uns auf einem blutigen und qualvollen Wege zur Internationale der Trivialität und zur Esperantokultur zu führen. Ich habe das schon in Deutschland und in Italien, angesichts der grauenvollen Unechtheit der Blubopropaganda vermutet, aber hier erst wird es mir fast zur Gewissheit.[61]

[59] See Steffan Davies, 'Exile and Reality in Erich Auerbach's *Mimesis*', in *From the Enlightenment to Modernism: Three Centuries of German Literature: Essays for Ritchie Robertson*, ed. by Carolin Düttlinger, Kevin Hilliard and Charlie Louth (Oxford: Legenda, 2022), pp. 333–46.

[60] Cited in Karlheinz Barck, '5 Briefe Erich Auerbachs an Walter Benjamin in Paris', *Zeitschrift für Germanistik*, 9.6 (1988), 688–94 (pp. 690–1).

[61] This letter is cited in full in Martin Vialon, 'Verdichtete Geschichtserfahrung. Erich Auerbachs Brief vom 3.1.1937 an Walter Benjamin', in *Raum der Freiheit. Reflexionen über Idee und Wirklichkeit. Festschrift für Antonia Grunenberg*, ed. by Michale Daxner and others (Bielefeld: Transcript, 2009), pp. 123–50. This is the fourth of five of Auerbach's letters to Benjamin from Istanbul (see Barck, '5 Briefe'); only one of Benjamin's responses has survived. See also Karlheinz Barck and Anthony Reynolds, 'Walter Benjamin and Erich Auerbach: Fragments of a Correspondence', *Diacritics*, 22.3/4 (1992), 81–3.

It is becoming increasingly clear to me that the present international situation is nothing but a ruse of providence designed to lead us along a bloody and torturous path to an international state of triviality and a culture of Esperanto. I suspected as much in Germany and Italy, in view of the dreadful inauthenticity of the 'blood and soil' propaganda, but only here has it almost reached the point of certainty.

The reference here is specifically to the Westernising reforms in Turkey throughout the 1930s. But Auerbach also laments the loss of meaning, complexity and correspondence in a world facing the perverse homogeneity of fascism. For Kader Konuk and Victoria Holbrook in *East West Mimesis*, Auerbach's psychic 'state of exile' pre-dates his actual emigration from Germany: they argue that his sense of detachment from his own historical environment was a life-long, and partially self-fashioned, identity (and that he was not, for example, as bereft of books in Istanbul as the epilogue to *Mimesis* suggests).[62] Undoubtedly there is lodged, in the groundwork for a study on 'the representation of reality in Western literature', a profound sense of detachment from Western culture.

Across its history as a literary concept, mimesis has been confronted with, or has emerged from, a state of exile. For Plato, mimesis is to be banished from the republic altogether. Auerbach and Benjamin, writing far from home, both broadly understand mimesis as a set of oscillating detachments and reattachments between the subject and his or her contextual reality. For Auerbach, as we have seen, mimesis is a sensory mode borne out of Romantic thought, achieved in the tangible coming together of historical spirit and the individual body. For Benjamin, the mimetic faculty is an affective mode calling back to a pre-semiotic relationship between the self and its surroundings, and persisting fragmentarily in language. For both, their writing on mimesis is motivated, above all, by the aim of restoring forms of intelligibility and correspondence at a time when those forms are under threat. Mimesis becomes a mode in which alternatives to the given order of things may, or must, exist. It is, after all, a place of fiction.

Benjamin's esoteric thinking on mimesis is developed in the pair of essays mentioned above. The occult and magical linguistic ideas that characterise the first, 'Lehre vom Ähnlichen', are softened in the second, 'Über das mimetische Vermögen', which prioritises in their

---

[62] Kader Konuk and Victoria Holbrook, *East West Mimesis: Auerbach in Turkey* (Stanford, CA: Stanford University Press, 2010), pp. 29–30.

place a mimetic-naturalistic theory of language.[63] In reconstructing Benjamin's complex ideas, I will refer to both essays as a dialogic or chiasmic pair that reciprocally modify particular crucial points. Benjamin sets out from the Aristotelian assumption that mimesis is an anthropological category – a faculty innate to all human beings and essential to their learning and development, particularly to the task of making sense of the world and of others. The mimetic faculty can be defined as the perception and the production of similarities. It recuperates legibility from a world humming with potential corre-spondences – Benjamin calls them 'unsinnliche Ähnlichkeiten' (non-sensuous similarities) – which have been repressed in the modern world. It is the lasting instinctual remnant of a powerful compul-sion 'ähnlich zu werden und sich zu verhalten' (to become similar and behave mimetically). It is thus a faculty of *producing* as well as *registering* similarities and indicates, as such, a fleeting return to a primordial time prior to the instrumental division between object and subject.

Physiognomic reading – our interpretation of those 'similarities' that we perceive in faces – is one of the most common everyday manifestations of the mimetic faculty. But the similarities that occur in faces, Benjamin argues, are only a surface manifestation of 'unzählig vielen unbewußt oder auch gar nicht wahrgenommenen Ähnlicheiten' (countless other similarities perceived unconsciously or not at all).[64] In the past, humans were capable of detecting similari-ties that nowadays go unnoticed, such as the relationship that might persist between constellations in the stars and an individual human destiny.[65] The mystical act of reading stars and entrails and runes, ruled over by the mimetic faculty, persists in language. Language, for Benjamin, is not a system of arbitrary links between words and their objects, mired in convention. His language theory comes closer to the assumption (following Herder) of an essential relationship between words and the things they represent.[66] Knowledge of such

---

[63] Walter Benjamin, *GS* II.1, p. 950.

[64] Ibid., p. 205.

[65] Ibid., p. 206. Scholem, writing of conversations he held with Benjamin in Berlin in 1918, describes how for Benjamin, 'Die Entstehung der Sternbilder als Konfigurationen auf der Himmelsfläche' (the emergence of constellations of stars as configurations on the surface of the sky) represented, in effect, 'der Beginn des Lesens, der Schrift, die mit der Ausbildung des mythischen Weltalters zusammenfalle' (the beginning of reading, of script, which coincides with the education of the mythical world). Benjamin, *GS* II.3, p. 955.

[66] See Anson Rabinbach, 'Introduction to Walter Benjamin's "Doctrine of the Similar"', *New German Critique*, 17 (1979), 60–4 (p. 61).

relationships, once accessible to the augur or the priest, has made its way into language and writing, making language an archive of these lost experiences:

> Wenn nun dieses Herauslesen aus Sternen, Eingeweiden, Zufällen in der Urzeit der Menschheit das Lesen schlechthin war, wenn es weiterhin Vermittlungsglieder zu einem neuen Lesen, wie die Runen es gewesen sind, gegeben hat, so liegt die Annahme sehr nahe, jene mimetische Begabung, welche früher das Fundament der Hellsicht gewesen ist, sei in jahrtausendlangem Gange der Entwicklung ganz allmählich in Sprache und Schrift hineingewandert und habe sich in ihnen das vollkommenste Archiv unsinnlicher Ähnlichkeit geschaffen.[67]

> If, in the dawn of humanity, this reading from stars, entrails, and coincidences represented reading per se, and further, if there were mediating links to a newer kind of reading, as represented by the runes, then one might well assume that the mimetic faculty, which was earlier the basis for clairvoyance, quite gradually found its way into language and writing in the course of a development over thousands of years, thus creating for itself in language and writing the most perfect archive of non-sensuous similarity.

Benjamin's mimetic faculty, as we have seen, is the capacity to perceive and to produce similarities, and it persists, more than anywhere else, in the mystical activity of reading, in which similarities 'flüchtig [. . .] aus dem Fluß der Dinge hervorblitzen' (flash up fleetingly out of the stream of things).[68] But it is also seen in scenes of play, when children imitate not just other humans but objects; and it is preserved in gestural activities such as dance.[69] To behave mimetically, then, is to produce successive versions of the self as object, fully absorbed and at home in its own context: it is, for Michael T. Taussig, 'the capacity to Other'.[70]

For Elizabeth Stewart, Benjaminian mimesis rewrites subject–object relationships into 'dialogic structures' that might 'survive the deadening and reifying forces of modernity'.[71] His mimetic faculty draws from surrealist discourses of mimetic metamorphosis,

---

[67] Walter Benjamin, *GS* II.1, p. 209.
[68] Ibid., p. 209; Michael Jennings, *Dialectical Images: Walter Benjamin's Theory of Literary Criticism* (Ithaca, NY: Cornell University Press, 1987), p. 118.
[69] Walter Benjamin, *GS* II.1, pp. 210–11.
[70] Michael T. Taussig, *Mimesis and Alterity: A Particular History of the Senses* (London: Routledge, 1993), p. 19.
[71] Elizabeth Stewart, *Catastrophe and Survival: Walter Benjamin and Psychoanalysis* (London: Continuum, 2010), p. 78.

such as the work of Roger Caillois, a member of the Collège de Sociologie in Paris, at which Benjamin attended lectures and seminars during the 1930s.[72] Caillois's 'Mimétisme et psychasthénie légendaire' (Mimicry and Legendary Psychasthenia, 1935) describes how camouflage and insectile mimicry entail a confusion of self with environment – a radical state of passivity that he terms a 'tentation de l'espace' (temptation by space).[73] This dispossession or mimetic assimilation into space is a movement into automatism, 'une sorte d'*instinct d'abandon* qui le polarise vers un mode d'existence réduite' (a sort of *instinct of renunciation* that orients it towards a mode of reduced existence) – towards what he calls '*l'inertie de l'élan vital*' (the *inertia of the élan vital*).[74]

This radical suspension of self, its assimilation into otherness, first glimpsed in the two mimesis essays, is a state to which Benjamin returns more fully in the sketches of *Berliner Kindheit um 1900*. The sketches of the *Berliner Kindheit* enliven the world through play, remembering a magical moment, still accessible to the child, that precedes instrumental reason and the subject–object split. One of these sketches, 'Die Mummerehlen' (The Mummerehlen), is a paradigmatic image of mimetic subject-formation. It shows a child-subject who comes into being through the formation of its perceived world when that formation looks like an *Entstellung*, a displacement or disfigurement. The character 'Muhme Rehlen' (Aunty Rehlen) of a children's song is misheard by the child narrator as the nonsensical word 'Mummerehlen'. This misunderstanding comes to redefine his understanding of the world around him: 'Das Missverstehen verstellte mir die Welt. Jedoch auf gute Art; es wies die Wege, die in ihr Inneres führten' (the misunderstanding distorted the world for me. But in a good way: it indicated the paths that led into its interior).[75] The mishearing, rousing up the alterity of things, gives rise to a set of experiences in which the world becomes both playground and mask, camouflage and costume: Benjamin's child learns 'in die Worte, die eigentlich Wolken waren, mich zu mummen' (to disguise myself in words, which really were clouds) – where his own lilting use of language, 'mummen'/'Mumme'/'Muhme', words of masking and

---

[72] See, for example, Joyce Cheng, 'Mask, Mimicry, Metamorphosis: Roger Caillois, Walter Benjamin and Surrealism in the 1930s', *Modernism/Modernity*, 16.1 (2009), 61–86; and Taussig, *Mimesis and Alterity*.

[73] Roger Caillois, 'Mimétisme et psychasthénie légendaire', *Minotaure*, 7 (1935), 4–10 (p. 4).

[74] Ibid., p. 9.

[75] Walter Benjamin, *GS* IV.1, p. 260.

misunderstanding, heightens the sense of an embracing alterity.[76] When he paints, he describes how 'die Farben, die ich dann mischte, färbten mich' (the colours I mixed would colour me). The subject, 'entstellt vor Ähnlichkeit mit allem, was hier um mich ist' (distorted by similarity with everything which surrounds me), laid low against the alterity of the world, is given form by that world and its alterity.[77] Mimesis returns upon the self.

Benjamin's texts gesture towards what I am describing as a phenomenological reading of mimesis: an attempt to understand and to account for the felt experience of a non-instrumental encounter with the world and the creation of meaning through that encounter, in which the creative self is necessarily also felt as being part of the world. Auerbach's and Benjamin's sensory rehabilitations of mimesis, made in exile, represent isolated moments of redemption within a twentieth-century literary history that has otherwise seemed set on the denunciation, expulsion or prohibition of mimetic theory from discussions of narrative. I turn now to a third point in this line of mimetic thinking, and one in whose writings this rethinking of mimesis is given a new and concrete figure.

Maurice Merleau-Ponty

This figure is one that may allow us to view a binary structure askance or anamorphically, and hence to allow that binary to appear to resolve itself. It is the figure of the chiasm. The chiasm is related to the Greek letter 'chi' (χ) and denotes the entanglement or interlacing of two poles which it simultaneously joins and holds apart from one another in a relationship of paradoxical reciprocity. Maurice Merleau-Ponty develops his notion of the chiasm in the fourth chapter of his unfinished book *Le Visible et l'invisible* (1968), as well as in his essay 'L'Œil et l'esprit' (The Eye and the Mind, 1961). Although Merleau-Ponty does not write explicitly of literary mimesis, through an investigation of painting 'L'Œil et l'esprit' reveals the chiasm as a helpful figure for understanding the embodied experience of making art.

As seeing and feeling bodies, we are enfolded into the acts of perception through which we come to know the world. Our eyes are housed within mobile, unstable bodies and are themselves made of

[76] Ibid., pp. 260–1.
[77] Ibid., pp. 262, 261.

soft, fleshy matter; the act of seeing is conditioned by an awareness of this corporeality. When we see a table, we can see it from only one angle at a time, and yet we continue to have a projective, proprioceptive sense of the table as a whole. *Le Visible et l'invisible* interrogates this experience of being in the world starting from Merleau-Ponty's premise of 'perceptual faith': our belief that perception gives us access to a shared world, even as that world is understood to be the private creation of individual bodies. The world does not pre-exist our perceptual experience of it. This situation solicits a rethinking of subjective experience. There is no way to inhabit another human's sensory experience of the world – we must simply have faith that it corresponds in some way with our own. But occasionally we become aware of another person's perceptions of the world and a kind of doubling occurs:

> La chose perçue par autrui se dédouble: il y a *celle qu'il perçoit* Dieu sait où, et il y a celle que je vois, moi, hors de son corps, et que j'appelle la chose vraie, – comme il appelle chose vraie la table qu'*il voit* et renvoie aux apparences celle que je vois.[78]

> The thing perceived by the other is doubled: there is *the one he perceives*, God knows where, and there is the one I see, outside of his body, and which I call the true thing – as he calls true thing the table *he sees* and consigns to the category of appearances the one I see.

In such moments, a hole is torn momentarily in the fabric of our private world and we must abandon any solipsistic notion of subjective sovereignty. By the same token we become aware of ourselves as visible object for the other: 'je me sens vu' (I feel myself seen).[79] We must, then, recognise that we, as subjects, are also objects – a 'chose parmi les choses' (thing among things) as well as 'celui qui les voit et les touche' (what sees and touches those things).[80] These moments, which punctuate our lives, define our existence as interrelational and intersubjective. They are, as the beginnings of imagining the internal world of another, also the beginnings of empathy and of fiction. Subject and object are the condition of the other's existence: the perceiving subject solicits, encroaches on and completes the objects of his or her perceived surroundings just as those objects solicit, encroach on and complete his or her presence amongst them. We exist as subject *and* object, even in private moments: this is attested

---

[78] Maurice Merleau-Ponty, *Le Visible et l'invisible* (Paris: Gallimard, 1964), p. 25.
[79] Ibid., p. 108.
[80] Ibid., p. 178.

in particular by Merleau-Ponty's well-known image of one hand touching the other, in which the body is both the touching subject and the felt, tangible object within the same act of touching. In the fourth chapter, 'L'entrelacs – le chiasme' (The Intertwining – The Chiasm), this subject–world relationship is described as a criss-crossing or 'chiasmic' exchange, one that leads Merleau-Ponty to formulate his notion of a shared intersubjective 'flesh':

> Encore une fois, la chair dont nous parlons n'est pas la matière. Elle est l'enroulement du visible sur le corps voyant, du tangible sur le corps touchant, qui est attesté notamment quand le corps se voit, se touche en train de voir et de toucher les choses, de sorte que, simul-tanément, *comme* tangible il descend parmi elles, *comme* touchant il les domine toutes et tire de lui-même ce rapport, et même ce double rapport, par déhiscence ou fission de sa masse.[81]

> Once again, the flesh we are speaking of is not matter. It is the coiling over of the visible upon the seeing body, of the tangible upon the touching body, which is attested in particular when the body sees itself, touches itself seeing and touching the things, such that, simultaneously, as tangible it descends among them, as touching it dominates them all and draws this relationship and even this double relationship from itself, by dehiscence or fission of its own mass.

Perception happens at the site of crossover between the seeing and the visible, toucher and touched: it is a point at which the self is doubled.

'L'Œil et l'esprit' offers a close description of chiasmic perception at work in the act of painting. Painting registers the complex act of vision within which the seeing body is enfolded as a visible thing. The essay describes a body that is familiar to the reader of *Le Visible et l'invisible*: a body defined as 'un entrelacs de vision et de mouve-ment' (an intertwining of vision and movement), and that sees itself seeing, touches itself touching: 'au nombre des choses, il est l'une d'elles, il est pris dans le tissu du monde et sa cohésion est celle d'une chose' (a thing among things, it is caught in the fabric of the world, and its cohesion is that of a thing).[82]

A painted image, Merleau-Ponty shows, is not a second-order rep-resentation of an object fixed in that body's gaze. Rather, the things or objects to be painted are already implanted within the artist's body by virtue of perception, in what he calls a 'formule charnelle'

---

[81] Ibid., p. 189, p. 146.
[82] Maurice Merleau-Ponty, 'L'Œil et l'esprit' (Paris: Gallimard, 1964), p. 19.

(carnal formula).[83] A painting does not aim to reconstruct things as they are, 'out there', but rather offers the traces of this interior vision. The conventions of painting such as shadows, perspective and, most significantly for this book, lines and outlines, are not part of what we see but register *how* we see. In this way, the seeing body is part of the painting. Painting exists in a perpetual crossing-over between the subject and the world, offering up both the act of seeing objects and that seeing's return on the subject. A painting of a mountain, for example, is not a copy of a real mountain but a continual project of 'dévoiler les moyens, rien que visibles, par lesquels la montagne se fait montagne sous nos yeux' (unveiling the means, visible and not otherwise, by which it makes itself a mountain before our eyes).[84]

The visual arts – particularly painting and photography – are intrinsic models for any discussion of literary mimesis. Balzac refers to the author quite casually, in his *Avant-propos*, as a 'peintre plus ou moins fidèle' (more or less faithful painter) (B I 10). By the nineteenth century literature and painting were, despite Lessing's attempt to hold them apart in the *Laokoon*, fully established interlocutors – whether as bickering sisters or as collaborators in the emergence of new forms, such as the illustrated book. If literary realism often calls upon the language of the visual arts as a kind of pretext, by way of self-expla-nation – as if pictorial realism were somehow closer to nature itself, given its supposed freedom from the arbitrary signifiers of language – pictorial realism, too, turns out to be a complicated kind of texture of conventions, such that, as Roman Jakobson shows, 'it is necessary to learn the language of painting in order to "see" a picture'.[85] The vicissitudes of convention in visual art are helpfully narrated in Ernst Gombrich's *Art and Illusion* (notwithstanding critiques of his own essentialising of certain forms of Renaissance convention, such as perspective), and I will make use of his helpful gloss of those conven-tions as 'schemata' elsewhere in this book.[86] The literary texts I will discuss here frequently reflect upon their status as literature through intermedial interjections: whether to proclaim their own superiority, or – as in, for example, the model of the 'verbal sketch' – to coyly intimate their own inferiority, and in either case mediating a complex

---

[83] Ibid., p. 22.

[84] Ibid., pp. 28–9.

[85] Cited in Andrew Hemingway, 'The Realist Aesthetic in Painting: "Serious and com-mitted, ironic and brutal, sincere and full of poetry"', in *A Concise Companion to Realism*, ed. by Beaumont, pp. 121–42 (p. 122).

[86] E. H. Gombrich, *Art and Illusion: A Study in the Psychology of Pictorial Representation* (London: Phaidon, 1996).

and embodied experience of the art form. I am attuned here, in particular, to Hoffmann's penetrative understanding of the visual arts, as a practitioner himself – an experienced caricaturist, painter and consummate doodler – as well as to his understanding of the distortive effects of visual technologies such as eyeglasses and the like.

Merleau-Ponty's description of the act of painting in 'L'Œil et l'esprit' provides a helpful intertext, then, to inform the readings that I have begun to explore in this chapter: readings of a mimesis that is freed from the charge of dutiful imitation (whatever that might be) and understood as an attempt to negotiate a felt encounter with those objects. The artistic and literary mode most associated with phenomenology is not realism but impressionism, which is associated with the 'filtering' of experiences 'through the medium of human consciousness', and indeed of the representation of 'the interaction between human consciousness and the objects of that consciousness': with reality as individual sensory experience.[87] Literary impressionism is associated with literary modernism – above all with Joseph Conrad – and with its departure from nineteenth-century realism and its apparent simplification of human sensory reality. This book will show that Hoffmann and Balzac – particularly in Chapter 4, which investigates their treatment of non-representational visual artworks – open up an early prefiguring of an impressionist account of experience, in which reality is *felt* rather than known.

Because of Merleau-Ponty's insistence that such encounters also involve a recognition of the subject's status as object for others, the figure of the chiasm can be helpful for thinking about moments of self-reflexivity in literary texts, moments that often accompany representations of the act of writing or drawing. One such moment occurs in a scene in Hoffmann's tale *Die Abenteuer der Silvester-Nacht* (The New Year's Eve Adventure). At this point in the narrative, the narrating protagonist, the travelling Enthusiast, has fled a party after having encountered, and been scolded by, his ex-lover Julie; and has also fled a scene in an inn, where he encountered the two other main characters of the tale: Peter Schlemihl, who has lost his shadow (a character lifted from Adelbert von Chamisso's fairy tale *Peter Schlemihls wundersame Geschichte*), and Erasmus Spikher, who has lost his reflection. The three characters find themselves strangely bound together in an unsettling state of connectedness and reflection

---

[87] John G. Peters, *Conrad and Impressionism* (Cambridge: Cambridge University Press, 2001), p. 3, p. 16.

that seems to revolve around the narrator's own foundational, and rather more intangible, sense of incompleteness.

The Enthusiast books himself a night in another inn. Entering his room and examining his reflection in the mirror, where he sees another vision of Julie, he discovers that the room is already occupied by the diminutive Erasmus Spikher:

> Juliens Bild war verschwunden, entschlossen ergriff ich ein Licht, riß die Gardinen des Bettes rasch auf und schaute hinein. Wie kann ich dir denn das Gefühl beschreiben, das mich durchbebte, als ich den Kleinen erblickte, der mit dem jugendlichen wiewohl schmerzlich verzogenen Gesicht da lag und im Schlaf recht aus tiefer Brust aufseufzte: Giulietta – Giulietta – (H II.1 338)

> The image of Julie had disappeared, and resolutely I seized a candle, ripped the curtains of the bed apart, and looked inside. How can I describe my feelings to you when I saw before me the little man, lying there with youthful features which were contorted in pain, sighing in his sleep, 'Giulietta – Giulietta!'

A few moments later, the Enthusiast, having thrown Spikher out and gone to bed himself, wakes up to see – in a moment of explicit chiasm or crossover – Spikher dramatically illuminated by candlelight and writing frantically at the desk:

> Es mochte wohl schon Morgen sein, als ein blendender Schimmer mich weckte. Ich schlug die Augen auf und erblickte den Kleinen, der im weißen Schlafrock die Nachtmütze auf dem Kopf, den Rücken mir zugewendet am Tische saß und bei beiden angezündten Lichtern emsig schrieb. Er sah recht spukhaft aus, mir wandelte ein Grauen an; der Traum erfaßte mich plötzlich. (H II.1 340)

> It must have been early morning when a glaring light woke me. I opened my eyes and saw the little man, in his white dressing gown and with a nightcap on his head, sitting at the table with his back turned to me, writing busily by the light of the two candles. There was a ghostly look about him, horror came over me, and suddenly I was seized by a dream.

Illuminated before his own half-dreaming eyes, the narrator is witness to the act of writing as it takes place before him. The text Spikher is composing will form the final section of the tale: it narrates his own tale of loss, both of his reflection and of the beloved Giulietta, in an explicit but altered reflection of the life stories of both Schlemihl and the narrating Enthusiast. The narrator feels himself suddenly transformed into a narrative object, marked by the passive construc-tions of that final sentence: caught and fixed not by the gaze of the other, for Spikher does not look at him, being fully absorbed in his own world, but rather in the radical possibility of the other's mind, the other's narrative. Even the source of light is reversed: it is emitted first by the Enthusiast's candle, where it falls on Spikher's sleeping face, and second by Spikher's own dazzling candles. These moments of unexpected, chiasmic synchronicity are part of the tale's perva-sive sense that one character lives, acts out or dreams what another tells. It is in this sense, like many of Hoffmann's tales, a tale closely concerned with the reversibility of the roles of narrative subject and narrative object in the making of narrative or in writing about the self, and is in that way an unsettling staging of mimesis.

***

When Eric Downing argues for the importance of restoring 'an awareness of the dual, conflictual, and even self-deconstructive nature of realism' in the face of some of the critiques of realism mentioned earlier in this chapter, he aims to take seriously the pos-sibilities of literary mimesis as a concept for helping us to understand what texts can do, but also for helping us to understand how texts themselves think about or reflect upon what they do.[88] The chiasm, which simultaneously solicits and resists the notion of a principle split between subject and object, is for this reason a helpful figure for the self-reflexive and conflictual relationship between subject and object implicated in the sensory readings of mimesis presented in this chapter.

Christopher Prendergast writes of this sustaining conflictuality as the '"anxiety of representation" which arises when the security of the assumptions which underpin the mimetic project is called into question'.[89] One of the most surprising things for the reader of nineteenth-century realist novels, and for the reader of Balzac, is just how often such fraught self-questioning occurs in those novels: how inappropriate the description of such works as 'passive recording' turns out to be, and how accurate the description 'strenuous art'.[90] Reproducing reproduction, and staging the mimetic act in a set of performances or displays that Pirholt calls 'metamimetic', is one of

---

[88] Eric Downing, *Double Exposures*, p. 13. Downing, too, theorises a 'chiastic' realism – this time in the context of a chapter on Adalbert Stifter – although he does not explicitly refer to Merleau-Ponty's chiasm.
[89] Prendergast, *The Order of Mimesis*, p. 69.
[90] Levine, 'Literary Realism Reconsidered', p. 14.

the ways in which realist and proto-realist fiction thinks about itself. It is my aim in this book to show that one of the particular ways in which Balzac's works reflect on the problems of representation can be traced through a set of encounters with Hoffmann.

I therefore approach the texts in this book, most of which exist in a twilight zone of Romanticism and emergent realism, as betraying a compulsion to thematise mimesis, to raise it to the level of plot. I do not mean to collapse mimesis into sheer self-referentiality. It is a consistent characteristic of all variations on mimetic thought that mimesis presupposes *something* external to the work, although that something is rarely ontologically fixed. But that something that is external to the text might be no less near-at-hand than the hand of the writer, the writer's body and mind, and it may be less outside the text than tangled up within it. It is thus defined by its interrelational quality. There is no better expression of this idea than the lines I consider in Chapter 2.

The aim, then, is not to dilute mimesis so completely as to claim that it means nothing at all or everything at once but rather to show, as this chapter has begun to do, that mimesis has always been a troubling and troublesome concept, for the obvious reason that our relationship to reality has never been a simple one. I wish to contribute to a sense of how Hoffmann and Balzac – writers who are both deeply invested in the representation of reality – contribute, in their fictions, to mimetic thinking, to playing with its edges and limits. They do this frequently through engaging the prevailing tropes of the time: hence the proliferation of mirrors and mirror-scenes, as we saw in the scene of Balzac's 'Théorie du conte' in the Introduction, as well as in the scene taken from *Abenteuer*, above, and in another scene sketched out below. My selected readings of Balzac and Hoffmann in what follows work as narratives of a chiasmic mimesis, offering in changing formulations a view onto a subject who 'returns' upon himself (it is, without exception, *him*self in these works) in the act of making art or writing a narrative. As a point of conscious return, and as a point of explicit connection, furthermore, the chiasm will also appropriately furnish the scene for comparative work. As I follow the narrative line through three distinct variations, it will become clear that the bounding line of narrative is a singularly troubled figure, prone to looping back on itself and to finding itself in tangles. I will return explicitly, in Chapter 5, to the image of the cross, but throughout the book I will seek to show that a chiasmic intertwining characterises all of the other 'bounding lines' here, which function not just as symbols of narrative movement, but also as traces of the author's writing body, and as thresholds onto the world, with the potential to take the self beyond itself.

I turn finally, now, to another passage by Balzac, taken this time from *Illusions perdues*, and which Prendergast discusses in detail. It is the description of the fairground booth in the Galeries du Bois. The booth in question promises to its customer the spectacle of 'ce que Dieu ne saurait voir' (that which God cannot see):

> Une fois entré, vous vous trouviez nez à nez avec une grande glace. Tout à coup une voix, qui eût épouvanté Hoffmann le Berlinois, parlait comme une mécanique dont le ressort est poussé. 'Vous voyez là, messieurs, ce que dans toute l'éternité Dieu ne saurait voir, c'est-à-dire votre semblable. Dieu n'a pas son semblable!' Vous vous en alliez honteux sans oser avouer votre stupidité. (B V 359)

> Once inside, you found yourself nose-to-nose with a large mirror. Suddenly a voice that would have terrified Hoffmann of Berlin himself spoke like a mechanical contrivance when a spring is pressed. 'You see there, gentlemen, that which God in all eternity will never be able to see, which is to say your resemblance. God has no resemblance!' You left ashamed, unable to admit your idiocy.

Prendergast's reading of this scene locates within it the Platonic fear of a hall of illusions prey to 'an uncontrolled and degraded *mimesis*'. As mise-en-abyme, the scene in the booth 'sums up the whole of the Galeries', which in turn 'sum up the whole of *Illusions perdues*', for 'the Galeries admit to the city everything and everyone that would be rigorously banished from Plato's city; they realise Plato's nightmare of an invasion of the body politic by the charlatan and the magician, the disturbance of hierarchy by the circulation of false images and deceptive signs'.[91] It is a nightmare that corresponds to that infamous Balzacian view of an emergent capitalism in which signs and values are no longer fixed. And in *Illusions perdues*, a novel about the manufacture of books and of words, the promise of making meaning through the work of writing is continuously bounced back into the threat of reflection and repetition. Lucien, the Romantic poet of the provinces who desperately changes his name, costume and political allegiance in order to succeed first as a poet and then as a journalist in Paris, discovers that language is a commodity to be produced, bought and sold. In the fairground booth, as the narrator switches into the mocking second-person voice, the viewer-turned-reader-turned-customer is duped by the promise of knowledge, pays

---

[91] Prendergast, *The Order of Mimesis*, p. 92.

the entry toll, and meets only the familiar blank face of his or her own ignorance.

What has not yet been commented on is the presence of E. T. A. Hoffmann 'le Berlinois' in this important scene, as in many others across *La Comédie humaine*. Such moments contain, in Auerbach's terms, the 'demonic' traces of a Romantic impulse in order to intensify an atmosphere of unease. But there is something more here. Balzac refers specifically to Hoffmann in the context of an empty spectacle: a kind of sham mimesis, a bad and disappointing joke in which the customer is left out of pocket, having encountered, as spectacle, only their own reflection in the mirror. In the disembodied, Hoffmannesque voice, a mechanical contraption is encountered in the place of spiritual knowledge. The most fantastic illusion, then, is ultimately empty; even Hoffmann, the 'chantre de l'impossible' (B VII 956), master of illusions – produces only a set of reflections, for he too deals in the stuff of the everyday, the dulled reality of the self, in the mechanised repetitions of mimesis.

Chapter 2

A Brief History of Undulating Lines

The line has long served as a figure for the movement of narrative. The 'story line' fixes the experience of narrative in pictural form, approximating it as a single, sweeping progression from a starting point to a finishing point, via any number of turns, twists and loops. In *Ariadne's Thread*, J. Hillis Miller interrogates the 'story line' by means of the image of Ariadne unwinding a spool of thread as she moves through the labyrinth. 'The thread is the labyrinth,' he writes, 'and at the same time it is a repetition of the labyrinth'.[1] The narrative thread works as a visual figure for reading because it is a simulation or a double of the route it marks. As readers, we follow the turns of a plotted line which repeats or indicates a path but which is nonetheless held at a remove from that path.

The motif of the line has in other contexts – notably psychoanalysis and surrealism – acted as a pretext for narrative, being not quite, or not yet, legible as lettering, and thus in some sense a pre-mimetic figure, teasing at the edges of intelligibility. In D. W. Winnicott's 'squiggle game', child and analyst take turns to trace a spontaneous 'squiggle' – 'some kind of an impulsive line-drawing' – which the other player then articulates into a recognisable image.[2] The game encourages the reading of narrative from random forms, purporting to let analysis be guided by the will of the thread: 'to play and see what might happen'.[3] For Maurice Merleau-Ponty in 'L'Œil et l'esprit', the undulating line, once divested of its servitude as borderline or outline, is freed, and in being freed it no longer contains

---

[1] J. Hillis Miller, *Ariadne's Thread: Story Lines* (New Haven, CT: Yale University Press, 1992), p. 19.

[2] D. W. Winnicott, 'The Squiggle Game', in *Psycho-Analytic Explorations*, ed. by Claire Winnicott, Ray Shepherd and Madeleine Davis (Cambridge, MA: Harvard University Press, 1989), pp. 299–317, p. 302.

[3] Ibid., p. 311.

but constitutes the narrative impulse in an image.[4] Such a line, in Paul Klee's famous phrase, is a point that has transformed into 'ein Spaziergang um seiner selbst willen' (a stroll for its own sake), inviting its viewer's eyes along for the walk.[5] By bringing the act of reading a text up against the act of viewing an image, the hand-drawn line traces the fluid border' between verbal and visual modes of representation.

This chapter will serve as an introduction to my readings of Hoffmann and Balzac by following the course of a single waving line that appears to have held intense imaginative attraction for both of them. It is on the basis of this particular line, which I read as a 'reverse ekphrastic' figure – a pictorial expression of the shape of text – that I will move to study a number of other lines as textual motifs in the following chapters. The line I consider in this chapter is originally drawn by Laurence Sterne as an exuberant flourish made with a walking stick in a now ubiquitous passage of *Tristram Shandy* (Fig. 3). Sterne's line is copied, first by Hoffmann, in a little-known early piece, 'Fragment eines humoristischen Aufsatzes' (Fragment of a Humorous Essay, 1795–1800, Fig. 4); and second, more famously, by Balzac, as the epigraph to *La Peau de chagrin* (Fig. 5). The image, drawn and redrawn in three ways, by virtue of its being continuous with lines of text, either encapsulated within a narrative or set as its epigraph, comes to resemble a contradictory story-line: one that mimics the twisting shape of narrative development whilst refusing to de-lineate in a precise way. Being not text but a picture of text, one that is itself set within the body of the text, the line seems to want to be read. At once text, image, gesture and bodily outline, the drawn and redrawn line is presented as a sensuous motif for writing, both representing and displacing written words. The attitude encapsulated in the sweeping gesture of the line is repeated, in varying fictional forms, across the works discussed in the following chapters of this book. Lines appear as energetic arabesques in Chapter 3; as bold, though erratic, scribbles and flourishes in Chapter 4; and finally, in Chapter 5, as a cross scored violently across the body.

The three pictured lines reproduced in this chapter form a triangulated relationship of imitation that takes place across two centuries, three countries and three languages. In each case, the line, when

---

[4] Maurice Merleau-Ponty, 'L'Œil et l'esprit' (Paris: Gallimard, 1964), p. 74.

[5] Cited in Toni Hildebrandt, 'Die tachistische Geste 1951–70', in *Bild und Geste: Figurationen des Denkens in Philosophie und Kunst*, ed. by Ulrich Richtmeyer, Fabian Goppelsröder and Toni Hindebrandt (Bielefeld: Transcript Verlag, 2014), pp. 45–64 (p. 52).

drawn into dialogue with narrative style, troubles a set of assumptions about the mechanics of reading. Where elsewhere these writers draw from the lexicon of the artist or the art critic, engaging a style we might call 'ekphrastic' or 'pictorial' – paying particular attention to the line or stroke of the painter's brush – here, their inclusions of a pictured line shift the experience of reading into the experience of viewing an image. The gestural and performative impetus behind that shifting, in turn, gives a heightened sense of the author's presence within the text. The extravagant sweep of the copied line becomes emblematic for my comparative approach: it gathers up within itself questions concerning authorship, concerning the representational and non-representational possibilities of art, and concerning the logic of words that function like images, and of images that function as text.

The three lines form a single knot within a more expansive carpet of lines that function as representations of narrative, charted more thoroughly in works such as those by Joseph Hillis Miller and Tim Ingold.[6] Hoffmann's and Balzac's lines are tightly interwoven with each other's, as much as with Sterne's: all three are indebted to William Hogarth's line of beauty, with which I will begin my reading. The line copied and adapted, first by Hoffmann and then again by Balzac, has the rare advantage of working as a visual emblem of an intertextual relationship, resembling something like a signature or imprint. It reflects a practical influence, then, by unfolding a history of reading, at the same time as it gestures towards a set of shared interests in text, in pictures and in mimesis.

No narrative concerned with nineteenth-century lines can be free of the influence of William Hogarth. Hogarth's reconceptualisation of the Renaissance 'figura serpentinata' as the 'line of beauty' resonated across art and literature of the eighteenth and nineteenth centuries. Of the seven lines that he depicts in the chapter 'Of Lines' in his *Analysis of Beauty* (1772, Fig. 2.1), it is number four – an S-shaped strand, composed of 'two curves contrasted' – that he names the 'line of beauty'.[7] The two dominant attributes of this line, its intricacy and its variety, are absent, Hogarth claims, from its neighbours, which he denounces as 'deviations into stiffness and meanness on one hand, and clumsiness and deformity on the other'.[8] The line of beauty finds its counterpart in the line of grace, which snakes into

---

[6] Miller, *Ariadne's Thread*; Tim Ingold, *Lines: A Brief History* (London: Routledge, 2007).

[7] William Hogarth, *The Analysis of Beauty: Written with a View of Fixing the Fluctuating Ideas of Taste* (London: W. Strahan, 1772), p. 38.

[8] Ibid., p. 49.

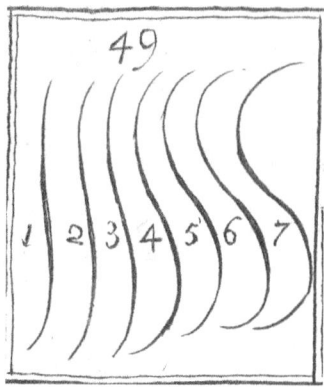

Figure 2.1 Detail from William Hogarth, *Analysis of Beauty*, Plate 1 (1753). © The British Library Board 31.b.231, Plate 1

three dimensions, as in the figure of a serpent curling up a staff or of a wire wrapped around a cone. Hogarth's material universe is saturated with such lines: they occur in natural objects, like horns and branches, and in the human frame – in its bones, sinews and muscle fibres. The line of beauty denotes both the contours of these shapes and their seduction of the eye or hand that follows them: shaped like 'winding walks' and 'serpentine rivers', Hogarth presents them as flowing and shifting figures that stir themselves up within our vision. It is precisely the ability of such a line to rouse the free play of our attention and curiosity, as it leads us on 'a wanton kind of chace', that 'intitles it to the name of beautiful'.[9] The line of beauty is, therefore, also explicitly a figure of reading: a compact form indicating an energetic course, as in 'the well-connected thread of a play, or novel, which ever increases as the plot thickens'.[10]

In this, Hogarth also gestures towards a tradition of treating the lines and lineaments of the human form as readable, like script. One of his most commanding images in this vein is that of pressing a pliable wire against the outside edge of the human body to take an impression of its profile. He notes how much more smooth the resulting line would be when pressed against a well-shaped body or statue than against one stripped of skin or fat: 'how *gradually* the changes in its shape are produced; how imperceptibly the different curvatures run into each other, and how easily the eye glides along

[9] Ibid., p. 25.
[10] Ibid., pp. 24–5.

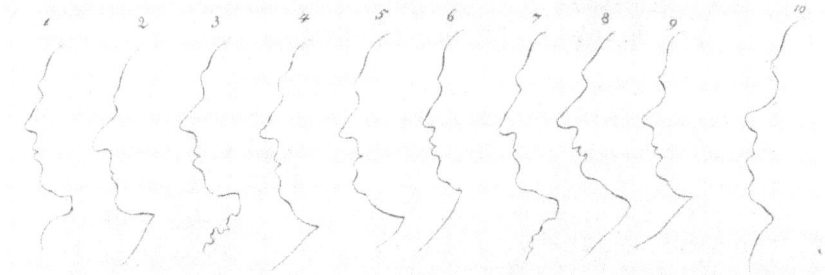

Figure 2.2 Johann Caspar Lavater, 'Zehn Gränzumrisse männlicher Gesichter' (Ten Outlines of Male Faces), *Physiognomische Fragmente, zur Beförderung der Menschenkenntnisze und Menschenliebe.* Leipzig und Winterthur: Weidmanns Erben, 1775–8. © ETH-Bibliothek Zürich, Rar 9206, https://doi. org/10.3931/e-rara-1099 / Public Domain Mark

the varied wavings of its sweep'.[11] This kind of line prefigures Johann Caspar Lavater's concern for the physiognomic profile line as an approximation of the body's sweeping outermost edge. In Lavater's enormously popular *Physiognomische Fragmente zur Beförderung der Menschenkenntnis und Menschenliebe* (Physiognomic Fragments for the Advancement of the Knowledge and Love of Humans), the lines he extracts from the human body form the basis of a system of 'reading' internal character from fixed external features of the body. Diagrams such as the one above (Fig. 2.2) are testament to the significance of the singular, waving line in Lavaterian thinking.

This set of altered variations of a face, an echo of Hogarth's seven-part series, offers ten shifting, evolving accounts of the undulating line as a signifier of type. For both thinkers, the single and infinitely variable line is the arbiter of multiple shapes and narratives. By virtue of its lack of fixity, the undulating line is a kind of shorthand for the moves we make in deducing meaning from form. For William Blake, similarly, the 'bounding line' (that is, both the moving line with its bounding energy, and the boundary line), which does not exist in nature but only as a necessary ingredient of visual representation, does not trace *what* we see but *how* we see. The 'bounding line' traces a visual process, distinguishing a figure from its background whilst fusing them together. 'Leave out this line,' Blake warns, 'and you leave out life itself; all is chaos again'.[12]

[11] Hogarth, *The Analysis of Beauty*, p. 61.
[12] William Blake, 'A Descriptive Catalogue of Pictures', in *The Complete Poetry and Prose of William Blake*, ed. by David V. Erdman (New York, NY: Anchor, 1988), pp. 529–51 (p. 550).

Critics such as W. J. T. Mitchell, Andrew Piper and Miranda Stanyon have shown how Hogarth's line of beauty shapes, and takes shape within, the literary works of Romanticism.[13] For Piper, the Romantic period saw the emergence of a specifically wavy inter-medial line that marked the crossover of text and image, reading and seeing. It is '*the* image of the interaction between text and image' specific to the medial conditions of the Romantic period: the emergence and diffusion of visual culture and its encroachment into literature, particularly in illustrated books, including Lavater's *Physiognomische Fragmente* and Balzac's visual epigraph. 'The romantic interest in the line', Piper writes, 'was a way of exploring the possibility of textual and visual simultaneity, a simultaneity that nevertheless always bordered on illegibility at the moment of such synthesis.'[14] The risk of illegibility is a fundamental characteristic of the Hoffmannesque and Balzacian versions of Hogarth's line of beauty. In what follows I will suggest that their copied lines both interrupt and draw attention to the act of reading by making a picture of a line of text. Such an image, as an intervention into the crossover between modes of writing and drawing, comes to represent a new figure for what James Heffernan has termed 'the struggle for power – the paragone – between the image and the word'.[15]

The image reproduced in Figure 2.3, taken from Laurence Sterne's *Tristram Shandy*, as parody of Hogarth's line of beauty, represents the inked trace of Corporal Trim's flourish with his walking stick as he digresses wordlessly on the celibate life of the bachelor: 'Whilst a man is free – cried the Corporal, giving a flourish with his stick thus—'.[16] The flourish is often cited in discussions of Sterne's typo-graphical eccentricities in *Tristram Shandy*: eccentricities which are understood as part of wider bibliographic practices that underscore the material status of the text, coding a 'performative textuality'

---

[13] W. J. T. Mitchell, 'Metamorphoses of the Vortex: Hogarth, Turner, and Blake', in *Articulate Images: The Sister Arts from Hogarth to Tennyson*, ed. by Richard Wendorf (Minneapolis, MN: University of Minnesota Press, 1983), pp. 125–69; Andrew Piper, *Dreaming in Books: The Making of the Bibliographic Imagination in the Romantic Age* (Chicago, IL: University of Chicago Press, 2009); Miranda Stanyon, 'Serpentine Sighs: De Quincey's *Suspiria de Profundis* and the Serpentine Line', *Studies in Romanticism*, 53.1 (2014), 31–58.

[14] Piper, *Dreaming in Books*, pp. 185, 189.

[15] James A. W. Heffernan, *Museum of Words: The Poetics of Ekphrasis from Homer to Ashbery* (Chicago, IL: University of Chicago Press, 1993), p. 136.

[16] Laurence Sterne, *The Life and Opinions of Tristram Shandy, Gentleman: The Text*, ed. by Melvyn New and Joan New, 2 vols (Gainesville, FL: University Presses of Florida, 1978), II, p. 743.

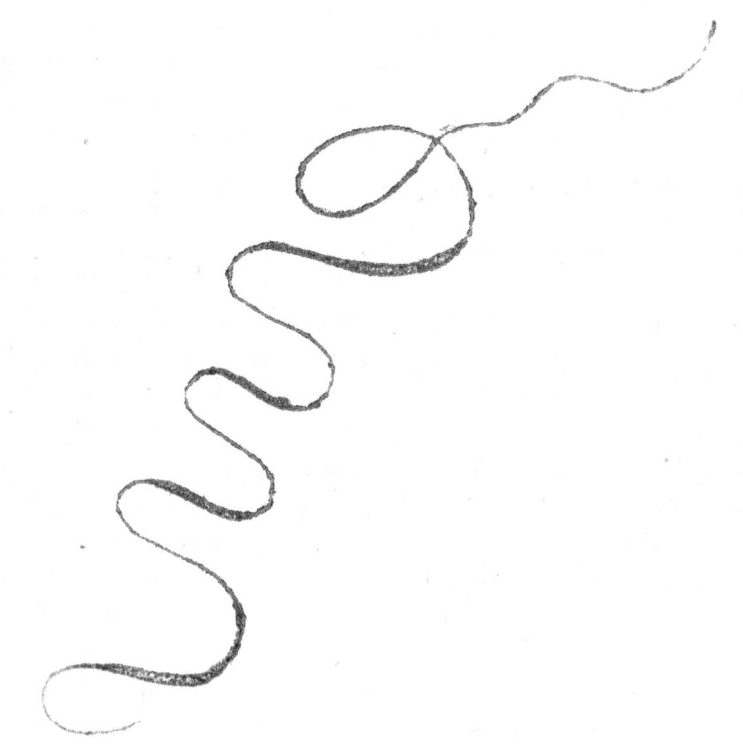

Figure 2.3 Corporal Trim's flourish. Laurence Sterne, *Tristram Shandy*
© The British Library Board Ashley1770 vol. IX, p. 17

drawing from the Scriblerian tradition.[17] Besides the flourish, these
include an entirely black page memorialising the character Yorick;
a marbled page, which appeared in a slightly different variation in
every edition, though which is now reproduced in a uniform design;
a page left entirely blank, which the reader is instructed to fill for
him- or herself with a visualisation of the widow Wadman – 'Sit
down, Sir, paint her to your own mind—'; and a series of horizontal
lines which, more explicitly than Trim's flourish, playfully map the
non-linear narrative development of each volume.[18] These devices
are typically seen to contribute to a thickening of the page as material

[17] See Christopher Fanning, 'Sterne and Print Culture', in *The Cambridge Companion
to Laurence Sterne*, ed. by Thomas Keymer (Cambridge: Cambridge University Press,
2010), pp. 125–41 (p. 129).
[18] Sterne, *Tristram Shandy*, I, pp. 37–8; 269–70; II, pp. 566–7; 570–1.

– so as to make the act of our reading into the object of our reading. A comment made by Roger Moss on the related phenomenon of Sterne's unconventional use of punctuation is particularly fitting in the case of the walking stick's flourish. 'Just as you cannot be conscious of the mechanics of walking without being in danger of tripping up', he writes, 'so these devices, once focused on, make reading dangerously ludicrous and uncomfortable.'[19] Sterne's paratextual eccentricities contribute to a meditation on reading by interrupting its course. The flourish thus represents an energetic encounter with what Christopher Fanning calls the narrator's 'textual presence' as it crystallises in the formal elements of the text in a movement of 'performance and reflection', as the narrator gesticulates to interrupt the flow of text and, 'thus', to make himself known.[20]

Yet if we take the form of Trim's squiggle seriously – its being a line, and not, say, a circle or a spiral, or some other shape – then its role within the text becomes more complicated, being not a mere interrupter of the text but also a depiction of it. The squiggle functions as an ironic approximation of narrative form, highlighting the arbitrariness of the linear narrative figure; and, furthermore, as a challenge to the representational capacity of words in the face of pictures: 'A thousand of my father's most subtle syllogisms', remarks Shandy, 'could not have said more for celibacy.'[21] By demanding of his reader a switch from reading to looking, the squiggle reflects on other moments in the text when Sterne calls upon the 'visual imagination' of his readers through his use of painterly or pictorial rhetoric. Most apposite here is a passage from Shandy's introduction of Corporal Trim, which foregrounds the figurative line made by the artist:

> I have but one more stroke to give to finish Corporal Trim's character, – and it is the only dark line in it. – The fellow loved to advise, – or rather to hear himself talk; his carriage, however, was so perfectly respectful, 'twas easy to keep him silent when you had him so; but set his tongue a-going, – you had no hold of him – he was voluble; – the eternal interlardings of your Honour, with the respectfulness of Corporal Trim's manner, interceding so strong in behalf of his elocution, – that though you might have been incommoded, – you could not well be angry. My uncle Toby was seldom either the one or

[19] Roger B. Moss, 'Sterne's Punctuation', *Eighteenth-Century Studies*, 15.2 (1981–2), 179–200 (p. 194).
[20] Christopher Fanning, 'Small Particles of Eloquence: Sterne and the Scriblerian Text', *Modern Philology*, 100.3 (2003), 360–92 (p. 361).
[21] Sterne, *Tristram Shandy*, II, p. 744.

the other with him, – or, at least, this fault, in Trim, broke no squares with them. My uncle Toby, as I said, loved the man; – and besides, as he ever looked upon a faithful servant, – but as an humble friend, – he could not bear to stop his mouth. – Such was Corporal Trim.[22]

This passage features a number of key features of Sterne's literary pictorialism: a style in which the narrator mediates the reader's impression of a character or scene by giving details in a highly visual mode, primarily through the co-option of the vocabulary of the visual arts and aesthetic theory and through reference to real artists and their works. Now writer, now painter, the narrator reflects on his status by playing at changing guise. What is most significant in this passage is that the 'one more stroke' that the narrator-artist adds to his picture, the 'dark line' of Trim's character, is Trim's verbal incontinence, his propensity to speak more than his status might ordinarily allow. The figurative dark line here, like the literal line cast by Trim's stick, and the compulsive return to the interrupting dash, are the inarticulate symbols of Trim's digression, conveying not speech itself so much as the sense of speech. Both narrator and character, Shandy and Trim, defer to the motif of the inked line as they point towards the potential of narrative itself to turn arbitrary – to show where lines of text turn into flourish, into pure line.

Sterne's innovations in pictorialism, as with so many of his innovations of the novel's formal elements, were not inventions or transformations so much as invigorating consolidations of existing literary trends. Sterne's appeal to the figure of the absent artist is a convention found in works by Fielding and Swift, each of whom make explicit appeals to Hogarth in their works. Pat Rogers, who documents these appeals to the absent artist, has called them a 'towel-throwing exercise', by which the author pretends to abdicate his authority through allusion to something off the page and out of hand.[23] The trope also engages the rhetorical prowess of the *non finito*, as channelled through the visual or verbal sketch, a form to which Richard C. Sha has credited the 'artful rhetoric of denied rhetoricity'.[24] The artist William Gilpin's late eighteenth-century treatise on the art of sketching expresses this sense of the

---

[22] Sterne, *Tristam Shandy*, I, pp. 109–10.

[23] Pat Rogers, '"How I want thee, humorous Hogart": The Motif of the Absent Artist in Swift, Fielding and Others', *Papers on Language and Literature*, 42.1 (2006), 25–45 (p. 25).

[24] Richard C. Sha, *The Visual and Verbal Sketch in British Romanticism* (Philadelphia, PA: University of Pennsylvania Press, 1998), p. 3.

sketcher's prowess: 'when the enthusiasm of his art is upon him, he often produces from the glow of his imagination, with a few bold strokes, such wonderful effusions of genius, as the more sober, and correct productions of his pencil cannot equal'.[25] This rhetorical downplaying of the sketcher's own representational capacity mirrors other Romantic forms of the *non finito*, such as the fragment and the *Umriss* or outline drawing (more of which will be detailed in Chapter 4). To give a sketch of a character, scene or argument means to arrive at the barest and most essential detail – and also to emphasise the process of extraction, delineating what is lost or discarded in the process as the 'sketching' narrator appears to strain for the least mediated, and most efficient, kind of mimesis. Some sense of that is given by Sterne in the following:

> Such were the out-lines of Dr. Slop's figure, which – if you have read Hogarth's analysis of beauty, and if you have not, I wish you would; – you must know, may as certainly be caricatured, and conveyed to the mind by three strokes as three hundred.[26]

In this passage, Sterne makes a yet more insistent call upon the reader's sensibilities to collaborate in the visual scene, insisting boisterously on the 'less is more' ideal implied by Hogarth's singular line of beauty by noting that 'three strokes' might do as well as 'three hundred'. Elsewhere, Sterne takes the appeal to the artist a step further, transforming the trope into a whole new kind of correspondence with the arts, in what Rogers calls 'a literalization of the motif', by actually writing to Hogarth, via Richard Berenger, to ask him to illustrate a scene from his novel.[27] What Sterne specifically asks for in his letter is a sketch: 'the Loosest Sketch in Nature'.[28] Again he opens up a specifically intermedial sensibility: the will to turn the world into words and words into pictures – and finally, perhaps, into life itself.

All three authors – Sterne, Hoffmann and Balzac – engage in a comparable pictorial style, characterised above all by the motif of the artist's painted line, which proves in each case a clue to a particular intermedial sensibility. This pictorialism has implications for our

---

[25] William Gilpin, 'The Art of Sketching Landscape', in *Three Essays: On Picturesque Beauty; on Picturesque Travel; and on Sketching Landscape; to which is added a poem, on Landscape Painting* (London: Blamire, 1794), p. 62.

[26] Sterne, *Tristram Shandy*, I, p. 121.

[27] Rogers, '"How I want thee, Humorous Hogart"', p. 35.

[28] Melvyn New and Peter de Voogd (eds), *The Letters of Laurence Sterne: Part 1, 1739–1764* (Gainesville, FL: University Presses of Florida), p. 130.

understanding of their inclusion of the squiggle. As wry reflections of one another, their flourishes reflect back on the act of composition through a performative, intermedial gesture of authorial presence.

E. T. A. Hoffmann, one of Sterne's most notorious German admirers, is his equal in matters of narrative play. Steven Paul Scher and Duncan Large have explored some of Hoffmann's most 'explicit Sternean references' and 'obvious Shandyisms' with particular reference to his disconcerting masterpiece, *Die Lebensansichten des Katers Murr* (The Life and Opinions of Tomcat Murr, 1819–21), the very title of which indicates its indebtedness to Sterne.[29] Yet their analyses offer only a brief acknowledgement of Hoffmann's most visually immediate 'parodic plagiarism' of Sterne: his reproduction of Trim's flourish in an essay fragment composed some twenty years earlier.[30] Hoffmann's scribble, which has been almost entirely ignored in scholarship, offers an energetic new account of what Duncan Large calls the author's 'derived lines', and of Scher's arguments concerning both writers' eschewal of narrative linearity: their refusal 'to invent and realize a coherent plot' in favour of circularity, giving continuity to their texts not by linearity but by an 'omnipresent, self-reflective authorial consciousness'.[31] Hoffmann's appropriation of Sterne's line in his 'Fragment eines humoristischen Aufsatzes', a scrap of work originally intended for a collaborative *Taschenbuch* with his friend Theodor von Hippel, reproduced in Fig. 2.4, is surely the clearest trace of his encounter with Sterne's work.[32] He even echoes Trim's defiant 'thus' when he introduces it: 'hier bat der Corporal Trim sein Freyheits-System einzurücken und es geschieht also' (Here Corporal Trim asked to engage his system of freedom, and it happens thus) (H I 780). The fragment in which the line appears is an unpublished piece of writing, composed years before Hoffmann's first real successes as a writer from 1809, but this fact does not diminish its relevance for a study of Hoffmann. On the contrary, it proves the intensity and duration of his engagement with Sterne.

---

[29] Steven Paul Scher, 'Hoffmann and Sterne: Unmediated Parallels in Narrative Method', *Comparative Literature*, 28.4 (1976), 309–25 (p. 311).

[30] Duncan Large, 'Derived Lines, Received Opinions: Parodic Plagiarism in Sterne and Hoffmann', *New Comparison: A Journal of Comparative and General Literary Studies*, 35/36 (2003), 66–77 (p. 76).

[31] Scher, 'Hoffmann and Sterne', pp. 321–2.

[32] The image is reproduced, with commentary, in Dietmar Ponert, *E. T. A. Hoffmann – Das bildkünstlerische Werk: Ein kritisches Gesamtverzeichnis*, 2 vols (Petersburg: Michael Imhof Verlag, 2012). Hoffmann's plans for the *Taschenbuch* with Hippel are discussed in I, p. 106.

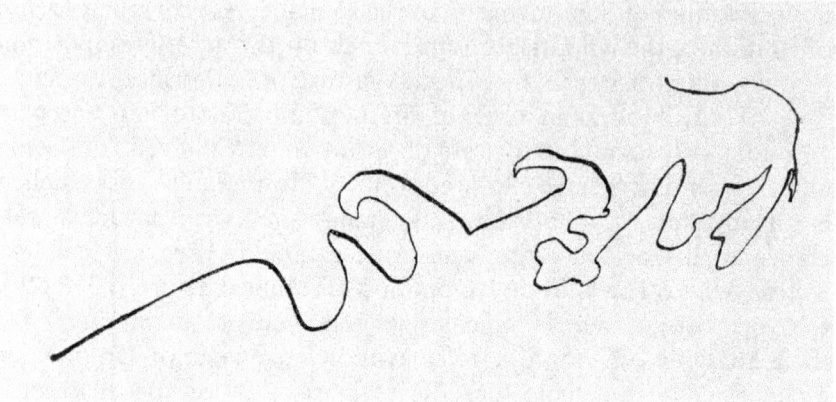

Figure 2.4 Detail from E. T. A. Hoffmann's 'Fragment eines humoristischen Aufsatzes' (Fragment of a humorous essay), 1795–. © Staatsbibliothek Bamberg L.g.o.391-e(B19, p. 348

According to Hartmut Steinecke, the fragment may be dated to the latter half of the 1790s, the period of Hoffmann's closest friendship with Hippel and the height of his interest in Sterne, whose *Tristram Shandy* he read in the popular German translation by Johann Joachim Christoph Bode (see H I 1316). The inclusion of the Shandyean flourish is followed by a brief and rather confusing reflection on what Hoffmann calls Trim's 'system' – the free life of the bachelor:

> Seyn Sie so gütig den Tristram Shandy nachzulesen, und Sie werden Sich von der Vortrefflichkeit des Trim-schen Systems noch mehr überzeugen – ich hätte auch weniger Gründe dafür angeben können – *argumenta ad hominem – ad crumenum* pp. – indessen bin ich von dem Gegentheile überzeugt; oder mit anderen Worten: seit der Zeit daß ich Noten und Zoten schreiben lernte, scheinen mir die Angriffe auf die Unsterblichkeit der Seele nur Windbälle für feuersprühende Batterien in diesem elenden PißWinkel der Santa Hermandad der Menschheit zu seyn (H I 780–1).

> Be so gracious as to read Tristram Shandy, and you will be further convinced of the excellence of Trim's system – I could also have stated lesser reasons – *argumenta ad hominen – ad crumenum*, etc. – meanwhile, I am convinced of the opposite; or, in other words: since learning to write notes and crude jokes, assaults on the immortality of the soul seem to me only fodder for fire-spraying batteries in this miserable piss-corner, the holy fraternity of humanity.

If there were a way of formulating a line of ugliness, surely Hoffmann's scribbled version, with its bulbous protrusions and sharp ridges, would be it. Despite its lack of that sweeping quality that suggests, for Hogarth, the graceful, fleshy contours of the body, its bumps and knots suggest bodily or facial outlines. In this light the squiggle is reminiscent of those faces that appear from disturbing and unexpected places in Hoffmann's fiction. One of the clearest examples of this is the shifting landscape as viewed by Nathanael from the phantasmagoric *Ratsturm* in *Der Sandmann* (The Sandman, 1816). As Andrew Webber shows, this scene, through activating metonymic elements – namely the grey bushes that recall earlier descriptions of Coppelius's eyebrows, as well as Hoffmann's own mock-Lavaterian self-portraiture – evokes the 'physiognomy of the monster showman', be it that of the Sandman or of the author.[33]

Hoffmann's line of ugliness bespeaks an interest, which he shared with Hogarth, Lavater and other caricaturists, in 'low, vicious and distorted physiognomies'.[34] Indeed, further into this same essay fragment, Hoffmann experiments more exuberantly with the Lavaterian method, as we see in Figure 2.5. In this visual pun, the 'Spießbürger-Köpfe' (heads of philistines) are 'aufgespießt' (skewered) like pieces of flesh ripe to be read. The line is disentangled from its meaningful contortions in the profiles of faces and transformed into the grotesque image of the skewer holding those faces together, allowing them to be read as a series, and clinching the pun which arises specifically in the fusion of word and image. It was on the basis of Hoffmann's impulse towards caricature – that interest in exaggerated ugliness – that Goethe criticised him on mimetic grounds, for caricaturists, according to Goethe, disfigure the truth of natural forms.[35] And yet, as E. H. Gombrich and Ernst Kris argue, caricature's own paradoxical-seeming trick is to produce 'a likeness more true than mere imitation could be'.[36] Its distortive effects do not deviate from the truth but actually reveal a more essential truth by deviating from what is strictly available within the visual field; by reproducing reality as

---

[33] Andrew Webber, 'About Face: E. T. A. Hoffmann, Weimar Film and the Technological Afterlife of Gothic Physiognomy' in *Popular Revenants: The German Gothic and its International Reception, 1800–2000*, ed. by Andrew Cusack and Barry Murnane (Rochester, NY: Camden House, 2012), pp. 161–80 (p. 168).

[34] David Kunzle, 'Goethe and Caricature: From Hogarth to Töpffer', *Journal of the Warburg and Courtauld Institutes*, 48 (1985), 164–88, p. 165.

[35] Ibid., p. 168.

[36] E. H. Gombrich and Ernst Kris, 'The Principles of Caricature', *British Journal of Medical Psychology*, 17 (1938), 319–42, p. 319.

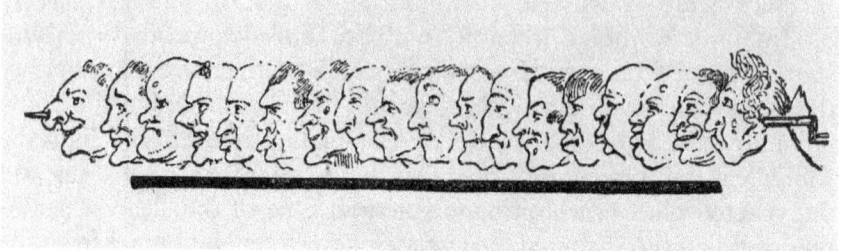

Figure 2.5 Detail from E. T. A. Hoffmann's 'Fragment eines humoristischen Aufsatzes' (Fragment of a humorous essay), 1795–. © Staatsbibliothek Bamberg L.g.o.391-e(B19, p. 348

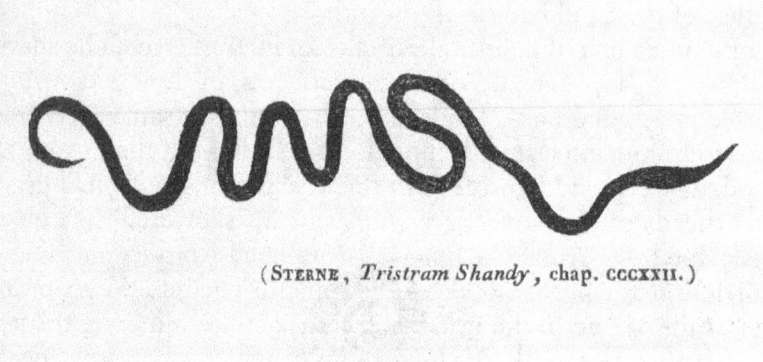

(STERNE, *Tristram Shandy*, chap. CCCXXII.)

Figure 2.6 Epigraph, Honoré de Balzac, *La Peau de chagrin* (1831). © The British Library Board C.59.d.13, title page

filtered through the mind and wit of the caricaturist. It is in that sense a neat case study into the expanded sense of mimesis narrated in the previous chapter and glossed by Gerhard Neumann as a specifically 'anamorphic' form of realism.

It is almost certainly impossible that Balzac, himself a great admirer of Sterne, would have encountered Hoffmann's Shandyean line. That both writers should have lighted upon the idea to copy out Sterne's flourish is striking. It is tempting to read the different versions – two reconfigurations of the same raw graphic material – within the framework of Winnicott's 'squiggle game', as the un-meaning line is modified by each player into a new meaningful form. Houssiaux, a later publisher, famously took a turn in this game by turning the squiggle into a snake; and the modern Penguin edition has offered a further altered variation.

Balzac's version of the Shandyean flourish (Fig. 2.6) has proved more fertile for criticism than has Hoffmann's. Often accused of referring to a nonexistent chapter of *Tristram Shandy*, 'CCCXXII', in fact the epigraph – as demonstrated by the work of Jeri Debois King – shows that his most probable source, the 1818 volume of Sterne's works translated by Frenais and de la Baume, did include Trim's flourish in a Chapter 322, as a result of how the translators had ordered the volumes. That this edition also included the aprocryphal *Les Mémoires de Sterne* by Richard Griffith, as King points out, proves that 'Balzac's idea of Sterne was based, in part at least, on an inauthentic work,' and that the translations of Sterne that inspired him 'simultaneously acted as screens to conceal the real Sterne from Balzac'.[37] The squiggle is thus, as a trace of Balzac's own reading, a figure for the inevitable distortion that accompanies the act of citation: not only in its deliberately altered form, but in the history of reading and translation that it accidentally unfolds.

The course traced by Balzac's Shandyean line across *La Peau de chagrin* will be the subject of the following chapter, but that line appears in another novel by Balzac that deserves some attention here. In the final scene of Balzac's *Le Colonel Chabert* (1831), Chabert, condemned to end his life in a hospice and reduced to the nameless state of the prisoner, 'numéro 164, septième salle' (number 164, seventh room), playfully scribbles a line in the air with his cane:

> Il se mit au port d'armes, feignit de les coucher en joue, et s'écria en souriant: 'Feu des deux pièces! vive Napoléon!' Et il décrivit en l'air avec sa canne une arabesque imaginaire. (B III 372)

> He ported arms, pretended to take aim at them, and shouted with a smile: 'Fire! Both arms! Vive Napoleon!' And he drew an imaginary arabesque in the air with his cane.

This 'arabesque imaginaire' (imaginary arabesque), as physical gesture, is far closer to Trim's original exuberant flourish than is the epigraph of *La Peau de chagrin*.[38] The fictional gesture made by the bachelor with his cane in *Tristram Shandy* and recorded by Sterne in the form of an inked drawing is transformed back into a movement made in the air by a bachelor with his cane. In this sense, the arabesque traces the passage taken by gesture into a figure that

---

[37] Jeri DeBois King, *Paratextuality in Balzac's* La Peau de chagrin: The Wild Ass's Skin (Lewiston, NY: Edwin Mellen, 1992), pp. 52, 58.

[38] This is noted by Peter Brooks in 'Narrative Transaction and Transference (Unburying "Le Colonel Chabert")', *NOVEL: A Forum on Fiction*, 15.2 (1982), 101–10, p. 108.

resembles writing, and its passage back again; it records the alchemic transformation of movement into a legible figure.

As a figure for the act of writing, the line is also a gesture of writing's flimsiness, its potential for dissolution into empty words. On file, Chabert is dead, recorded in the *Victoires et Conquêtes* as having fallen at the 1807 Battle of Eylau (B III 323). Returning to Paris after a long and grisly escape from Germany, Chabert finds not only that he is supposed, by all accounts, not to exist, but that his wife has re-married le comte Ferraud, become la comtesse Ferraud, and has liquidated Chabert's fortune. As a hero of the Napoleonic Wars, a remnant of the Empire returned to a greatly changed Restoration-era society, Chabert must now undergo a living death within a society that has expelled him. He finally refuses to commit his signature to the settlement contract offered to him by his former wife, thus refusing the final paper identity offered to him: essentially a bribe that would pay the Colonel to stay legally dead. The unguided arabesque that he draws in the epilogue functions as the reflection or empty mockery of meaningful etched lines: the signatures made on legal contracts that signify birth, marriage and death. It is in that sense a parody of such writing, line reduced to sheer form.

It is the specific characteristic of the lines examined in this chapter that, as non-linguistic notations, they can open up a channel of intertextuality unhampered by questions of translation. It is no wonder, then, that the squiggle, as idiosyncratic and as resistant to reproduction as a handwritten signature – the Derridean figure that apparently confers originality and authorial presence, but paradoxically signifies the author's absence, and gains meaning only through being imperfectly repeated – undergoes significant and deliberate changes in being copied from Sterne by Hoffmann and by Balzac. The most significant change, introduced by both, is that whereas Sterne's line is drawn vertically, from bottom left to top right, both of theirs run more or less horizontally, from left to right, rendering the squiggle explicitly as a line of text. I have shown how, in each case, the act of picturing text reflects back upon the writer's use of pictorial language. In this light, it is tempting to speak of the squiggles in terms of a reverse pictorialism, or even of a 'reverse ekphrasis'. This latter term, which may be defined as the visual representation of a verbal representation, to invert a standard definition of ekphrasis, is introduced by Murray Krieger in the foreword to *Ekphrasis: Illusion of the Natural Sign*, when he writes of two 'fully ingenious, yet equally vain, attempts to represent visually Homer's description of the shield of Achilles in book 18 of the *Iliad*'.[39] For Krieger, the incommensurability of these visual representations with their verbal counterparts only 'justifies our conviction that such a thing' – a poetic representation – 'could never be rendered adequately, so that any attempt at a reverse *ekphrasis* [. . .] must be in vain'.[40] In this way, they prove a paradoxical tangle within ekphrastic discourse: the ekphrastic text attempts to reproduce the visual experience of an object that may only be comprehended in its textual form. If ekphrasis always seems to describe a sense of incommensurability – in the inability of the visual structure to match the verbal, or vice versa – then these three 'reverse ekphrastic' manoeuvres playfully compound that (non-)sense.

Perhaps the most seriously sustained exploration of the term 'reverse ekphrasis', and the sense of incompleteness or sketchiness that it engenders, is given in Garrett Stewart's study of painted scenes of reading, *The Look of Reading*. A painting of a reading figure, for Stewart, 'offers up the rendering of verbal *reception* rather than execution', with its focus on the reader rather than on the text being read.[41] What makes these three squiggles significant, then, is that the reception is absent from the image, leaving only the barest indication of text, or, in Hogarth's terms, the movement of our eyes across it. They resemble what Stewart calls elsewhere, in a brief reference to a work by Henri Michaux, a kind of 'choreographed doodling'.[42] The 'doodle', which is etymologically associated with the verb 'dawdle', is an apt label for the handwork of the squiggle, which interrupts and slows the pace of text. The seductive energy that Hogarth and Blake deduce from bounding lines is countered by the doodle's intentional purposelessness. Like doodles, these lines are figures of excess. Being not quite illustrations, they are secondary to textual meaning, suggesting narrative rupture or narrative subversion; or alternative narratives, as shorthand for what Stewart terms 'narratives untold'.[43]

An ekphrasis is a mimesis of a mimesis: that is, a version of mimesis whose representational object is itself a work of art. A reverse ekphrasis, as embodied in one of these lines, is also a mimesis

---

[39] Murray Krieger, *Ekphrasis: Illusion of the Natural Sign* (Baltimore, MD: Johns Hopkins University Press, 1992), p. xiii.

[40] Ibid., pp. xiv–xv.

[41] Garrett Stewart, *The Look of Reading: Book, Painting, Text* (Chicago, IL: University of Chicago Press, 2006), p. 82.

[42] Garrett Stewart, 'Painted Readers, Narrative Regress', *Narrative*, 11.2 (2003), 125–76, p. 136.

[43] Stewart, *The Look of Reading*, p. 85.

of a mimesis: its representational object is not, say, a painting or sculpture, but a narrative. But these lines are also indicative of the mimetic impulse, the urge to write or draw, reduced to a single mark. In citing the three squiggles here as emblematic figures that enter into dialogue with narrative technique, this chapter has aimed to introduce the little-known version drawn by Hoffmann into long-standing discussions of Balzac's arabesque and Sterne's flourish, thus inserting a third stage into this particular history of citation and distortion. That Hoffmann also copied Sterne's flourish contributes to a new understanding of the relationship between Hoffmann and Balzac. Both writers, through the mediating influence of Sterne, reflect on the act of writing through distancing themselves to it by playing with the insertion of a literal narrative line. The lines they draw underscore, first, a preoccupation with the interrelatedness of word and image, and with the cross-transformations between these two media. Second, as counterparts of the figurative pictorial lines so often employed in their narratives, their squiggles constitute a meditation on mark-making. The squiggle, protean and infinitely variable, opens up new configurations of the figure of the narrator, not just as writer or artist, but as scribbler, as doodler – always seeking out new ways to mediate between the world and the object of their art.

Part II

Lines

Chapter 3

Arabesque: *Der goldne Topf* and *La Peau de chagrin*

The undulating lines introduced in Chapter 2 as 'reverse-ekphrastic' pictures of text stage the scene of reading as a site of interplay between legibility and illegibility. This chapter returns to one of these lines – to Balzac's visual epigraph to *La Peau de chagrin* – and recontextualises it by placing it in dialogue with Hoffmann's 'modern fairy tale' *Der goldne Topf*. In this I take seriously the label sometimes applied to Balzac's squiggle: arabesque.

Perhaps *the* motif of nineteenth-century Orientalism, the arabesque – frequently described as a Western appropriation of decorative tendril patterns found in Arab art and architecture, primarily by Venetian artists of the Renaissance – had long been established, by the nineteenth century, as a fully Western, vaguely exoticising design that had 'detached [itself] from any reference point in the Islamic world'.[1] A few major, interrelated characteristics feature in the arabesque's oscillations in and out of favour in eighteenth- and nineteenth-century aesthetic theory and will in turn be important for the discussion here: first, its marginal status, as border-work with the tendency to creep from the framework into the picture (as in rococo designs); second, its nonconformity to nature or non-representationality; and, third, its haphazard or nonsensical quality. The somewhat surprising levels of vitriol directed towards the arabesque by certain rationalist and classicist thinkers of the eighteenth century are evident in Adolf Riem's polemic 'Ueber die

---

[1] Margaret S. Graves, 'Spatchcocking the Arabesque: Big Books, Industrial Design, and the Captivation of Islamic Art and Architecture', in *Arabesque without End: Across Music and the Arts, from Faust to Shahrazad*, ed. by Anne Leonard (Abingdon-on-Thames: Routledge, 2022), pp. 19–55 (p. 19). For an outline of the history of the arabesque, see Günter Oesterle, 'Arabeske', in *Ästhetische Grundbegriffe: Historisches Wörterbuch in sieben Bänden*, ed. by Karlheinz Barck and others (Stuttgart: Metzler, 2000), I, pp. 272–86.

Arabeske' (On the Arabesque) (1788), in which he calls arabesques 'die bloße Mißgeburten und Ungeheuer einer regellosen Imagination' (nothing but the monstrous productions of an unbridled imagination), objects whose nonconformity to natural beauty mires them in the state of 'nichts bedeutende Sudeleyen' (meaningless scribbling).[2] 'Sudeleyen' is a provocative, because fully intermedial, term. The Grimm-Wörterbuch aligns it with both visual art, as 'pfuscherhaftes, minderwertiges oder unsorgfältiges kunstwerk, besonders gemälde' (botched, inferior or careless art, especially paintings) and writing, as 'unsauber, flüchtig geschriebenes schriftstück' (grubby, hastily composed writing), whilst Winfried Menninghaus's translation as 'scribbling' is suggestive of a scriptural register, but also of that sheer exuberant form, hovering between meaning and disarray, that I examined in the preceding chapter.[3]

This intermedial quality was an important additional characteristic of the Romantic arabesque as it seeped into the space of the illustrated book and took on textual form. By the end of the nineteenth century the arabesque would become a fully multimedial figure, moving capriciously from visual art and architecture into literature, music, dance and beyond. Menninghaus pins the beginning of this medial diffusion at a crucial moment in aesthetic history: in Kant's formulation of the parergon's relationship to the ergon in the *Critique of Judgment*, in which Kant discusses arabesque designs, without naming them as such, as exemplars of aesthetic autonomy, of 'free' as opposed to 'adherent' beauty, having no object and no directly representational or conceptual baggage. This revaluation of the border-work *as* border-work incited a new enthusiasm for the arabesque. For the Romantics, from Runge to Schlegel to Tieck to Hoffmann, the arabesque opened up new possibilities in form: extending beyond a simple motif, it became a 'formal principle that manifests itself across all levels of artistic expression'.[4] With lines that double, branch out and twist back on themselves, arabesque shapes are self-engendering, self-shaping, self-fulfilling figures, appearing

[2] Adolf Riem, 'Ueber die Arabeske', in *Monatsschrift der Akademie der Künste und Wissenschaften zu Berlin* (Berlin: König. Preuß akad. Kunst- und Buchhandlung, 1788), pp. 117–37 (p. 128).

[3] 'Sudelei', in *Deutsches Wörterbuch von Jacob Grimm und Wilhelm Grimm* <https://woerterbuchnetz.de/?sigle=DWB#1> [accessed 10 October 2022]; Winfried Menninghaus, 'Hummingbirds, Shells, Picture-Frames: Kant's "Free Beauties" and the Romantic Arabesque', in *Rereading Romanticism*, ed. Martha B. Helfer (Amsterdam: Rodopi, 2000), pp. 27–46 (p. 30).

[4] David E. Wellbery, 'Poet, Artist, Arabesque: On Peter Cornelius's Illustrations to Goethe's *Faust*', in *Arabesque without End*, ed. by Leonard, p. 62.

to gesture towards infinity. In the writings of Friedrich Schlegel, the arabesque's qualities of plenitude, self-reflection and unfixity, as 'künstlich geordnete Verwirrung' (artfully ordered confusion), raise it to a figure for production whose primary literary analogue is the *Märchen*, the fairy tale, for its imaginative exuberance and use of interlacing narrative threads or interlocking frames.[5]

Accordingly, the two works I will discuss in this chapter are variations on the *Märchen* or *conte*: Hoffmann's *Der goldne Topf* and Balzac's *La Peau de chagrin*. In these tales, the fantastic mode is generated through Orientalising impulses. For Balzac, the arabesque is the visual form of the novel's epigraph, its framing emblem and point of departure. For Hoffmann, the structure of the tale itself, with its criss-crossing narrative threads, traces the protagonist's initiation into a new plane of existence as one that suggests the experience of an Oriental artwork. As the marker of a switch from a realist into a fantastic mode, and as a motif of writing or drawing, the curling lines of the arabesque trace the tendency of the text to turn back on itself, in questioning self-reflection.

In the two tales I will examine here, the task of reading and copying a text (for Anselmus) or of narrating a life (for Raphaël) – the will to render a story legible – betrays a concern about narrative communication: about who is reading and who is narrating, and about whether the narrative will be understood or disregarded as little more than 'Orientalischer Schwulst' (Oriental bombast) (H II.1 246). In both works, this communicative anxiety is pictured in the written lines of an Eastern script. If the Western anxiety about the wilful non-representationality of arabesques seems excessive, then it might highlight to us that mimesis – often assumed a literary commonplace – is a specifically Western convention; that 'no cultures outside the West', as Matthew Potolsky reminds us, 'have regarded realism as an important goal'.[6] The arabesques here accordingly dis-orient the texts, becoming the locus of a set of shifts between the intelligible and the arcane, between meaning and meaninglessness, never quite crystallising into the first nor dissolving into the second. The appropriation of a marginal Eastern form as a motif for the fantastic and for the illegible Other allows for a reflection on the premises of the Western reading self.

---

[5] Friedrich Schlegel, 'Rede über die Mythologie', in *Friedrich Schlegel: Kritische Ausgabe seiner Werke*, ed. By Ernst Behler and others, 32 vols (Paderborn: Brill/Schöningh, 1966–), II, 312–29, p. 318.

[6] Matthew Potolsky, *Mimesis* (London: Routledge, 2006), p. 94.

Der goldne Topf

One of the primary charges that Walter Scott levels against Hoffmann's tales relates to a tendency towards ornament and excess that Scott, essentially rehashing eighteenth-century critiques of the arabesque, designates not just as irrational and distasteful, but as morally reprehensible:

> The reader must be contented to look upon the gambols of the author as he would behold the flying leaps and incongruous trans-mutations of Harlequin, without seeking to discover either meaning or end further than the surprise of the moment.[7]

Scott explicitly goes on to compare such 'fantastic extravagances' to the arabesque:

> In fact, the grotesque in his compositions partly resembles the arabesque in painting, in which is introduced the most strange and complicated monsters, resembling centaurs, griffins, sphinxes, chimeras, rocs, and all other creatures of the romantic imagination, dazzling the beholder as it were by the unbounded fertility of the authors' imagination, and sating it by the rich contrast of all the varieties of shape and colouring, while there is in reality nothing to satisfy the understanding or inform the judgment.[8]

In this rich description, which seems to bely a certain grudging admiration for Hoffmann's imaginative capacities, Scott highlights precisely those aspects of the arabesque that appealed to the Romantic imagination: its meaninglessness (or freedom from meaning), its imaginativeness and its unboundedness. Here, I seek to pursue that sense of unboundedness through *Der goldne Topf*, Hoffmann's most 'arabesque' work and his work arguably most aligned with early Romantic thought. In doing so, and in following Günter Oesterle's important essay on arabesques in this work, I will show how the text unleashes the repressed energies of the marginal flourish in 'dazzling' shifts between meaning and meaninglessness, fixity and infinity, by engaging the repetitiousness, symmetries and contrasts of arabesque designs on a formal level, and by moving the narrative frame

---

[7] Walter Scott, 'On the Supernatural in Fictitious Composition; and particularly on the Works of Ernest Theodore William Hoffmann', *Foreign Quarterly Review* 1 (1827), 60–98, p. 72.

[8] Ibid., p. 74, pp. 81–2.

repeatedly towards the centre of its form.[9] In doing so, Hoffmann narrates a near-ekphrastic encounter with a specifically Eastern work of art, one that is not straightforwardly legible to the Western eye. He thus frees up his work from the restrictive obligation of making sense – and of ending – and gives expression to one of his most significant tropes: the doubled or serial self. Repetition, finally, emerges as an uneasy substitute for resolution.

At the centre of *Der goldne Topf* is the seduction of the protagonist by an Eastern line. This line, a refiguring of the Renaissance 'figura serpentinata', coiling and calligraphic in its movements, is the form taken by Serpentina, the daughter of the salamander Archivarius Lindhorst, who is invoked as the living projection of his scripts. The protagonist Anselmus – Lindhorst's hapless amanuensis, who finds himself caught between the prosaic streets of Dresden and a lofty realm of poetic experience, Atlantis, unable to consolidate the one within the other – may be understood as a precursor of Balzac's Raphaël de Valentin, the hero of *La Peau de chagrin*. Both young men, scholars of Eastern languages, find themselves initiated into a new and fantastic existence which unfolds in impossible shapes within the context of their everyday lives. Anselmus's initiation is triggered by his transcription of Arabic and Coptic scripts under the tutelage of the magical archivist Lindhorst. As the creation myths of Atlantis emerge from Lindhorst's manuscripts and from Anselmus's copies, the seductive line of Serpentina, and the possibility of artistic transcendence, grow more distinct – a process that is fatally interrupted by the interferences of the witchy Liese, who is associated with Anselmus's fatal mistake as he spills ink on his manuscript. In paying attention to both line and inkblot, my reading here will aim to offer an alternative account to those readings that ascribe to the tale a kind of teleological linear logic, as an account of Anselmus's snaking path from 'Schreiber' (writer) to 'Schriftsteller' (author), and thus as something like a '*Bildungsroman* in fairy-tale form'.[10] Instead, I will place the motif of the non-utilitarian line in the context of an arabesque design.

Scholarship has lingered over the question of whether the tale's careful depiction of Dresden betrays the social critique of an

[9] Günter Oesterle, 'Arabeske, Schrift und Poesie in E. T. A. Hoffmanns Kunstmärchen "Der goldne Topf"', *Athenäum*, 1 (1991), 69–107.

[10] Uwe Wirth, 'Der goldne Topf', in *E. T. A. Hoffmann: Leben – Werk – Wirkung*, ed. by Detlef Kremer (Berlin: De Gruyter, 2009), pp. 114–24 (p. 118). See also Hartmut Steinecke's commentary in H II.1, p. 770, and James McGlathery, 'The Suicide Motif in E. T. A. Hoffmann's "Der goldne Topf"', *Monatshefte*, 58 (1966), 115–23 (p. 115).

emergent realism, or whether that 'realist' narrative style is only mounted against a fantastic alternative as part of what Daemmrich calls a 'Stilmittel der zweifach Optik' (stylistic method of double optics), to show in clearer distinction the plight of the artist, for whom reality itself is only another filmy and insubstantial layer of experience.[11] Consensus has largely gathered around this second option. For John Reddick, Hoffmann's lucid portrayal of Dresden life incidentally 'points to the beginnings of the German realist tradition', but its more important role is to contribute to a 'systematic irony' by showing up 'the decidedly uncertain nature of everything else that is silhouetted against it' and questioning the certainty of any given reality.[12] Manfred Momberger argues that Hoffmann engages the referential codes of realism precisely to show the status of reality as a shimmering spectacle of appearances. By establishing neither true realism nor a pure flight of fancy, Hoffmann produces narrative experience itself in a text that, by oscillating between framing and enframed narrative levels, attempts to yield an insight into 'die Produziertheit, die Fiktionalität der "Wirklichkeit" selbst' (the produced and fictional status of 'reality' itself).[13] In true arabesque style, the framework and the enframed content threaten to flip positions. A question taken from *Prinzessin Brambilla*, addressed to the reader, serves nicely to illustrate this: 'und du wähntest, nur jener Traum sei dein eigentliches Sein, was du aber sonst für dein Leben gehalten, nur der Mißverstand des betörten Sinns?' (And did you not dare to think that the dream alone was your true existence, and that what you had previously taken for life was only the delusion of your befuddled senses?) (H V 793).

Joanna Neilly's account of *Der goldne Topf* recasts the binary model of Anselmus's existence as an Oriental (and implicitly arabesque) pluralism, in which multiple contradictory understandings of the world allow the artist's work to emerge in the final form of the text *Der goldne Topf* itself. This chapter will follow Neilly in suggesting that Hoffmann's ambivalent attitude towards the 'Orient as utopian ideal' is critically invested in the acts of writing and

---

[11] Horst Daemmrich, 'Wirklichkeit als Form: ein Aspekt Hoffmannscher Erzählkunst', *Colloquia Germanica*, 4 (1970), 36–45, p. 43.

[12] John Reddick, 'E. T. A. Hoffmann's "Der goldne Topf" and its "Durchgehaltene Ironie"', *MLR*, 71.3 (1976), 577–94, p. 579.

[13] Manfred Momberger, *Sonne und Punsch: Die Dissemination des romantischen Kunstbegriffs bei E. T. A. Hoffmann* (Munich: Fink, 1986), p. 94.

inscription that underpin that ideal.[14] The emergence of the Oriental 'elsewhere' – which exists both as an escape from, and as part of, the everyday world; as a fiction – is accompanied by a self-critical attention to the act of its depiction. My reading here thus pays attention to the marks made in writing and copying and to their participation in systems of reading and knowledge. The process of writing, in the tale, is neither easy nor assured. The form of Serpentina – the singular beautiful line – is joined on the page by another inky mark, the accidental inkblot associated with the analphabetic and unaesthetic Liese, and which threatens both to ruin the legibility of the manuscript and to scupper Anselmus's chance at transcendence. In this chapter I put forward a case for this work less as a *Märchen*-like *Bildungsroman* than as an experiment in freeing up a narrative from the strictures of sense-making. A reading that incorporates both the line and the inkblot, the one within the other, to engage a skewed optic appropriate to a reading of Hoffmann – approaching the model of anamorphosis, as in Gerhard Neumann's account, discussed elsewhere in this book – will also allow for a closer examination of two of Hoffmann's most overlooked female characters, Veronika Paulmann and Liese.[15] As a doubled, duplicitous form, the anamorphic image incorporates a disfiguration within the pictorial field, such that understanding is accompanied by the lingering threat of illegibility. Like arabesque designs, the curvilinear motif in this work is foregrounded, but it does not follow a 'linear' logic – in the sense of a teleological or rational one – so much as it disperses meaning in an illusionist gesture towards endlessness.

The Line

Arabesque forms structure *Der goldne Topf* as traces of Anselmus's changing vision. In Lindhorst's library, Anselmus stops short at the sight of 'der vielen Pünktchen, Striche und Züge und Schnörkel, die bald Pflanzen, bald Moose, bald Tiergestalten darzustellen schienen' (the many little points, lines and strokes and flourishes, which appeared now to represent plants, now mosses, now animal figures) (H II.1 286). These endlessly reflecting patterns are also reflected across the pages he is instructed to copy, where they

---

[14] Joanna Neilly, *E. T. A. Hoffmann's Orient: Romantic Aesthetics and the German Imagination* (Oxford: Legenda, 2016), p. 27.

[15] Gerhard Neumann, 'Anamorphose. E. T. A. Hoffmanns Poetik der Defiguration', in *Mimesis und Simulation*, ed. by Andreas Kablitz and Gerhard Neumann (Freiburg im Breisgau: Rombach, 1998), pp. 377–417, p. 399.

dazzle and overwhelm his vision: 'so viele sonderbare krause Züge und Schnörkel durcheinander, die, ohne dem Auge einen einzigen Ruhepunkt zu geben, den Blick verwirrten, daß es ihm beinahe unmöglich schien das alles genau nachzumalen' (so many strange curling strokes and flourishes tangled together, which, by failing to give the eye a single point to rest on, confused one's view, such that it seemed to him almost impossible to reproduce it all exactly) (H II.1 301). These patterns are self-reflecting, self-repeating and seemingly non-representational: like arabesque designs, they overwhelm the eye by refusing it a single point of focus. But, as Anselmus discovers, they can be copied, and as he begins to copy them, they offer the potential for new understanding:

> War ihm schon vor dem Essen das Kopieren der arabischen Zeichen geglückt, so ging die Arbeit jetzt noch viel besser von Statten, ja er konnte selbst die Schnelle und Leichtigkeit nicht begreifen, womit er die krausen Züge der fremden Schrift nachzumalen vermochte. [. . .] Da wehte es wie in leisen, leisen, lispelnden Krystallklängen durch das Zimmer: ich bin dir nahe – nahe – nahe! – ich helfe dir! – sei mutig! – sei standhaft, lieber Anselmus! – ich mühe mich mit dir, damit du mein werdest! Und so wie er voll innern Entzückens die Töne vernahm, wurden ihm immer verständlicher die unbekannten Zeichen – er durfte kaum mehr hineinblicken in das Original – ja es war, als stünden schon wie in blasser Schrift die Zeichen auf dem Pergament, und er dürfe sie nur mit geübter Hand schwarz überziehen. (H II.1 274)

> If he had been doing well in copying these Arabic symbols before dinner, now the work was proceeding even better: in truth, he could not understand the speed and the ease with which he was able to transcribe the curling strokes of these foreign characters. [. . .] Then soft, low, undulating tones of crystal wafted through the room: 'I am near, near, near! I will help you. Be brave, be steadfast, dear Anselmus! I will give you my help so that you may be mine!' And as Anselmus heard these sounds with inner rapture, the unfamiliar characters grew ever more intelligible to him, and he hardly needed to look at the original script at all; in fact, it seemed as if the characters were already outlined on the parchment in pale ink and there was nothing more for him to do but fill them in with black.

The lines of script here move fluidly between the incomprehensible curlicues of a foreign language, through the sinuous lines implied by the body and sibilant words of Serpentina, into legible lines of script that appear 'ever more intelligible' to him, thus tracing the process of reading as form becomes meaningful.

Anselmus lives in a strictly linearised and bounded world. The inhabitants of Dresden are greatly preoccupied with the cutting and casting of their silhouettes, paying particular attention to appendages such as wigs, hats and cloaks: when Veronika dreams of her future marriage to Anselmus, she pictures herself in a fashionable hat and 'neue[r] türkische[r] Shawl' (new Turkish shawl) (H II.1 259). Hoffmann's narrator accordingly mimics physiognomic discourse, engaging the assumption that the body is inherently meaningful in its shape and that its meaning may be extracted through the correct interpretation of its bounding lines. With mock-Lavaterian sincerity, he claims that Anselmus's idiosyncratic appearance gives him 'einen gewissen magistermäßigen Styl, dem sich nun wieder Gang und Stellung durchaus nicht fügen wollte' (a certain schoolmasterish air which was at odds with his gait and bearing) (H II.1 230).

For Lindhorst, it is precisely Anselmus's awkwardness and misalignment, his 'kindliches poetisches Gemüt' (childish, poetic temperament) (H II.1 291), that make him a suitable apprentice and potential son-in-law. As a hybrid being who appears in turn as a man, vulture, and a bush of fire lilies, Lindhorst rules over an entirely different regime of legibility from the one embraced by philistine Dresden society. Accordingly, when Anselmus first hands over a sample of his handwriting to Lindhorst in the blue library, his lines appear distorted and stripped of meaning:

> Anselmus wurde wie vom Blitz getroffen, als ihm seine Handschrift so höchst miserabel vorkam. Da war keine Rfinde in den Zügen, kein Druck richtig, kein Verhältnis der großen und kleinen Buchstaben. (H II.1 273)

> Anselmus was struck as if by lightning, his handwriting appearing to him now so utterly wretched. There was no shape to his strokes, the pressure was all wrong, capital and small letters were indistinguishable from one another.

Anselmus's passage from 'Schreiber' to 'Schriftsteller' may be read as a disambiguation of the Orientally inflected line from within a bourgeois society committed to a comparatively impoverished regime of legibility. As we saw in Chapter 2, Andrew Piper has traced the emergence of the sinuous Romantic line – a serpentine line, with its roots in the Hogarthian line of beauty – as a figure distinct from other kinds of line that might function, in science or geography, as a 'marker of either distinction (the outline) or linearity (teleology)'. He places the emergence of the Romantic line, 'as *the* image of the interaction between text and image', at a time of 'an increasingly sophisticated intermedial sensibility', which inspired new fascination for outline drawings, *Umrisse*, silhouette drawings, *Schattenrisse*, and for illustrated books.[16] The Romantic line emerges from the crossover of text and image, marking 'the possibility of textual and visual simultaneity'.[17] Maurice Merleau-Ponty offers a similar narrative in his discussion of lines in art in 'L'Œil et l'esprit', this time in the context of modernist painting. In the works of a painter like Klee, the descriptive or contouring line is replaced by a freer, undulating 'ligne flexueuse' (serpentine line).[18] In these different contexts, the non-utilitarian, undulating line is unshackled from its servitude to the terminal outline or contour, no longer describing the visual but participating in visibility.

Lindhorst, and his visual projection in the calligraphic curves of Serpentina, the living embodiment of the Romantic line, comes to resemble the guardian of an arcane or magical reading. The Dresdeners' denunciations echo the rationalist-classicist critique of arabesque forms: Paulmann claims that he is 'nur kurios in absonderlichen Redensarten' (simply odd in his bizarre phraseology) (H II.1 250), and Heerbrand, pointedly, that his stories are '*orientalischer* Schwulst' (*Oriental* fabrication, my emphasis) (H II.1 246). To follow this line of thought would be to read Anselmus's forays in the blue library as a discovery of *Dichtung* within a world of bored prose, an untangling of Romantic significance from a stale reality via the inspiration of Eastern stories. This untangling happens by means of a shift into Orientalism, an unfurling of Eastern stories mediated through the figure of the arabesque, poised between image and lettering. The convergence of pictorial and textual modes is geared towards a representation of the coming into being of legibility – from visible lines into legible letters. The precariousness and riskiness of that process – the danger of its lapsing back into illegible form, and the final renunciation of a transcendent arabesque realm – is embodied in the character of Liese.

[16] Andrew Piper, *Dreaming in Books: The Making of the Bibliographic Imagination in the Romantic Age* (Chicago, IL: University of Chicago Press, 2009), p. 185.

[17] Ibid., p. 189.

[18] Maurice Merleau-Ponty, 'L'Œil et l'esprit' (Paris: Gallimard, 1964), p. 72.

The Inkblot

For Friedrich Kittler, who likens Anselmus's tutelage under Lindhorst to the practice of standardising handwriting in German schools at the turn of the nineteenth century, Liese is an impediment to the system of reading represented by Lindhorst: she does, after all, rip the pages from his books.[19] And she is associated with the inkblot that Anselmus drops on the manuscript. Known variously as 'das Äpfelweib' (the apple woman) who tells fortunes by the Dresden gates, as 'die alte Liese' (old Liese), Veronika Paulmann's childhood nurse, and as 'die Rauerin', Lindhorst's sworn enemy, she is also, according to Lindhorst's mythology, the hybrid child of a 'schnöde Runkelrübe' (dirty beet) and a 'lumpichter Flederwisch' (ragged feather brush) (H II.1 298). As a mixed and messy figure – a figure of formlessness – introduced when Anselmus upturns her apple-cart and spills her apples (which she refers to as her sons), and associated repeatedly with *Ge-* nouns, such as 'Gekrächze' (croaking) and 'Gepiepe' (squeaking) and 'Gesindel' (rabble), (H II.1 264–5), she is nonetheless, as fortune-teller, a guardian of a particular kind of knowledge. For it is Liese's mantic line to Anselmus at the beginning of the tale – 'Ins Krystall bald dein Fall' (into the crystal you will fall) (H II.1 229) – that spells out the tale's trajectory: when Anselmus is disillusioned from his task and spills his ink, Lindhorst punishes him by encasing him in glass. As much as she is associated with mess and indecipherability, then, Liese mirrors Lindhorst by introducing an alternative and explicitly female logic into the text, one associated with a strange scene of equinoctial witchcraft and with her devotion to the lovelorn Veronika Paulmann and Angelike Oster. Finally, like the moving figures of Lindhorst's scrolls and the emergence of Serpentina from a tree, Liese too appears as a re-vitalisation of prosaic lines when her face emerges from Lindhorst's door-knocker (H II.1 243–4).

As such, Liese assumes a marginal position in a peculiar art history: the art of blotting. Günter and Ingrid Oesterle and Caroline Schubert, amongst others, have traced a genealogy of artists who engaged in blotting methods from the eighteenth century onwards.[20] These range from Alexander Cozens and his landscape paintings to

[19] Friedrich Kittler, *Aufschreibesysteme 1800–1900* (Munich: Fink, 2003), pp. 110–11.

[20] Günter and Ingrid Oesterle, 'Der Imaginationsreiz der Flecken von Leonardo da Vinci bis Peter Rühmkorf', in *Signaturen der Gegenwartsliteratur, Festschrift für Walter Hinderer*, ed. by Dieter Borchmeyer (Würzburg: Königshausen und Neumann, 1999), pp. 213–38; Caroline Schubert, *Defiguration der Schrift: Tintenkleckserei, Makulatur*

the fantastic experiments of Justinus Kerner's *Klecksographien* and Victor Hugo's incantatory stain paintings, and to the exploitation of such techniques in the twentieth century in psychoanalysis (Hermann Rorschach) and abstract expressionism (Jackson Pollock).[21] All of these blotters take as the basis for their art the fact that what looks like accidental formlessness also looks like it might have a secret meaning. It is, in that sense, a kind of wry representational game. For Alexander Cozens, the 'accidental forms without lines' made by spilled ink are 'conformable to nature' – which makes his blotting, like the sketching techniques touted by William Gilpin and others, into a more quintessential kind of mimetic work. Justinus Kerner's inkblots, on the other hand, supposedly forego representation altogether, allowing instead for the real manifestation of dark spirits on the page. All of these blotting methods take seriously Leonardo da Vinci's advice for artists to seek out, as inspiration for their works, the figures that seem to spring from crumbling patches of walls, the formlessness of stains or the wisps of clouds. Hoffmann himself – if not a practitioner of such methods, then perhaps an interested party – includes, in his *Kunzischer Riß* (see Figure 3.1), an impertinent 'Kleks' in amongst the strange mixture of real and fictional characters who populate his imaginative plan of the Gendarmenmarkt. Far smoother than an accidental blot, surely – with its rounded body, its nose and tail – by labelling the blot *as* blot, Hoffmann turns it into a mediator between the brutely material dimension of the drawing and its legibility as diagram.

In *Kater Murr*, blotting paper or the *Makulaturblatt*, set against the typeset page, is the interlocutor and mirror-space of Johannes Kreisler's sanctioned written spaces. Blots both here and elsewhere (as in games of 'blotto' or 'Klecksographien') encourage the folding of paper to summon up symmetrical designs. Liese, too, has a specifically reflective role to play in the text. As a mirror of Lindhorst, Liese presides over her own specifically female strand of the story. Veronika Paulmann, like Anselmus, is haunted by fantastic spirits that intervene in her life – this time in the form of a domestic imp emerging from household objects, who mocks her bourgeois daydreams of becoming 'Frau Hofrätin' (Mrs Privy Councillor) (H II.1 261). Veronika's narrative, which develops in

---

und Schreibfehler bei E. T. A. Hoffmann und Nikolaj Gogol' (Berlin: De Gruyter, 2021), pp. 118–19.

[21] Alexander Cozens, 'A New Method of Assisting the Invention in Drawing Original Compositions of Landscape', reprinted in A. P. Oppé, *Alexander & John Robert Cozens* (London: Adam and Charles Black, 1952), pp. 165–87 (p. 170).

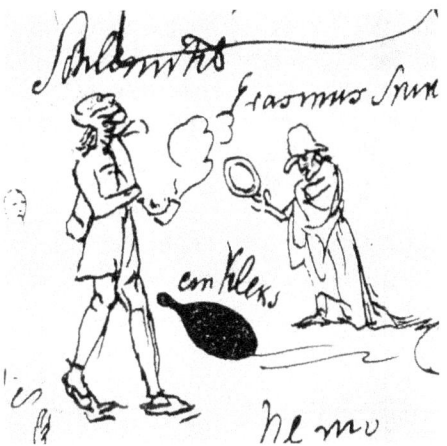

Figure 3.1 Detail from E. T. A. Hoffmann, *Kunzischer Riß*. © Staatsbibliothek Bamberg L.g.o.390(1

the fifth and the seventh vigils and which is followed, on both occasions, by Anselmus's first experiences in Lindhorst's library (in the sixth and the eighth vigils), both neatly interlaces with and reflects Anselmus's narrative, therefore, in an arabesque intertwining of narrative threads. Like Anselmus, Veronika suffers delusory fantasies that threaten to wrench her out of her ordinary life, though they are more prosaic-seeming fantasies than his – as befits the future housewife rather than the future artist. It is appropriate, then, that what Veronika receives from Liese, in place of a spoken prophesy, is a small mirror. This mirror is given central status in the tale when Anselmus peers into it over her shoulder and their faces appear framed within it together:

> Da kam ihm aber wieder einmal der Dämon des Ungeschicks über den Hals, er stieß an den Tisch und Veronika's niedliches Nähkästchen fiel herab, Anselmus hob es auf, der Deckel war gesprungen, und es blinkte ihm ein kleiner runder Metallspiegel entgegen, in den er mit ganz eigner Lust hineinschaute. [. . .] Da war es dem Anselmus als beginne ein Kampf in seinem Innern – Gedanken – Bilder – blitzten hervor und vergingen wieder – der Archivarius Lindhorst – Serpentina – die grüne Schlange – endlich wurde es ruhiger und alles Verworrene fügte und gestaltete sich zum deutlichen Bewußtsein. (H II.1 295)

But once again the demon of awkwardness possessed him, and he stumbled against the table, Veronica's sweet little sewing box tumbling to the floor. Anselmus picked it up: the lid had fallen open and

> a small round metallic mirror shone up at him, which he looked into
> with special pleasure. [. . .] Anselmus felt as if a battle were com-
> mencing in his soul: thoughts and images flashed before him and
> disappeared again – Archivarius Lindhorst – Serpentina – the green
> snake – until it finally abated and all the chaos rearranged itself to
> assume a clearly comprehensible shape.

In the new configuration of shapes in Veronika's mirror, the narrative subject recognises himself as an object: first, as a character
in Veronika's own fantasy narrative; and, second, as a pawn in
the mysterious battle played out between Liese and Lindhorst.
Anselmus's momentary insight into Veronika's experience effectively decentralises his position in the overall shape of the tale,
which is now exposed as a collection of inter-reflecting arabesque
patterns in which the singular narrative line is confounded by the
blossoming and branching outwards of multiple possible lines
and symmetrical offshoots – to include, for example, Heerbrand's
vision of a dancing 'lateinische Frakturschrift' (Latin Gothic
script) (H II.1 240). By creating the impression of endless further
interlocking narratives, the tale engages something akin to what
Gombrich calls the illusionist 'etc. principle' in the context of visual
art: 'the assumption we tend to make that to see a few members of a
series is to see them all'.[22] In Romantic terms, it follows the logic of
the fragment and other forms of the *non finito* that gesture towards
a more totalising ideal. The once-central protagonist is exposed as
endlessly repeatable; only one of so many paper dolls, each one
a wistful Romantic hero of his or her own more or less mundane
private fantasies.

Veronika's mirror provokes a shift in Anselmus's perception
that will cast the world's visual register back into the prosaic
lines and shapes of which it consisted before the introduction of
Serpentina, until Anselmus 'konnte sich nicht genug wundern wie
ihm das Alles sonst so seltsam und wundervoll habe vorkommen
können' (could not help but wonder at how all of it had once
appeared to him to be so strange and marvellous) (H II.1 300). It
is in this disenchanted state that Anselmus makes the fatal inkblot
on his manuscript:

> Aber er sah auf der Pergamentrolle so viele sonderbare Krause
> Züge und Schnörkel durcheinander, die ohne dem Auge einen

---

[22] E. H. Gombrich, *Art and Illusion: A Study in the Psychology of Pictorial Representation*
(London: Phaidon, 1996), p. 175.

einzigen Ruhepunkt zu geben den Blick verwirrten, daß es ihm beinahe unmöglich schien das Alles genau nachzumalen. Ja bei dem Überblick des Ganzen schien das Pergament nur ein bunt geaderter Marmor oder ein mit Moosen durchsprenkelter Stein. – Er wollte dem unerachtet das Mögliche versuchen und tunkte getrost die Feder ein, aber die Tinte wollte durchaus nicht fließen, er spritzte die Feder ungeduldig aus und – o Himmel! ein großer Klecks fiel auf das ausgebreitete Original. (H II.1 301)

But on the roll of parchment he saw a number of strange curling strokes and flourishes tangled together, which confused one's view by not giving the eye a single point to rest on, such that it seemed to him almost impossible to reproduce the whole thing exactly. Indeed, on surveying it the parchment resembled only a brightly mottled slab of marble or a stone flecked with moss. He nevertheless resolved to do his very best and confidently dipped his pen in the ink, but no matter his efforts, the ink would not flow. He impatiently flicked the point of his pen and – oh heavens! – a large blot fell onto the outspread original.

The 'krause Züge' from before are now just that, curling strokes or lines, without also being the arcane imprints of something else. Franz Fühmann, in his bleakly realist reading of the tale through the figure of Veronika, states of her behaviour: 'ins Tiefste zu schaun und nichts daraus zu ziehen als ein Mittel, schneller Frau Hofrätin zu werden, ist das nicht furchtbar? – Es ist alltäglich' (To see into the depths and to take nothing from it but a means to more quickly become the wife of the Privy Counsellor – is that not dreadful? – It is everyday life).[23] Veronika's and Liese's magic is 'alltäglich' because if the narrative act can lead to transcendence, that act can also be reversed, rehabilitating the domestic shapes that once appeared threatening and turning Lindhorst's blue library back into a normal building. Significantly, the manuscript now resembles a slab of marble or a moss-flecked stone: that is, precisely the kind of natural form from which Leonardo encouraged artists to seek their inspiration. This does not have to mean that in the final reading things are bland and meaningless – after all, the *Märchen* ends in a vision of transcendence – but rather that things are both fantastically significant and meaningless at once: that the states of enchantment and disenchantment are coexistent and dependent on one another, and that

23 Franz Fühmann, *Fräulein Veronika Paulmann aus der Pirnaer Vorstadt oder Etwas über das Schauerliche bei E. T. A. Hoffmann* (Munich: Deutscher Taschenbuch Verlag, 1984), pp. 89–90.

in this tale Hoffmann is attached to the precariousness of the first state, warning that the second is never far behind it. The possibility of understanding is accompanied by an inevitable lapse into illegibility, mimetic form attended by its own potential undoing.

Ornamental Frames

The tale's shifting levels reach a higher intensity in the context of its narrative frame, in which the narrator pauses at several points to confess the difficulties he has faced in telling his story. The twelfth vigil is given over to the longest of these confessions:

> Ich härmte mich recht ab, wenn ich die eilf Vigilien, die ich glücklich zu Stande gebracht, durchlief und nun dachte, daß es mir wohl niemals vergönnt sein werde, die zwölfte als Schlußstein hinzuzufügen, den so oft ich mich zur Nachtzeit hinsetzte um das Werk zu vollenden, war es, als hielten mir recht tückische Geister (es mochten wohl Verwandte – vielleicht Cousins germains der getöteten Hexe sein) ein glänzend poliertes Metall vor, in dem ich mein Ich erblickte, blaß, übernächtig und melancholisch wie der Registrator Heerbrand nach dem Punsch-Rausch. (H II.1 316)

> When I looked over the eleven vigils, which are now fortunately completed, it grieved me to the heart to think that inserting the Twelfth Vigil, the very keystone of the whole, would never be permitted me, for whenever I tried during the night to complete the work, it was as if mischievous spirits (they might indeed be relatives or even blood cousins of the slain witch) were holding a polished and gleaming piece of metal before my eyes in which I could behold my own self – pale, worn out, and melancholy, like Registrar Heerbrand after his bout with the punch.

This second mirror sequence again exposes the criss-crossing arabesque structure of entwinement and repetition in the alternating experiences of disenchantment and dream, this time coupling together the narratives of Heerbrand and the narrator. In the case of *Der goldne Topf*, the young artist-to-be – who is at first seduced by his visions and then disenchanted by them – is revealed as no more than an ornamental figure in the work of a narrator busily confessing his own hungover anxieties about representation, as if the inkblot cast by Anselmus on his work functions less as a superficial stain on a manuscript than as a stone thrown into the surface of a lake, or a rip in a tapestry, disrupting the work layer by layer from the centre outwards.

In one of the very strangest images of the tale, the archivist Lindhorst offers the narrator a glass of punch and then climbs into the glass himself before the narrator takes a sip:

> Tragen Sie keine Sorge mein Bester, rief der Archivarius, warf den Schlafrock schnell ab, stieg zu meinem nicht geringen Erstaunen in den Pokal und verschwand in den Flammen. – Ohne Scheu kostete ich, die Flamme leise weghauchend, von dem Getränk – es war köstlich! (H II.1 318)

> 'Have no fear, my good fellow,' Archivarius Lindhorst called, then quickly cast off his robe and, to my great amazement, climbed into the goblet and disappeared into the flames. Without hesitation I softly blew back the flame and took a sip – it was delicious!

In this intricate textual flourish, the narrator, it is suggested, drinks the fictional character he has produced, in the context of a scene in which that character has ostensibly become a real one, thus perpetuating the sense of tales engulfed within tales, and the continuous moves to swap centre and margin, that have played out across the twelve vigils. The narrator re-absorbs into himself the narrative he has produced, delineating the fictional character as object, as production – but he does so on the whim and instruction of that very object. The living object is articulated through and against the porous borders of the narrative body, which has in turn become an engine of textual production and consumption.

The cohabitation and co-engulfment of Dresden and Atlantis mirrors the experience of text-making itself, as layers of significance and legibility are superimposed on one another. By bringing the romantic line to the centre of the page, then partnering it with the inkblot, and then fracturing and multiplying the narrative branches across the fantasies of Veronika and the writing narrator, Hoffmann engenders the illusion of an arabesque design as the figure for a narrative continually engaged in self-reflection. This design, brimming with potential significance, is also suggestive of the experience of looking at a form that does not readily yield to the Western eye. The twelve sections of *Der goldne Topf* participate in a shifting tapestry of reflecting portions, meditating on itself through a seemingly endless series of internal reflections and repetitions. In doing so, repetition is introduced as a proxy for resolution, as the tapestry draws its readers into its ongoing meditation, engulfing and fracturing endlessly as it continues to unfurl.

La Peau de chagrin

Though steeped in the historical detail of any Balzacian fiction, *La Peau de chagrin* is marked out by its status as the only full-length fantastic novel in *La Comédie humaine*. According to his notes, Balzac originally conceived the novel as a 'conte oriental' (Oriental tale), an epithet which he used again in a pseudonymous review.[24] In another review, Philarète Chasles refers to it as a 'conte arabe' (Arabic tale); and in a pseudonymous article published in *La Caricature* in 1830, Balzac calls it 'mon célèbre conte fantastique' (my famous fantastic tale), a phrase which, as we have seen, had distinctly Hoffmannesque connotations at that time, not least because Hoffmann's *Fantasiestücke* had appeared under the title *Contes fantastiques*.[25] Whilst these labels were discarded on the novel's integration into *La Comédie humaine* as one of the *Études philosophiques*, the novel's strange dual identity has led Sandy Petrey to ask a vital question: 'How can this key document of realism also be a fairy tale?'[26]

If the *roman philosophique* was indeed originally intended as a *conte*, the structure of the text – a swollen frame narrative which nearly engulfs its centre – is characterised by the temporality of a Hoffmannesque *Märchen*, with a plot shaped less by progression than by the collapsing inwards of interlocking frames. The narrative is sifted into two distinct temporal modes. The present frame in parts I and III is introduced in succinct journalistic staccato: 'Vers la fin du mois d'octobre dernier' (Towards the end of last October, beginning of Part I); 'Dans les premiers jours du mois de décembre' (In the last days of the month of December, beginning of Part III). The enframed middle portion, on the other hand, is entirely taken up by Raphaël's own first-person account of his life. This temporal fracturing is superimposed over a fracturing of generic mode – Parts I and III deal with a fantastic, Faustian–Oriental contract, and Part II with Raphaël's entirely non-fantastic account of his life – such that the novel may be

---

[24] Honoré de Balzac, *Pensées, Sujets, Fragments*, ed. by Jacques Crépet (Paris: Blaizot, 1910), p. 669; Honoré de Balzac, 'La Peau de chagrin, Roman philosophique par M. de Balzac', *Œuvres diverses*, ed. by Pierre-Georges Castex and others, 2 vols (Paris: Gallimard, 1990–6), II, pp. 849–50 (p. 850).

[25] In Alfred Coudreux [Honoré de Balzac], 'Les Litanies romantiques', *La Caricature*, 6 (9 Dec 1830), *Œuvres diverses*, II, 822–7, p. 823.

[26] Sandy Petrey, *In the Court of the Pear King: French Culture and the Rise of Realism* (Ithaca, NY: Cornell University Press, 2005), p. 59.

said to be founded upon the kind of 'chronic dualism' that has long been associated with Hoffmann's tales.[27] Such a reading is intensified in a brief but significant sequence in Part II, when Raphaël describes a turning point in his life through a reference to the figure of the specifically German *Doppelgänger*: 'Après des courses vagabondes, j'allais, comme le double d'un Allemand, revenir à mon logis d'où je n'étais pas sorti, pour me réveiller moi-même en sursaut' (After much wandering, I would return, like a German double, to my lodgings, which I had never left, and would wake with a start) (B X 42). As if dreaming, Raphaël is both inside and outside himself at once, as both narrator and character of his own tale.

The central figure for the novel's doubled structure is the eponymous skin, first discovered strung up on a wall in the midst of a chaotic antique shop. The novel takes on the double meaning of *chagrin*, which refers first to the piece of shagreen, the magical skin purchased by Raphaël, and second to the emotional state of *chagrin* which dominates the life story narrated by Raphaël in the middle part of the novel. Referring both to the skin, the organ of touch, and to an affective state akin to melancholy, it signifies both touch and feeling. If one *chagrin* – a life of poverty, paternal tyranny and rejection by Fœdora – has already turned Raphaël into the errant orphan of a harsh and unfeeling world, the second – the figure of the skin – does the same in taking harsh stock of his desire and literalising the descent into the undesiring half-life of the novel's part III. The skin makes of the text a self-reflexive fold, with Raphaël's own history of his *chagrin*-as-misery couched within the encompassing frame-narration about the *chagrin*-as-skin. The novel, then, is structured like skin on skin – touching feeling, feeling touch. Indeed, in something of a Hoffmannesque (or arabesque) movement from margin to centre, the novel's fantastic portion takes the position of the frame surrounding the 'realist' narrative, in a reversal of what we might expect of dream sequences and the like. A closer examination of this narrative form will be central to the reading that follows.

La Peau de chagrin opens, in Part I, 'Le Talisman', with the wretched Raphaël de Valentin by the Seine, in a neat reflection of the wretched Anselmus, who is introduced to us on the banks of the Elbe. Raphaël, following a spell of impoverishment and a series of failed intrigues with the ruthless courtesan Fœdora, plans to drown himself. After losing his last few coins in a gambling den, and intending only to postpone his death a little longer, he enters an antique

---

[27] The term is taken from E. T. A. Hoffmann's *Prinzessin Brambilla* (H V 311).

shop. The distinctly Mephistophelian antique seller he meets inside offers to sell him a scrap of magic skin. Etched into the skin in Arabic is a pact promising to fulfil its owner's desires at the expense of his continued life: Raphaël acquiesces to the purchase, and his fate is sealed.

Every new turn of Raphaël's extraordinary lifeline, supposedly realised by the magic skin – a surprise inheritance, romance, illness, death – is an event that might occur in any human life, as the merchant advises him. Any fantastic interpretation of events is thus closely shadowed by a more rational one. Indeed, Raphaël is in some ways only another version of the ambitious young male *arriviste* seeking to rise up in Parisian society, embodied in the figures of Eugène de Rastignac, who makes his first appearance in *La Peau de chagrin*, or of Lucien de Rubempré of *Illusions perdues*, who discovers for himself that the journalist possesses the 'puissance fantastique accordée aux désirs de ceux qui possèdent des talismans dans les contes arabes' (fantastic power granted to the desires of those who possess talismans in Arabic tales) (B V 462). In Raphaël's case, the erotically charged energy of male ambition is literalised: the verbalisation of his desires in the form of an expression like 'je souhais' (I wish), or 'je veux' (I want), actually brings, or seems to bring, those desires about, and as they are realised, the skin shrinks. The talisman is thus turned into an index charting the dwindling lot of life left to Raphaël. To take seriously the significance of the skin and its capacity to represent life means to take seriously the fantastic gambit of the novel, making the talisman a kind of cipher for writing itself. It is even described as a 'feuille' (as in 'leaf' but perhaps also 'page') at a late stage in the novel, by which point it has shrivelled considerably, and the novel, too, has nearly run out.

Raphaël's first wish is for an evening of excess in the form of a debauched party – one that is described as a 'féerie digne d'un conte oriental' (enchantment worthy of an Oriental tale) (B X 107). In its hazy aftermath, he begins to narrate the story of his life to a drunken and sleeping audience. This narration forms the content of the novel's Part II, 'La Femme sans cœur' (The woman without a heart), in which he recounts his history, focusing on the domineering rule of his father and the frustrated attempts at courtship with Fœdora which precipitate his suicidal state at the beginning of the novel. In Part III, 'L'Agonie' (The Agony), we are rushed back to the present temporal frame, in which the promise of Raphaël's pact has caught up with him, the skin having shrunk to almost nothing, and Raphaël, in fear of expressing any desire at all, withers away into a vegetative state of seclusion. Committed either to an existence of desire without life, or of life without desire, he makes a desperate attempt at the latter option, retreating into an existence that approaches an object-like state. The impossibility of living in this way is definitively proven on his re-encounter with Pauline, once a friend and now his lover, and he dies in throes of desire for her in the novel's florid final scene.

The energy structuring and animating the novel is Raphaël's desire to make himself legible: to narrate and to be understood. In the antique shop, he laments 'des souffrances inouïes et qu'il est difficile d'exprimer en langage humain' (the untold sufferings which it is difficult to express in human language) (B X 81); later, he sighs melodramatically to Émile: 'si tu connaissais ma vie' (if you only knew my life) (B X 119). The yearning for narrative intelligibility – to account for the self – runs alongside a fear of illegibility and dissolution registered by the novel's hieroglyphic epigraph, the line that does not conform to lettering. For Peter Brooks, the novel charts the path of narrative desire: it traces a forward-moving propulsion both spurned on and checked by the death drive, hurtling 'toward the end which would be both its destruction and its meaning'.[28] This propulsion is mirrored, in his account, by Balzac's transformation of Sterne's digressive narrative line into one that more closely signals the bounding movement of text. But in an alternative account – one that recognises the doubled-over structure of the novel as I have just outlined it – that skewed arabesque line might be seen as indicative of the anamorphic or kaleidoscopic vision implied by a fantastic narrative: the hallucinatory gambols of an imagination that Balzac himself describes, in the preface to the novel, as a 'miroir concentrique' (concentric mirror) (B X 1193). The line, in this reading, does not chart the journey of a narrative to its finish but, instead, the unravelling of a meaningful mark into disarray.

In what follows I will first outline E. T. A. Hoffmann's paratextual presence within and around *La Peau de chagrin* before returning to a fuller reading of the doubleness that structures the novel. As I will show, the forward-bounding arabesque line, as a symbol of narrative energy, is joined in equal measure by the threat of illegibility. Running simultaneous to this is a reading of Raphaël's own double status, as both subject and object of his narrative.

---

[28] Peter Brooks, *Reading for the Plot: Design and Intention in Narrative* (Cambridge, MA: Harvard University Press, 1992), p. 58.

Conte hoffmannien

From the earliest days of its reception *La Peau de chagrin* was called a Hoffmannesque work. In August 1831, the writer Charles de Bernard published a review in which he explicitly termed it an imitation of Hoffmann:

> La masse d'esprit qui circule dans la société tue l'originalité indivi-duelle. On vit sur le fond commun, au lieu de travailler sur le sien. Vient-il, à de longs intervalles, quelqu'un de ces hommes forts qui ouvrent eux-mêmes leur route, chacun se jette dans la voie qu'il a frayée, et glane sur sa trace, au lieu de chercher une moisson vierge.
>
> Voici encore un homme de talent qui va demander, au foyer du voisin, une étincelle pour allumer le sien. Cette fois, le voisin, c'est Hoffmann, auteur de génie et d'inspiration, qui a creusé lui-même sa mine, et qui doit faire école. Tant qu'il n'inspirera que des ouvrages comme *la Peau de chagrin*, nous n'aurons pas à nous plaindre. Il y a originalité dans cette copie, création réelle dans cette imitation. Comme dans Hoffmann, une trame surnaturelle et fantastique s'y déroule au milieu des événements de la vie positive.[29]

> The mass of spirit that circulates in society kills individual original-ity. We live off the common reserves rather than working on our own. On the rare occasion that there arrives one of those strong men who blazes his own trail, everyone rushes to follow the route that he has cleared, gleaning from his tracks instead of seeking out a new harvest.
>
> Here again is a talented man who will ask for a match at his neigh-bour's hearth in order to light his own. This time, the neighbour is Hoffmann, that author of genius and inspiration who discovered his own seam to mine, and who will surely have a lasting influence. As long as he inspires only works like *La Peau de chagrin*, we will have nothing to complain about. There is originality in this copy, real cre-ativity in the imitation. As in Hoffmann, a supernatural and fantastic plot unfurls from within the events of life as it *is*.

Public debates such as these had a significant role to play in the crafting of Balzac's authorial image, as he worked simultaneously to defend himself against accusations of mimicry and to engage the fashionable and profitable forms of the time. De Bernard, who

---

[29] Charles de Bernard, '*La Peau de chagrin*, par M. de Balzac', originally published in *Gazette de Franche-Comté*, 13 August 1831. Cited in Charles Spoelberch de Lovenjoul, *Histoire des œuvres de H. de Balzac* (Geneva: Slatkine, 1968), pp. 355–7 (p. 355).

praises Hoffmann for his genius and originality, addresses the line between homage and imitation, response and repetition, with some generosity. Balzac's reply is a firm rebuttal grounded in nationalist sentiment, defending the similarities between their works by invoking a model of intertextuality based on the inevitability of influence and reflection:

> Vous accusez peut-être légèrement la jeune littérature de viser à l'imitation des chefs-d'œuvre étrangers. Croyez-vous que le *fantastique* d'Hoffmann n'est pas virtuellement dans *Micromêgas*, qui, lui-même, était déjà dans Cyrano de Bergerac, où Voltaire l'a pris? Les genres appartiennent à tout le monde, et les Allemands n'ont pas plus le privilège de la lune que nous celui du soleil, et l'Écosse celui des brouillards ossianiques. Qui peut se flatter d'être inventeur? Je ne me suis vraiment pas inspiré d'Hoffmann, que je n'ai connu qu'après avoir *pensé* mon ouvrage; mais il y a dans ceci quelque chose de plus grave. Nous manquons de patriotisme entre nous, et nous détruisons notre nationalité et notre suprématie littéraire, en nous démolissant les uns les autres.

> Perhaps you accuse contemporary literature too lightly of aiming to imitate foreign masterpieces. Do you not think that Hoffmann's *fantastic* is potentially to be found in *Micromégas*, which itself was already in Cyrano de Bergerac, from which Voltaire took it? Genres belong to everybody, and the Germans have no more claim to the moon than we to the sun, nor Scotland to Ossianic mists. Who can pride himself on being an inventor? I truly took no inspiration from Hoffmann, whom I did not come to know until after having *conceived* my work; but there is something more serious at play here. We lack mutual patriotism, and we do damage to our nationality and to our literary supremacy when we pull one another down.

The cascade of literary borrowings here is reminiscent of a playful note made some ten years earlier in the margin of *Cromwell*: 'Vers de Racine que j'ai pris sans scrupule à Racine qui l'avait pris à Corneille, qui l'avait pris à Rotrou' (Verse by Racine which I have unscrupulously taken from Racine, who took it from Corneille, who took it from Rotrou).[30] And whilst critics have taken Balzac's refutation of the Hoffmannesque influence at face value, Balzac's claim to have discovered the works of Hoffmann only after having 'conceived' his work – 'après avoir *pensé* mon ouvrage' – is tellingly vague. After all,

---

[30] Balzac, *Œuvres diverses*, I, pp. 1683–4.

Balzac himself had advertised the text as a 'conte fantastique' before its publication in full knowledge of what that label signified.

Balzac's coy rebuttal resembles a direct echo of another author's confrontation with Hoffmann: that of Samuel Taylor Coleridge, who published a rewritten version of *Der goldne Topf* in *Blackwood's Edinburgh Magazine* in January 1822. He titled it 'Historie and Gests of Maxilian', and the first instalment (the story was never completed) comprises what he calls a 'free imitation' of the first portion of Hoffmann's *Der goldne Topf*. In a lengthy introduction to the piece, Coleridge's narrator makes the strange claim that *he* had first come up with the original story himself, but that by a process of animal magnetism, the disembodied spirit of a German named Frederick Miller was able to hear him discussing it with his friends before returning to his body to write his own version in the language of 'high Dutch'. Julian Knox, following H. J. Jackson, has noted have suggested that the foreword plays on Coleridge's previous experiences with accusations of plagiarism.[31] Like Balzac, though in far more extravagant terms, Coleridge claims to have thought up Hoffmann's works before Hoffmann himself had a chance to. Both responses endorse what Robert Macfarlane has called those 'recombinative theories of literary creation' that gained ground across the nineteenth century: theories of writing as a craft of assimilation and reassemblage of existing material, far removed from the image of the solitary creation of the artwork *ex nihilo*, a trope often associated with Romanticism, though complicated by Romantic artworks themselves.[32]

Hoffmann's works offer an explicit meditation on such topics. As I have shown above, *Der goldne Topf*, with its depiction of an artist trapped between a humdrum Dresden and a lofty Atlantis, reveals the recycled state of the literary self, spiralling inwards as the narrator writes of Anselmus who writes of Atlantis, to suggest an endless swarm of possible tales within the tale. We saw much the same thing in *Abenteuer der Silvester-Nacht*, in which Hoffmann brazenly lifts the character of Peter Schlemihl from Adelbert von Chamisso's *Peter Schlemihls wundersame Geschichte* into a story in which every character appears to be repeating the story of another. The recycling and self-citation of these works comes to determine the format of

[31] Julian Knox, 'Coleridge's "Cousin-German": *Blackwood's*, Alter-Egos, and the Making of a Man of Letters', *European Romantic Review*, 21.4 (2010) 425–46, p. 428.

[32] Robert Macfarlane, *Original Copy: Plagiarism and Originality in Nineteenth-Century Literature* (Oxford: Oxford University Press, 2007), p. 5.

Die Serapionsbrüder, a cycle which is predicated, as Andrew Piper
has shown, on a poetic strategy of repetition and reproducibility.[33]
Autopoeic originality and novelty are displaced by the artwork's
dependence on different kinds of similitude and sameness.

To return to the question of Balzac's own imitations, it is in
keeping with his commentary of the state of the book market in
the early 1830s that in his response to Charles de Bernard, Balzac
wants simultaneously to profit from literary fashions and to distance himself from the figure of the hack. And this is symptomatic
of a more general contradiction: his 'willingness to engage fully
with the literary market while at the same time trying to redeem his
work from the commodification this entailed'.[34] In his journalistic
writings, Balzac voices clear anxieties about the expanding literary market of the 1830s, to whose voracious appetite underpaid
writers had to cater – an enterprise that was financially insecure
because of the hefty cuts demanded by publishers and because of
the rise of lending libraries. Concessions to fashion had to be made.
In 'De la mode en littérature', published in *La Mode* in May 1830,
Balzac writes of the demands of the reading populace in terms that
clearly foreshadow the publication of *La Peau de chagrin*: 'Il faut
aujourd'hui à ce public fantasque des feux d'artifice en littérature,
comme un monde elegant et toujours paré, comme des boutiques
brillantes, et de bazars magiques: il veut *Les Mille et une Nuits*
partout' (Today's fanciful public demands fireworks in literature,
as they demand that high society be always elegant and dressed for
the ball, boutiques brilliant, and bazaars magical; they want *The
Arabian Nights* everywhere).[35] Balzac's ironic distancing of himself
from his forthcoming novel – the article is signed only 'H.' – places
La Peau de chagrin, his own version of the *Thousand and One
Nights*, as part of a critical response to the rabble's taste for fantastic literature.

La Peau de chagrin explicitly continues this response to the fantastic genre on the level of narrative, and it does so in part through
its engagement with Hoffmann. For Timothy Lewis, Hoffmann is
called up as 'the novelist's chosen interlocutor': a suggestion that
is tempered by José-Luis Diaz, who notes that Balzac's preoccupation with Hoffmann 'semble plutôt signe de rivalité que d'adoption'

---

33 Piper, *Dreaming in Books*, p. 66.
34 Sotirios Paraschas, '*Illusions Perdues*: Writers, Artists and the Reflexive Novel', in
   The Cambridge Companion to Balzac, ed. by Owen Heathcote and Andrew Watts
   (Cambridge: Cambridge University Press, 2017), pp. 97–110 (p. 107).
35 Balzac, *Œuvres diverses*, II, p. 757.

(seems more a sign of rivalry than of adoption).[36] Fantastic elements punctuate the text. In one particularly wry moment, an attendee at Raphaël's first grand party cries out: 'Voilà des petits pois *délicieusement* fantastiques!' (Here are some most *deliciously* fantastic peas!) (B X 101). Two further examples of Balzac's engagement with the fantastic mode will be illustrative here.

The first is an episode of part III in which Raphaël takes his talisman to be investigated by a trio of scientists – a naturalist, a physicist and a chemist – all of whom claim to be able to explain away its mysteries, and all of whom fail in varyingly spectacular fashion. Lavrille, the naturalist, narrates to Raphaël what is essentially a captivating exotic *conte*, interspersed with foreign words and fragments of legend, in his description of the ass of whose hide the skin is supposedly a scrap: 'le roi zoologique de l'Orient' (the zoological king of the Orient). Shortly after this, Planchette's explanation of mechanics so seduces Raphaël that he is described as being 'charmé comme un enfant auquel sa nourrice conte une histoire merveilleuse' (charmed like a child to whom a nurse is telling a marvellous story). Finally, before the third scientist's forge, he feels himself 'transporté dans le monde nocturne et fantastique des ballades allemandes' (transported into the nocturnal and fantastic world of German ballads) (B X 299). To the reference to German ballads (presumably to Goethe) is added the German name of this third scientist – Spieghalter. The scientists' materialist accounts of the skin are glossed as exotic fantasies, only so many further internalised narratives. The wry comedy contained in the notion that science can be flipped into fantasy – or rather, perhaps, that it can only hold a mirror up to Raphaël, reflecting his extraordinarily dismal fantasy back to him – is clinched when, in his attempt to re-stretch the skin and prolong Raphaël's life, Spieghalter's forge explodes.

Still further into the final part of the novel is a more explicitly Hoffmannesque scene in which Raphaël uses a magical 'lorgnette' (a pair of opera glasses), which disfigures the world so as to make it, and Fœdora, less desirable – and thus, again, to prolong Raphaël's life:

> La vie de Raphaël dépendait d'un pacte encore inviolé qu'il avait fait lui-même, il s'était promis de ne jamais regarder attentivement

---

[36] Timothy W. Lewis, *The Influence of E. T. A. Hoffmann on Balzac* (unpublished doctoral thesis, University of London, 1991), p. 337; José-Luis Diaz, 'Ce que Balzac fait au fantastique', *L'Année balzacienne* 13 (2012), 61–83, p. 71.

aucune femme et pour se mettre à l'abri d'une tentation, il portait un lorgnon dont le verre microscopique, artistement disposé, détruisait l'harmonie des plus beaux traits, en leur donnant un hideux aspect. (B X 225–6)

Raphaël's life depended on a pact as yet unbroken which he had made with himself: he had promised himself to never gaze at any woman, and to shield himself from temptation he carried a pair of opera glasses the microscopic lens of which, artistically disposed, destroyed the harmony of the most beautiful features, giving them a hideous appearance.

This brief sequence – in which a magical object is introduced, never again to be mentioned in the narrative, disappearing as quickly as it emerges – explores the potential of a multiperspectival and artificially mutable vision. The *lorgnette* is reminiscent of Hoffmann's many optical devices: the telescope purchased by Nathanael in *Der Sandmann* in order to spy on the automaton Olimpia, for example, or the magical spectacles sold to the actor Giglio Fava in *Prinzessin Brambilla* to aid him in a search for the prince Cornelio Chiapperi. Elsewhere, Balzac seems to muse on the possibilities of a realist method understood as a kaleidoscopic or magical vision, such as in *Petites Misères de la vie conjugale:* 'Ô civilisation! ô Paris! admirable kaléidoscope qui, toujours agité, nous montre ces quatre brimborions: l'homme, la femme, l'enfant et le vieillard sous tant de formes, que tes tableaux sont innombrables!' (Oh civilisation! Oh Paris! Admirable kaleidoscope which, when shaken, offers us these four trinkets: man, woman, child and aged person, in so many forms that your tableaux are innumerable!).[37]

Might we return to the serpentine line of Balzac's epigraph, then, and re-envision it as a kaleidoscopic or anamorphic line, simultaneously legible (as symbol of plot) and illegible (as arabesque), describing the meanderings not just of fate, fortune and plot, but perhaps also of vision? It is an irony apparent only to the modern reader that the line has become a symbol of Balzac's own lack of sight – for Balzac, who could not have known about Hoffmann's version of the same line as shown in Chapter 2, has unwittingly, even blindly, evoked him once again in his epigraph. And so the line appears as an appropriately hallucinatory encounter in the form of another kind of frame narrative, firmly positioning the fashionable fantastic and *la vogue d'Hoffmann* as its discursive context: as

---

[37] Balzac, *Œuvres diverses*, II, p. 809.

antagonistic 'interlocutor', as Lewis would have it, or as a haunting visual presence.[38]

Chagrin

By means of an allegorical fantasy, *La Peau de chagrin* explores Raphaël's relationship to his own narrative act. Much existing criticism on the text responds to it broadly in this vein. Patrick M. Bray has argued that the text 'inscribes within its pages a theory of its own writing'; that the piece of skin is 'a fiction, which allows a theory of willpower to become materialized in a tangible object'.[39] The text is central to accounts of Balzac's language given by Martin Kanes, for whom 'the *shrinking* of the skin can represent nothing other than the possibility that language skews the relationship of the mind to the world'; and by Dorothy Kelly, who shows that the skin marks the meeting of signifier (the size of the skin) and the signified (the length of Raphaël's life), such that 'language and the real coincide'.[40]

Fewer critics have explicitly broached the topic of touch or feeling in this novel about a skin. Bray's focus, for one, is on the 'vicissitudes of theoretical visions' and the text's 'obsession with vision'.[41] Régine Borderie recognises the centrality of the body, 'le corps perturbateur' (the agitating body), for the individual who, alienated within a new market society whose universal index is money, finds himself or herself 'ramené d'abord à ce qu'il a de plus proche, sa peau, ses sens, son corps' (at first taken back to what is nearest, to his or her skin, senses, to the body).[42] But even this only begins to touch upon the lived, sensing body, not just as an allegorical figure but as the sensate envelope it is experienced as from within. The final part of this chapter will prioritise the novel's account of feeling and touch in relation both to vision and to the narrative act, in order to show, via a number of scenes of reading, how, in putting his life into narrative, Raphaël returns upon himself, in a phenomenological sense, as narrative object. This reading is rooted in the structures of doubling

---

[38] Lewis, 'The Influence of E. T. A. Hoffmann', p. 337.

[39] Patrick M. Bray, 'Balzac and the Chagrin of Theory', *L'Esprit Créateur*, 54.3 (2014), 66–77 (pp. 66, 68).

[40] Martin Kanes, *Balzac's Comedy of Words* (Princeton, NJ: Princeton University Press, 1975), p. 74. Dorothy Kelly, *Reconstructing Woman: from Fiction to Reality in the Nineteenth-Century Novel* (University Park, PA: Penn State University Press, 2007), p. 43.

[41] Bray, 'Balzac and the Chagrin of Theory', p. 75, p. 67.

[42] Régine Borderie, 'Le Corps de la philosophie: *La Peau de chagrin*', *L'Année balzacienne*, 12 (2001), 199–219 (pp. 201, 216).

owed to Balzac's explicit and implicit adoptions of Hoffmann and of the fantastic mode.

Let us turn first to one of the earliest and most well-known moments of the novel: Raphaël's entry into a gambling den. The payment exacted on his entry is his hat:

> Quand vous entrez dans une maison de jeu, la loi commence par vous dépouiller de votre chapeau. Est-ce une parabole évangélique et prov-identielle? N'est-ce pas plutôt une manière de conclure un contrat infernal avec vous en exigeant je ne sais quel gage? [. . .] Est-ce enfin pour prendre la mesure de votre crâne et dresser une statistique instructive sur la capacité cérébrale des joueurs? (B X 57–8)

> When you enter a gambling house, the law begins by removing your hat. Is it an evangelical and providential parable? Is it not, rather, a manner of concluding an infernal contract with you by demanding of you some kind of gauge? [. . .] Is it, finally, to take the measure of your skull and to set up instructive statistics on the cerebral capacity of gamblers?

Like Hoffmann's narrator in *Der goldne Topf*, Balzac's is prone to ironic approximations of Lavaterian discourse. The hat, as a marker of phrenological intelligibility, is a material toll for Raphaël's entry into the gambling den – and so, it turns out, into the novel. Hats, as in *Der goldne Topf*, are suggestive both of a social measure of class and of the measuring frenzy of phrenology: a pseudoscience based on the assumption that a human subject may be characterised by taking measure of the size and shape of the brain. It was, in this sense, together with physiognomy, 'a kind of diagnostic shorthand' for reading character, implying, together with other marginal pseudo-sciences like mesmerism, 'a world at once material and spiritual', in which body is the expression of spirit.[43] As a prosthetic mould for the head, the hat is an indexical sign confirming type and thus providing a way of reading Raphaël. As Raphaël offers himself up to the Cerberus-like doorkeeper of the gambling den and subsequently to the antique shop, another figure with a mask-like face, bearing 'l'apparence de ces têtes judaïques qui servent de types aux artistes quand ils veulent représenter Moïse' (the appearance of those Jewish heads which serve as models to artists when they want to make a representation of Moses) (B X 78), his body is drawn into a system of legibility and inscription.

---

[43] Lawrence Rothfield, *Vital Signs: Medical Realism in Nineteenth-Century Fiction* (Princeton, NJ: Princeton University Press, 1992), pp. 52–4.

The masked figures of the introduction cast echoes into the amorous plotline in the web of the possibilities and risks of reading with which Raphaël is confronted in the narrated section in Part II. Fœdora, the courtesan without a heart, the *fée d'or* (golden fairy) or the *faite d'or* (fact of gold); the marble and money 'statue de marbre' (statue of marble), 'statue d'argent' (statue of silver), and the 'incarnation de [s] es espérances' (incarnation of his hopes) (B X 159, 184, 146), embodies the upwards trajectory into elite society desired by Raphaël. And as he strains to read her features – 'Je voulais lire un sentiment, un espoir, dans toutes ces phases du visage' (I wanted to read an emotion, a hope, in every phase of her face) (B X 154) – this effort comes to be mirrored in the physiognomic forms of the world – 'Les arbres, l'air, le ciel, toute la nature semblait me répéter le sourire de Fœdora' (the trees, the air, the sky, everything in nature seemed to repeat back to me Fœdora's smile) (B X 167). Indeed, Fœdora's features seem to promise so much that in one scene Raphaël, anxious about what surfaces may or may not conceal and about the courtesan's continuous deflections, hides in her room to see her undress, 'pour examiner cette femme corporellement comme je l'avais étudiée intellectuellement, pour la connaître enfin tout entière' (in order to examine this woman corporeally as I had studied her intellectually, to finally know her completely) (B X 179). What follows is a sequence that stages an anxiety about reading and reading's possible failures. What worries Raphaël is that Fœdora's features will not yield what they seem to promise; that behind one inscrutable surface might only lie another. In the privacy of her room, Fœdora does indeed strip away a layer of social artifice: 'elle venait d'ôter un masque; actrice, son rôle était fini' (She had just removed a mask; an actress, her role was finished) (B X 182). But what is left beneath is no imperfection, as he fears. Instead, beneath the gauze of her shift, she is smooth, whole, 'comme une statue d'argent' (like a statue of silver) featuring 'nulle imperfection' (not a single imperfection) (B X 184). Glinting, intangible and associated explicitly with the smooth surface of coins, Raphaël, in struggling to understand the object of his desire, can gain no more purchase on her than he can on the money that so consistently slips from his grasp. Fœdora becomes the figure of a failed reading, a skin reduced to surface.

In an earlier version of the novel, Raphaël's fears about Fœdora are channelled through an apparent misreading of Hoffmann. In a passage included in the version of the novel published in 1831, and deleted in the 1834 version, Raphaël makes a direct but ambiguous reference to Hoffmann's *Prinzessin Brambilla* as he resolves to hide in Fœdora's room:

Je pensai tout à coup à la princesse Brambilla d'Hoffmann, à Fragoletta, capricieuses conceptions d'artiste, dignes de la statue de Polyclès. Je croyais voir ce monstre qui, tantôt officier, dompte un cheval fougueux; tantôt jeune fille, se met à sa toilette et désespère ses amans; puis, amant, désespère une vierge douce et modeste. Ne pouvant plus résoudre autrement Fœdora, je lui racontai cette histoire fantastique; mais, en elle, rien ne décela sa ressemblance avec cette poésie de l'impossible. (B X 179 var. a)

I thought at once of Hoffmann's princess Brambilla, of Fragoletta, capricious artistic visions worthy of the statue of Polycles. I thought I saw that monster who, now as an officer, tames a wild horse; now as a young girl, attends to her appearance and disheartens her lovers; now as a male lover, disheartens a gentle and modest virgin. Being unable to resolve the problem of Fœdora in any other way, I told her this fantastic story; but nothing in her reaction revealed her resemblance with this poetry of the impossible.

Here, Raphaël's more explicit fears about Fœdora's sexual identity cast the passage as a Freudian 'scene of infantile curiosity, a looking at and unveiling of the woman's sex'.[44] But Balzac's inclusion of Hoffmann's Brambilla as a counterpart to the hermaphroditic Fragoletta and to Polycles's statue – Hermaphroditus – is a confusing one. Hoffmann's Brambilla is an idealised woman: there is no ambiguity in the text concerning her sex or gender identity. This leads Timothy Lewis to suggest that Balzac's 'perusal of Hoffmann's text had been hasty' and that his later deletion of this passage was necessitated by a closer reading of Hoffmann's tale.[45] Lewis does not consider the possibility that the misreading might be significant on its own terms, or indeed that it might belong to Raphaël rather than to Balzac. If so, then the entire passage – which centres on Raphaël's anxiety about the legibility of his object of desire – is channelled through Raphaël's own suspicious, and erroneous, account of the central and idealised female figure in a piece of contemporary fantastic fiction.

The 'capricious artistic visions' could refer to those female characters of Hoffmann – Brambilla, Serpentina and perhaps most of all the automaton Olimpia – who appear as ideals to the desiring hero, often in the form of a dream or hallucination, but who either cannot be possessed by him or turn out, in the case of Olimpia, to have a fatal flaw. It is Olimpia in particular, that all-too-perfect human, who

---

[44] Peter Brooks, *Body Work: Objects of Desire in Modern Narrative* (Cambridge, MA: Harvard University Press, 1993), p. 86.
[45] Lewis, 'The Influence of E. T. A. Hoffmann', p. 47.

exemplifies the combination of seductiveness and unyieldingness that so frustrates Raphaël in Fœdora. There is something disquieting – even uncanny – about Fœdora's flawless body. When Raphaël goes on to tell Fœdora the 'histoire fantastique' (fantastic story) of *Fragoletta*, she listens to him 'comme un enfant écoutant une fable des *Mille est une nuits*' (like a child listening to a fable of the *Thousand and One Nights*). Brooks's 'scene of infantile curiosity' is reversed. The woman whose face Raphaël is so anxious to read, and who equally possesses the means to give him new meaning in society, turns from seductive storyteller into his rapt audience, with the sexlessness and innocence of the listening child. The Scheherazade framework of the *Thousand and One Nights*, in which the telling of tales is equated both with desire and with survival, is ironically flipped in these internalised scenes of reading and listening, which defer the possibility of achieving sexual knowledge in an unyielding readerly encounter where neither party has the capacity to satisfy the other.

This sexualised anxiety about reading and legibility reaches a climax at the end of part III when, in a final encounter with Pauline, Raphaël can no longer hold back the expression of his desires. This comes at the cost of his life and the end of his narrative (barring the coda-like postface continuing the stories of the two women). The narrative shifts to focus not on Raphaël but on Pauline, sidelining Raphaël into the object of her touch and vision:

> Un cri terrible sortit du gosier de la jeune fille, ses yeux se dilatèrent, ses sourcils, violemment tirés par une douleur inouïe, s'écartèrent avec horreur, elle lisait dans les yeux de Raphaël un de ces désirs furieux, jadis sa gloire à elle; mais à mesure que grandissait ce désir, la Peau, en se contractant, lui chatouillait la main. (B X 291–2)

> A terrible cry escaped from the young girl's throat, her eyes dilated, her eyebrows, pulled violently by an indescribable pain, parted with horror, she read in Raphaël's eyes one of those furious desires, which had once been her very glory, but as this desire grew, the contracting Skin tickled her hand.

As much as it is a parody of an erotic embrace, the scene is also a parody of reading.[46] Pauline's gargoyle-like expression as she comes to understand Raphaël's predicament – as she *reads* ('lisait') desire in his eyes, turning Raphaël back into a narrative object – could not be further removed from Fœdora's coy and indecipherable face.

---

[46] See Scott Sprenger, 'Death by Marriage in Balzac's *La Peau de chagrin*', *Dix-Neuf*, 11.1 (2008), 59–75, p. 59.

And here we find perhaps the most potent example of the relationship between the visual and the tactile as the note of desire glowing in Raphaël's eyes is felt in the skin contracting in Pauline's hand: a three-pointed encounter of eye on Skin on skin. The tickle she feels as she reads and the skin shrinks turns the experience of reading, again, into one that is *felt*, and played out on the level of the skin.

This scene of reading, where subject and world come together in a meaningful encounter – and are destroyed in that moment, as in a hallucination – is an appropriate climax for a novel which has both explicitly set its reader hunting for meaning ('tout y est mythe et figure' [everything there is myth and figure], as Balzac teases) and continually frustrates that activity by challenging how meaning might be drawn from an illegible figure.[47] By incorporating a flagrantly fantastic element, a magic piece of skin, within descriptions of Parisian life grounded in sociological and historical detail, perhaps the key tenet of this novel, which so singularly bridges 'le fantastique' of the fashionable *conte* and the descriptive realism of his later works, lies in the depiction of how the conditions of reality are felt. If the novel shows, as Gerard Cohen-Vrignaud has argued, that 'despite romance's attachment to the extraordinary, perhaps realism has its own way of mystifying' – or fantasising about – 'how things "really" happen', then those mystifications or fantasies are shown here to take distinctly sensory forms.[48]

* * *

Der goldne Topf and *La Peau de chagrin* interweave an Orientally inflected version of the fantastic genre with scenes from 'real' life in order to reflect upon the philosophical and narrative premises of that life. The arabesque – as motif or as structuring principle – is a symbol of narrative energy but also a marker of illegibility and, especially for Hoffmann, a figure of repetitiousness and reproducibility. Both engage an arabesque framework to address questions of legibility and illegibility, setting enframed narratives and scenes of reading within the main narrative. What emerges from those reflections is a sense of the self felt as narrative object, as the Merleau-Pontian subject whose own body is necessarily registered within the act of perception. In *Der goldne Topf*, this leads into a gesture of

[47] Balzac, *Correspondance*, I, pp. 396–7.
[48] Gerard Cohen-Vrignaud, 'Capitalism's Wishful Thinking', *Modern Language Quarterly*, 76.2 (2015), 181–99.

potentially endless fractured repetitions; in *La Peau de chagrin*, the self withers with the end of the text, as in a hallucination or dream.

The hallucinatory qualities of *Der goldne Topf* are clear: Anselmus is blowing smoke rings by the river when Serpentina and her sisters appear before his eyes, as if emerging from the landscape itself. But Raphaël of *La Peau de chagrin* also speaks of his internal narrative in the terms of hallucination. He begins his story with the following words:

> Je ne sais en vérité s'il ne faut pas attribuer aux fumes du vin et du punch l'espèce de lucidité qui me permet d'embrasser en cet instant toute ma vie comme un même tableau où les figures, les couleurs, les ombres, les lumières, les demi-teintes sont fidèlement rendues. (B X 120)

> I do not know, truth be told, whether or not I should attribute to the fumes of wine and punch the variety of lucidity which permits me to seize my whole life in this instant, like a tableau in which figures, colours, shadows, lights and shades are rendered true to life.

Few motifs could be more redolent of Hoffmann and of *Der goldne Topf* than the compelling images that emerge from the fumes of a narrator's glass of punch. Indeed, a warning about the narrator's alcoholism was attached to one early French translation of Hoffmann's tales. A footnote to the translation of Hoffmann's 'Don Juan' in *La Revue de Paris*, presumably by the translator Loève-Veimars himself, interrupts the text with the following digression:

> En lisant les souvenirs et les récits d'Hoffmann, il ne faut jamais oublier qu'il s'enivrait et qu'il puisait sa verve dans la bouteille: chaque image s'offrait à son esprit, colorée par les vapeurs du vin; de là le prisme fantastique qui, dans ses récits, environne toujours la réalité.[49]

> In reading the memories and the stories of Hoffmann, we must never forget that he drank and that he drew his flair from the bottle: every image offered itself to his mind coloured by the vapours of wine; thence the fantastic prism that always envelops reality in his tales.

In both cases the hallucinatory image, far from being an imperfect or distorted reflection of the real thing, is a consummate fiction: a compelling version of reality in its own right. In both cases, too, the hallucination can dissipate as suddenly as it emerges.

---

[49] Adolph-François Loève-Veimars, 'Une représentation de Don Juan, par E. T. A. Hoffmann', *La Revue de Paris*, 6 (1829), 57–69 (p. 57).

Chapter 4

Scribble: *Der Artushof* and *Le Chef-d'œuvre inconnu*

Given the intensive engagement with visual experience that has motivated the readings here so far, it is perhaps no great surprise that much existing comparative work on Hoffmann and Balzac has been devoted to the genre of the *Künstlergeschichte* or *conte artiste*: the tale that deals with the creation of visual art. This chapter draws together two such tales – Hoffmann's *Der Artushof* and Balzac's *Le Chef-d'œuvre inconnu* – that have been previously compared on the basis of a shared motif: the blank or botched canvas. What those tales share, beyond this motif and thematic complex, is the intrusion into the narrative of a self-conscious pictorial narrative style: a mode of writing that draws from the vocabulary of visual art, that concerns itself with the age-old trope of ekphrasis and that pays close attention to the execution of lines and strokes. In both, the narrating would-be artist relates an ironic detachment from his own work as he tells the story of a failed artwork. Chapter 4 investigates this narrative detachment as a rhetorical strategy that encourages reflection on the premises of mimesis in literature and visual art. In these two tales of unfinished artworks, the insufficiencies of the artistic method or medium are engaged, that is, *as* representational mode.

In Chapter 3, I alluded briefly to Balzac and Hoffmann's interest in physiognomic thought. For both, the human face is ripe for exploitation and magnification as a showplace of meaning, though Lavaterian thought is engaged primarily in an ironic manner. This is perhaps nowhere clearer for Hoffmann than in the playful physiognomic self-portrait he drew for his publisher Kunz in 1815/16 (see Figure 4.1), in which sections of his face are labelled according to the characteristics – material or fantastic – that supposedly underlie them. The 'd' scribbled onto his (presumably corpulent) cheeks, therefore, corresponds to the 'Beefsteak' and 'Portwein' of Dallach,

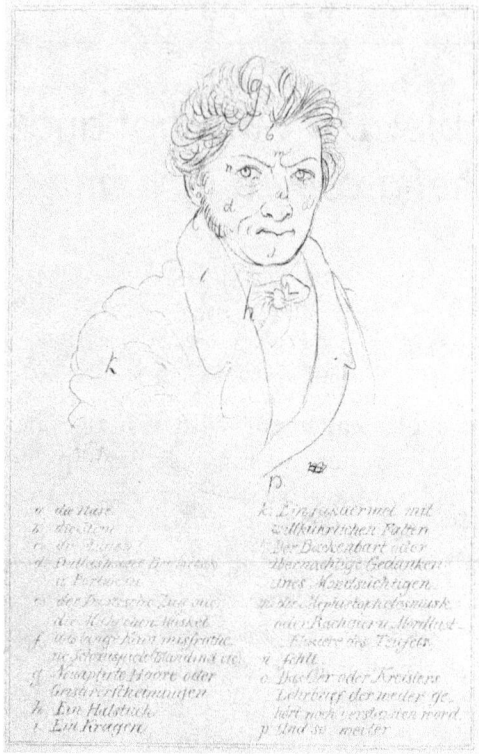

Figure 4.1 E. T. A. Hoffmann, portrait with physiognomic labels.
© Staatsbibliothek Bamberg L.g.o.390(1

a restaurant in Berlin, whilst the 'l' of his sideburns is labelled 'Der Backenbart oder übernächtige Gedanken eines Mondsüchtigen' (Whiskers, or the tired thoughts of a moonstruck man).[1] The portrait poses a whimsical challenge to Lavater's methodology and its conviction in the capacity of material forms to signify immaterial states. But it is also a meditation on the inked line. With the half-hidden 'g' coyly perched amongst the other strokes of his hair, looping down onto his forehead, and the 'e' that sits curled like a dimple by his mouth, Hoffmann's portrait flaunts the ability of the line to form both letter and picture, slipping from pictorial into textual meaning and back again. If the premise of Lavater's method is that the visual field of the body can be interpreted by a kind of 'readerly' methodology, engaging text and image as separate but related interlocutors, Hoffmann's

---

[1] For a full description of the image, see Dietmar Ponert, *E. T. A. Hoffmann – Das bildkünstlerische Werk: Ein kritisches Gesamtverzeichnis*, 2 vols (Petersburg: Michael Imhof Verlag, 2012), I, pp. 287–91.

response here is to draw out moments of fusion between visual and textual fields, such that the body can be understood as continuous with language: as a repository of meaning, experience, dream.

Balzac's method, predictably, is more rigorously materialist – and physiognomic – than Hoffmann's, but his too remains in an experimental and exuberant mode. As Peter Brooks notes, one of Balzac's major innovations in the nineteenth-century novel lies precisely in the 'new importance [he] attaches to the body as semiotic vehicle'.[2] In the theoretical texts originally intended to be published as the *Pathologie de la vie sociale* (Pathology of Social Life) he establishes a set of principles for decoding the outer details of human appearance in order to uncover their secret meanings; an elaborate 'vestignomie' (vestignomics) aligned with the principles of Gall and Lavater and which rests upon a faith in the legibility and interpretability of the human form. In *Théorie de la démarche* (Theory of the Gait), he writes that the human gait resembles 'la pensée en action' (thought in action); that 'un simple geste, un involontaire frémissement de lèvres peut devenir le terrible dénouement d'un drame caché longtemps entre deux cœurs' (a simple gesture, an involuntary quivering of the lips can become the terrible climax of a drama hidden long between two hearts) (B XII 280).

For Diana Knight, 'texts about paintings, painters and sculptors are obvious test cases for issues of representation'. In the case of these particular texts, art and eroticism interlock as versions of the Pygmalion myth, which 'conflates creative and erotic desire with mimetic representation'.[3] The Pygmalion myth both brings mimesis to a head, by forcing a resemblance so consummate that art equals life itself, but might equally be said to perform an inverse mimesis, by turning artifice into life. Both *Le Chef-d'œuvre inconnu* and *Der Artushof* are narratives concerned with how to bring images to life through the medium of text, and which relate the portrayal of impotent or deadened artworks. However, whilst both texts are founded upon an exploration of the insufficiencies of mimesis – art cannot equate to life; nor can it fulfil desire – they are not cautionary tales of a Pygmalionesque delusion, but rather explorations of a mimetic aesthetic that might be described in the terms of a sketch or a scribble, in which the fleetingness and incompleteness of the drawing is its

[2] Peter Brooks, *Body Work: Objects of Desire in Modern Narrative* (Cambridge, MA: Harvard University Press, 1993), pp. 66–7.
[3] Diana Knight, *Balzac and the Model of Painting: Artist Stories in 'La Comédie humaine'* (Oxford: Legenda, 2007), p. 1.

most potent characteristic. Both tales self-consciously undermine the fullness of the mimetic project in order to generate the object of art, finally producing an ambivalent relationship to the artwork.

Der Artushof

Der Artushof has so frequently been discussed as part of a series of Hoffmann's *Künstlernovellen* that, perhaps paradoxically, its salient distinguishing characteristic might be said to lie in its exemplary nature.[4] Experiences of seriality and sameness ripple across *Die Serapionsbrüder*, the cycle within which the tale is embedded. The frame narrative of the cycle is formed from the literary conversations of a group of six male companions who relate narratives to one another that they have previously written down. The foreword to the collection, written in the voice of a fictional editor, goes some way to explaining this combination of old and new material (for the majority of the tales had, in fact, been previously published in journals and magazines). The editor claims that his task is both to collect together 'verstreute Erzählungen und Märchen' (dispersed stories and tales) and 'Neues hinzufügen' (to introduce new material). He begs that the reader refrain from comparing his collection to the archetypal collection of Tieck's *Phantasus* – 'jenen ihm nachteiligen Vergleich *nicht* anzustellen' (*not* to draw him into this unfavourable comparison), an act that necessarily acknowledges the work's recycling of inherited models: not just of Tieck's *Phantasus*, but also of works such as Boccaccio's *Decameron* and Goethe's *Erzählungen deutscher Ausgewanderten* (Tales of German Refugees) (H IV 11).

From the outset, then, *Die Serapionsbrüder* is marked by its ambivalence towards imitation: the acknowledgement of a specific set of literary models comes simultaneously to a plea for the cycle to be read on its own terms. This ambivalence is worked through by the tales themselves and by their reflections of one another. Lothar Pikulik points out that the tangle of interrelations is registered by

---

[4] Wulf Segebrecht writes: 'Die Erzählung versammelt zahlreiche Motive und Konstellationen einer Künstlernovelle in E. T. A. Hoffmanns Manier' (the tale brings together several motifs and constellations of an artist novella in the manner of E. T. A. Hoffmann), in his commentary on the text (H IV, p. 1318). In a similar judgment, Christian Begemann writes: 'Zusammengenommen formieren diese Texte eine Reihe variierende Bearbeitungen der gleichen Grundproblematik' (Taken together, these texts form a series of varying adaptations of the same basic complex). 'Der Artushof (1816)', in *E. T. A. Hoffmann: Leben – Werk – Wirkung*, ed. by Detlef Kremer (Berlin: De Gruyter, 2009), pp. 93–6 (p. 93).

the reader as an experience of repeated recognition: 'je weiter man in den *Serapions-Brüdern* mit der Lektüre fortschreitet, desto besser erkennt man, wie sehr Hoffmanns Erzählungen Variationen einiger weniger Grundmuster sind' (the further one advances with his or her reading of *Die Serapionsbrüder*, the better one recognises that Hoffmann's tales are variations on a few basic patterns).[5] He goes on to compare the experience of reading *Die Serapionsbrüder* to the uncanny encounters and near-recognitions that occur to the protagonists of the tales themselves, suggesting that the reader undergoes repeated experiences of déjà vu in the same way that Hoffmann's characters themselves 'immer wieder auf schon Bekanntes oder doch in Ahnungen bereits früher vage Erfahrenes stoßen, das in der Wiederbegegnung konkretere Züge annimmt' (encounter, again and again, that which is familiar or that which has, according to vague memory, been experienced once before, and which takes on more concrete traits in being re-encountered).[6] The experience of reading *Die Serapionsbrüder* is tightly bound up with the experience of rereading and return. And, as Lothar warns in the very first line of the collection, no such return is ever complete: 'stelle man sich auch an wie man wolle, nicht wegzuleugnen, nicht wegzubannen ist die bittere Überzeugung, daß nimmer – nimmer wiederkehrt, was einmal dagewesen' (however you look at the question, the bitter conviction cannot be denied, nor banished, that what once was can never – never – be the same again).

Der Artushof is organised around one paradigmatically 'Serapiontic' experience, driven by the recurrence of a figure – or rather, of that figure's particular recognisable traits, her physiognomic 'Züge' – as the protagonist Traugott, on the hunt for his artistic ideal, must finally settle for a near match. Where the undulating arabesque lines of *Der goldne Topf* loosen themselves from the taxonomising bind of physiognomic discourse, the lines of *Der Artushof* are subjected to repetition and distortion such that the outline runs askew – following the model of the scribbled or scrawled hand drawing – forming an anamorphic effect, with unsettling consequences for the would-be artist. Through its narration of an incomplete and unsatisfactory recognition, the tale's form is enlisted to the service of reproducing the affective condition of the

---

[5] Lothar Pikulik, *E. T. A. Hoffmann als Erzähler: ein Kommentar zu den* Serapions-Brüdern (Göttingen: Vandenhoeck & Ruprecht, 1987), p. 84.
[6] Ibid., p. 84.

central character: namely, the reader is enlisted in the experience of an aesthetic disappointment or disillusionment.

Flourish

Traugott's artistic initiation begins with a line drawing, and that drawing begins with a single line. Poised in the act of writing out an official business letter in the Artushof in Danzig – a stock exchange by day whose frescoes seem to come to life in the 'magisches Helldunkel' (magic chiaroscuro) (H IV 177) of the evening – he finds himself instead sketching out one of the painted images in the hall:

> Er nahm ein Blatt, tunkte die Feder ein und wollte eben mit einem kecken kalligraphischen Schnörkel beginnen, als er, nochmals schnell das Geschäft von dem er zu schreiben hatte, überdenkend, die Augen in die Höhe warf. Nun wollte es der Zufall, daß er gerade vor den in einem Zuge abgebildeten Figuren stand, deren Anblick ihn jedesmal mit seltsamer unbegreiflicher Wehmut befing. [. . .] Niemals konnte er loskommen von dieser beider Anblick, und so geschah es denn auch jetzt, daß statt den Aviso des Herrn Elias Roos nach Hamburg zu schreiben, er nur das wundersame Bild anschaute und gedankenlos mit der Feder auf dem Papier herumkritzelte. (H IV 178–9)

> He took a sheet, dipped his pen in the inkwell, and was about to begin his letter of advice with a bold calligraphic flourish when, as he was reflecting again on what he had to write, he happened to cast his eyes aloft. As chance would have it, he was standing right in front of one of the represented figures in the procession whose appearance always filled him with a strange and incomprehensible melancholy. [. . .] He always experienced the greatest difficulty in tearing himself away from the sight of these two figures, and so it was now that, instead of writing Herr Elias Roos's letter of advice for Hamburg, he simply gazed at the marvellous picture and, without thinking what he was doing, began doodling with the pen across the paper.

Traugott's bold mark-making transforms, as if of its own accord, into a wayward doodle. His scrawls take the shape of two figures before him, 'in zierlichem kecken Umriß' (in delicately bold outline), led by the energy of the undeliberated line, later to be dismissed by his authorities as 'dumme Kinderstreiche' (childish scrawlings) (H IV 179–80). The flourish functions as an intermediary between two different kinds of notation: the detail of a business letter and an involuntary, even automatic, drawing. As the *Artushof* transforms from a daylit stock exchange into a ghostly evening gallery of living paintings, the space of the page allows line and number to unfold into a bold line drawing.[7] What the businessmen see as a childish act of de-figuration, a kind of graffiti, is for the artist an imaginative invigoration of commonplace lines. The adjective 'keck' (bold) is Hoffmann's favoured term for describing Jacques Callot, the seventeenth-century engraver and 'kecker Meister' (bold master) (H II.1 17) to whose 'manner' Hoffmann dedicates the foreword to the *Fantasiestücke*. Callot creates his figures 'oft nur durch ein paar kühne Striche' (often only by a couple of daring strokes), Hoffmann writes, which come alive such that 'jede schreitet, oft aus dem tiefsten Hintergrunde, [...] kräftig und in den natürlichsten Farben glänzend hervor' (each one strides out, often from the deepest background, powerfully and in the most natural colours) (H II.1 17). In their brevity, and in their reduction to only the quintessential lines, Callot's black-and-white drawings are able to evoke not just the sense of natural colour, but indeed of life itself. Here, too, Traugott's flourish marks the threshold at which observation or 'Beobachtung' slips into a Romantic vision, a seeing in double, wherein prosaic lines are charged with supernatural significance and life.

This passage is itself part of a series of two stages, for the wry narrator at the very beginning of the tale describes the magical double atmosphere of the *Artushof* by invoking the reader, 'Du, günstiger Leser!' (You, kind reader!), as witness (H IV 177). This interpellation, characteristic of Hoffmann, works as a preliminary narrative flourish, attempting to breach the divide between reader and fiction. The intersubjective 'Du', an interpolated figure existing somewhere between reader and fictional character, will read anew 'das seltsame Bild- und Schnitzwerk' (the strange picturings and carvings) in the evening light, he claims, such that its figures seem to come alive, becoming 'rege und lebendig' (animated and lively). 'Du' will accordingly feel, as does Traugott, the urge to reach for 'Tinte und Feder' (ink and pen) and 'jenen prächtigen Bürgermeister mit seinem wunderschönen Pagen abzukonterfeien' (to reproduce that splendid *Bürgermeister* with his handsome page) (H IV 178). 'Du' is

---

[7] For commentaries on the role of the outline in this tale, see Günter Oesterle, 'Romantische Urbanität? Börse und Kunst in E. T. A. Hoffmanns "Der Artushof"', in *'Hoffmanneske Geschichte': zu einer Literaturwissenschaft als Kulturwissenschaft*, ed. by Gerhard Neumann (Würzburg: Königshausen & Neumann, 2005), pp. 243–58; and Charlotte Kurbjuhn, 'E. T. A. Hoffmann: Umriss-Bilder und Serapiontisches Erzähl-Prinzip an der Grenze zwischen Kunst und Leben in *Der Artushof*', in *Kontur: Geschichte einer ästhetischen Denkfigur* (Ochsenfurt: De Gruyter, 2014), pp. 655–74.

thus called upon as a second writer or artist figure who shares with Traugott the compulsion to copy and to draw.

The curious premise of the tale – and this crucial point is left unexamined, such that it recedes into the background, contributing to the tale's dream- or sketch-like quality – is that the figures drawn by Traugott seem to come alive. Traugott, we remember, has not summoned these figures from his own creative imagination: it is an act of copying that has brought them to life. The figures who emerge from this first scene – images he discovers, furthermore, that he has drawn before as a child, 'in freilich verzerrten, jedoch sehr kenntlichen Umrissen' (in faltering but nonetheless very recognisable outline) (H IV 186) – come to occupy Traugott's every thought, such that he loses himself in the fictions he has created. As in the case of *Der goldne Topf*, in Chapter 3, then, the tale documents the emergence of a more vital kind of artistic experience from within the contours of an ordinary life. And here, too, the protagonist's predicament is given form by the presence in his life of two women: Felizitas, the painted ideal, and Christina, his altogether worldly fiancée and daughter of his boss, Elias Roos.[8] Unlike for Anselmus, however, the narrative here follows Traugott's confrontation with the reality that his artistic ideal cannot be seized in the context of his real life without its splitting into a series of second-rate versions.

Fiction

The figure that appears to have come to life as a result of Traugott's doodlings is not only a kind of living picture, but also himself an artist: the two-hundred-year-old painter Godofredus Berklinger, accompanied by his mysterious son. These two characters come to dominate Traugott's existence. After he catches sight of a certain Felizitas in one of Berklinger's paintings, apparently the artist's daughter, Traugott elevates her to the status of his ideal, abandoning his duties to his work and to Christina in order to dedicate himself more fully to his artistic career and to his pursuit of Felizitas.

Framed within Traugott's predicament – the fading of his daily reality beneath a vivid new artistic existence – is the more desperate predicament of Berklinger, an extreme portrait of the artist whose

---

[8] The antisemitic undertones of the tale, particularly in relation to the character of Elias Roos, are examined in Michael Mandelartz, '*Berganza* und *Der Artushof*: Poetische (Un-)Gerechtigkeit bei Lope de Vega, Cervantes, und E. T. A. Hoffmann', *Zeitschrift für interkulturelle Germanistik*, 8 (2017), 25–40 (pp. 31–8).

visions are shown to be irreconcilable with life. The critical scene in this regard comes when Traugott witnesses Berklinger's masterpiece:

> Der Jüngling, ganz altdeutsch gekleidet, öffnete ihm [Traugott] die Tür und führte ihn in ein geräumiges Gemach, wo er den Alten in der Mitte auf einem kleinen Schemel vor einer großen aufgespannten grau grundierten Leinwand sitzend antraf. 'Zur glücklichen Stunde,' rief der Alte ihm entgegen, 'sind Sie mein Herr gekommen [. . .]. Dies ist nun, wie Sie sehen, das wiedergewonnene Paradies, und sollte mir um Sie leid sein, wenn Sie irgend eine Allegorie herausklügeln wollten. Allegorische Gemälde machen nur Schwächlinge und Stümper; mein Bild soll nicht *bedeuten* sondern *sein*.' [. . .] Immer stärker, aber immer unverständlicher und verworrener wurde des Alten Ausdruck. (H IV 191)

> The young man, who was clad entirely in old German garb, opened the door for him and led him into a spacious room, in the centre of which he saw the old man sitting on a little footstool in front of a large canvas, primed in grey. 'You have come at a happy hour, my dear sir,' the old man called to him. [. . .] 'This, as you see, is Paradise Regained, and I should be much disappointed in you if you were tempted to wrangle some kind of clever allegory out of it. Only bad and bungling painters paint allegorical works: my picture is intended not to *signify*, but to *be*.' [. . .] His expression grew ever more forceful and ever more incomprehensible and confusing.

The central artistic delusion of Berklinger, nestled within the delusory narrative of Traugott, is a singular and fleeting scene, like a dream or a vision in which that central motif given only in a sparse three words – the 'grau grundierte Leinwand' (canvas, primed in grey) – disappears as soon as it is mentioned. Its presence, though vague and uncertain, intensifies the irony in Traugott's eagerness to seize Berklinger as his model, for although he initially believes the old painter to be 'von einem besonderen Wahnwitz befangen' (caught by a peculiar lunacy) (H IV 156), he later declares him 'mein Meister, mein Vater, mein Alles!' (my master, my father, my everything!) (H IV 199).

As a piece within *Die Serapionsbrüder*, *Der Artushof* offers a single point of entry into the much-discussed and debated Serapiontic Principle – the brethren's loosely theoretical point of departure for the creation of their fictions. A few points should be noted about this principle before its precise terms are explored. First, it is formulated by the characters from within the narrative, rather than by a narrator or by Hoffmann himself; second, it is not a didactic formula so much as a set of ideas discussed and modified erratically over the course of the narrative cycle; and third, it is a collaborative and sociable project, indeed, a project in criticism, that develops across the brethren's responses to one another's narratives.[9] These factors all heighten the irony with which it is introduced as literary-critical principle, and – perhaps most importantly – place it firmly within the realm of fiction, even as it sets about commenting on that fiction.

The principle is formed of two loose coordinates that are not fully reconciled with one another. These are, first, the principle of internal vision ('inneres Schauen') as the basis for the creation of art, exemplified by the hermit Serapion himself in the opening story *Der Einsiedler Serapion*, who is heralded as the brethren's patron saint; and, second, as corrective to this first principle, the principle of dualism. The principle of dualism remembers that Serapion's outlook is also a form of solipsistic madness that excludes him from all normal social standing, and insists on the artist's being grounded in a material environment, dependent on empirical experience. The lack of reconciliation between those two coordinates, and the resulting tension between an idealism driven into solipsism and a recognition of the artist's material conditioning, is part of how the method works in practice, and will strike a familiar note to the reader of any of Hoffmann's tales.

It is in response to the first two tales of the cycle, *Der Einsiedler Serapion* (The Hermit Serapion) and *Rat Krespel* (Councillor Krespel), that the discussion begins. In *Der Einsiedler Serapion* Cyprian describes his observations of a former German diplomat suffering from what the psychologically inclined Cyprian diagnoses as a 'fixe Idee': he is convinced that he is a Christian martyr, Saint Serapion, living not in provincial nineteenth-century Germany but in the Theban desert in the third century. He has sequestered himself away from society and reality and robustly defends his fantasy existence to Cyprian in terms that clearly draw from Fichtean idealism. Serapion insists on the supremacy of mind or spirit ('Geist') above all empirical experience: 'Ist es nicht der Geist allein, der das was sich um uns her begibt in Raum und Zeit, zu erfassen vermag?' (Is it not the mind alone which is able to comprehend the things that surround us in time and space?) (H IV 33–4). What Cyprian understands as a form of insanity also proves itself to be the basis of an unparalleled artistic talent, for in the course of their discussions Serapion relates

[9] Hilda Meldrum Brown, *E. T. A. Hoffmann and the Serapiontic Principle: Critique and Creativity* (Rochester, NY: Camden House, 2006), p. 2.

to Cyprian three dazzling tales: consummate artistic achievements, we are led to believe, which, in not being related back to the reader, attain a kind of ideal status as unknowable absences.

In the discussion following this narrative and the following one, *Rat Krespel*, Lothar remarks upon Serapion's predicament as follows:

> Armer Serapion, worin bestand dein Wahnsinn anders, als daß irgendein feindlicher Stern dir die Erkenntnis der Duplizität geraubt hatte, von der eigentlich allein unser irdisches Sein bedingt ist. Es gibt eine innere Welt und die geistige Kraft, sie in voller Klarheit, in dem vollendetesten Glanze des regesten Lebens zu schauen, aber es ist unser irdisches Erbteil, daß eben die Außenwelt, in der wir eingeschachtet, als der Hebel wirkt, der jene Kraft in Bewegung setzt. [. . .] Aber du, o mein Einsiedler! statuiertest keine Außenwelt, du sahst den versteckten Hebel nicht, die auf dein Inneres einwirkende Kraft; und wenn du mit grauenhaftem Scharfsinn behauptetest, daß es nur der Geist sei, der sehe, höre, fühle, der Tat und Begebenheit fasse, und daß also auch sich wirklich *das* begeben was er dafür anerkenne, so vergaßest du, daß die Außenwelt den in den Körper gebannten Geist zu jenen Funktionen der Wahrnehmung zwingt nach Willkür. Dein Leben, lieber Anchoret, war ein steter Traum, aus dem du in dem Jenseits gewiß nicht schmerzlich erwachtest. (H IV 68)

> Poor Serapion, in what did your madness consist, if not in the fact that some enemy star had robbed from you the recognition of that duplexity which is in fact the sole essential condition of our earthly existence. There is an inner world, and the spiritual faculty of seeing it with absolute clarity and in the most brilliant distinctness of active life; but it is our earthly lot that precisely the outer world within which we are encased functions as the lever that brings that faculty into play. [. . .] But you, happy hermit, lost sight of the outer world, and did not perceive the lever which set your inward faculty in motion; and when, with that gruesome acumen of yours, you declared that it is only the mind which sees, hears and takes cognisance of events and incidents, and that, as a consequence, whatever the mind takes cognisance of has actually happened, you forgot that it is the outer world which causes the spirit to exercise those functions which take cognisance. Your life was a continuous dream, from which your awaking in another world was assuredly not a painful one.

Serapion seems, in his own estimation at least, to have achieved what many of Hoffmann's artists strive towards: the complete reconciliation of internal and external worlds. But for Lothar, Serapion has lost sight of the fact that human beings are embodied – 'eingeschachtet' (enclosed) in the material universe – and that the achievements of the imagination, as vivid and potent as they may be, are dependent for their existence on our sensory entwinement with that universe. The image of the 'hidden lever' may point towards a Romantic interest in the search for an Archimedean point as a figure for self-knowledge.[10] Whilst the precise mechanical workings of the lever are irrelevant to Lothar, what remains is the idea that the achievements of the imagination may be activated or raised up by a point in the external universe that stimulates inspiration and creation. The lever, not unlike the chiasm, simultaneously joins together and holds apart those two forces that produce the work of art: the creative subject and the world in which he is embedded.

It is on the basis of the Romantic hermit's ambiguous achievements, which also constitute a desperate failure in terms of his status as a social being, that Lothar formulates a principle as a loose guideline for the brethren's narrative project. This gives rise to the most frequently cited version of the Serapiontic formula:

> Jeder prüfe wohl, ob er auch wirklich das geschaut, was er zu verkünden unternommen, ehe er es wagt laut damit zu werden. Wenigstens strebe jeder recht ernstlich darnach, das Bild, das ihm im Innern aufgegangen recht zu erfassen mit allen seinen Gestalten, Farben, Lichtern und Schatten, und dann, wenn er sich recht entzündet davon fühlt, die Darstellung ins äußere Leben [zu] tragen. (H IV 69)

> Let each of us try and examine well as to whether he has really seen what he has undertaken to describe before he dare put it in words. At least let each of us strive, most seriously, to get a clear grasp in his mind of the picture he is going to produce, with all of its forms, colours, lights and shadows; and then, when he feels himself thoroughly inflamed by it, to bring the representation out into external life.

Evidently, taking this statement out of the context of the prior discussion could risk leading to a simplified understanding of the Principle, because Lothar seems now to be returning to the notion that pure 'inneres Schauen' (internal vision) is the artistic ideal, and thus seems to be endorsing the equation of an artistic temperament with the kind of madness that leads us away from society. But Lothar has already emphasised the vital importance of remembering humans' embodied

---

[10] Jocelyn Holland, *The Lever as Instrument of Reason: Technological Constructions of Knowledge around 1800* (New York: Bloomsbury, 2019), p. 21.

state, and in this light his phrasing here can be reexamined: for what he is also saying, in this summary, is that sensory perception is the artist's most important tool, both in his careful observation of the world and in his careful attention to the colours, tones and forms with which to represent it.

The Serapiontic Principle has been termed explicitly 'antimimetisch'.[11] Certainly it reaches at a creative act that goes beyond the copying of natural forms or artistic models, though we know Hoffmann to be just as committed to the precise observation of everyday life as Jacques Callot, whom he praises for taking his subjects 'aus dem Leben' (from life). But, as a principle based on the conviction that art must arise from the recognition that internal being and external experience are related to but separate from one another, the Serapiontic Principle can be better understood as a corrective to neoclassical principles of imitating natural forms through received conventions, and as a (late) response to contemporary Romantic thought, which nonetheless, and crucially, operates within a framework that can be described as mimetic, in the important sense that it is related to the careful communication, through art, of individual sensory experience. The goal, for the group of narrators who discuss Serapion's predicament, is to become an artist who is faithful to his visions *without* giving up his place in society. If single-mindedly chasing the artistic ideal can prove antithetical to this goal (as it does in the case of Serapion and Berklinger), then Lothar's corrective is to acknowledge the empirical foundations of human experience – the intermingling of spirit and matter, our inescapable dependence on sensory perception for any expression whatsoever – and to make that acknowledgement the starting point for the work of art. This is a recursive, self-reflexive proposition: Lothar is suggesting that art should tackle the struggle to make art. It is, in that sense, a fitting description of Hoffmann's own method.

Figure

Der Artushof follows one set of strands that emerges from the tangled thematic complex of the Serapiontic Principle: the artist's loss of his ideal amongst the forms of the everyday. The blankness of Serapion's unnarrated ideal novellas is literalised in the form of the

---

[11] See Claudia Barnickel, 'Serapiontisches Prinzip/"Prinzip der Duplizität"', in *E. T. A. Hoffmann Handbuch: Leben – Werk – Wirkung*, ed. by Christine Lubkoll and Harald Neumeyer (Stuttgart: Metzler, 2015), pp. 395–9 (p. 395).

artist's blank canvas. The tale seeks to turn that loss into a formative principle of the narrative, in a Serapiontic sense: it tackles the experience of the work of art itself, where that experience is characterised as disillusionment. In order to show how this functions, it is worth turning first to a pictorial flourish inserted by the narrator, shortly after Traugott has first sketched out his figures, at a dinner hosted by Elias Roos:

> Wohl könnte ich dir, günstiger Leser! die fünf Personen, während sie bei Tische sitzen, bildlich vor Augen bringen, ich werde aber nur zu flüchtigen Umrissen gelangen, und zwar viel schlechteren als wie sie Traugott in dem ominösen Avisobriefe recht verwegen hinkritzelte, denn bald ist das Mahl geendet, und die wundersame Geschichte des wackern Traugott, die ich für dich, günstiger Leser! aufzuschreiben unternommen, reißt mich fort mit unwiderstehlicher Gewalt! (H IV 181)

> I wish I could, dear reader, offer to your eyes a picture of the five people sitting at that dinner table! – but I would achieve only fleeting outlines, far inferior to those daringly doodled by Traugott on that fateful letter of advice, for the meal will soon be over and the marvellous history of valiant Traugott that I have undertaken to write out for you, dear reader, urges me forward with irrepressible force!

Hoffmann, who is known for bringing his narrative voices in line with his characters (most notably in *Der Sandmann*, where the narrator is uncannily reminiscent of Nathanael), casts the narrator of *Der Artushof* as another doodler or sketcher next to Traugott. This passage is an apt example of that 'rhetoric of denied rhetoricity' characteristic of the nineteenth-century verbal sketch described by Richard C. Sha and discussed in Chapter 2 of this book,[12] and which August Wilhelm Schlegel detects in John Flaxman's line drawings, in which, he argues, 'die Phantasie wird aufgefordert to ergänzen' (the imagination is incited to complete the picture), as it is in poetry.[13] In this short passage the narrator claims that his description suffers because of the fact that his medium is that of narrative rather than painting. What it cannot be – a painted tableau – is turned into a negative rhetorical device that propels the narrative on. The apparent

---

[12] Richard C. Sha, *The Visual and Verbal Sketch in British Romanticism* (Philadelphia, PA: University of Pennsylvania Press, 1998), p. 1.

[13] August Wilhelm Schlegel, 'Über Zeichnungen zu Gedichten und John Flaxman's Umrisse' (1799), *Athenäum* II.2, pp. 204–5.

loss of the image, mediated through an ekphrastic switch, becomes the representational mode.

Traugott is so caught up in the recognisable outer forms of his ideal – failing, like Serapion, to understand that the ideal itself cannot be reconciled with reality – that the only plausible ending can be the triumph of the bad copy: 'er schaut das Ideal und fühlt die Ohnmacht es zu erfassen, es entflieht, meint er, unwiederbringlich' (he sees the ideal and feels the inability to grasp it, it flees from him, he thinks, irrevocably) (H IV 153). In turn, the tale's clunkily deceptive happy ending, in which all characters wind up cheerfully married, though not in the arrangements we might have expected (Christina to the accountant in her father's firm and Felizitas to Hofrath Mathesius), mediates an experience of the artwork as a loss of the ideal, or as a bathetic encounter of the ideal with the everyday. In this sense, the tale reproduces a sense of ambivalent distance from the artwork in a formal sense. For the punchline of *Der Artushof* is that Felizitas is, in fact, the male youth with whom Traugott has been familiar the whole the time. Recognisable clues to this are present everywhere in the text. In the presence of Berklinger's son, Traugott experiences a feeling of Felizitas's proximity, 'als stehe lichthell das geliebte Bild neben ihm, als fühle er den süßen Liebeshauch' (as though the beloved portrait were standing vividly beside him and he could feel its sweet loving breath) and the desire to embrace him: 'er hätte dann den Jüngling, als sei er die geliebte Felizitas selbst, an sein glühendes Herz drücken mögen' (he would have liked to have pressed the youth to his glowing breast as if he were the beloved Felizitas herself) (H IV 198). In this queer moment, recognisable traits are momentarily shifted from their usual rectilinear (and heterosexual) configurations, evidence that the ideal can be found in reality only in altered form. The distortive capacities of lines and outlines is at the centre of the tale.

When Traugott catches an illicit glimpse of Felizitas revealed as herself, Berklinger – desperate to hide his daughter from suitors on account of a hastily introduced ancient prophecy declaring that he will die as soon as she marries – whisks her away and they disappear without trace from the town. Traugott travels mistakenly to Italy to look for them, confusing the German town of Sorrent with its orthographic twin, the Italian Sorrent/Sorrento, a doubling of names that acts as a heavy-handed comment on the German artist's clichéd attraction to Italy, 'Land der Kunst' (land of art) (H IV 199). In Traugott's absence, Felizitas has married the bourgeois criminal counsellor Matthesius, become 'Frau Kriminalrätin'

(Mrs Criminal Counsellor), and has 'diverse Kinder in Cours gesetzt' (produced assorted children) (H IV 205), thus proving herself to be, in Traugott's eyes, similar to the earthly Christina, whose priorities in life include marrying well and perfecting her butter sauce (H IV 182). Berklinger, in accordance with the prophecy, dies in circumstances so grotesque and lurid as to be pantomimic. Meanwhile in Sorrento, Italy, Traugott discovers Dorina, a second-rate version of Felizitas, who is distinctly reminiscent of her: 'sie hatte die Züge der Felizitas, sie war es aber nicht' (she possessed the features of Felizitas, but it was not she) (H IV 201). The narrative, in accordance with the Serapiontic Principle, follows a series of scenarios in which Traugott finds himself landing back in each instance with only a painted copy of the ideal.

To read by means of *Züge*, individual traits, is to pay note to insignificant-seeming information. The *Zug* is a measure of difference, a marker of the idiosyncrasy of the individual, but when read as part of a series it is also a token of similitude and seriality, enabling recognition. Carlo Ginzburg, discussing Morelli's method of identifying paintings via their extraneous details, describes it as 'a method of interpretation based on discarded information, on marginal data, considered in some way significant'.[14] Drawing a constellation between Morelli, Sherlock Holmes and Sigmund Freud, Ginzburg postulates a 'conjectural paradigm' which developed in the nineteenth century alongside medical semiotics and police identificatory methods and which had its roots in an ancient impulse to hunt out and interpret the tracks and traces left behind by animals. In Hoffmann's tale of reappearing 'Züge', the identificatory work of the trait or trace is troubled when it returns as part of a series. Traugott does not, in fact, recognise the individual herself but rather the patterning of sameness and difference that he sees in a set of faces. Dorina forms just one part of a series of which Felizitas is one necessary other part: 'Sie war in der Tat beinahe Felizitas selbst, nur schienen ihm die Züge starker, bestimmter, so wie das Haar dunkler. Es war dasselbe Bild von Raphaël und von Rubens gemalt' (She was, indeed, almost Felizitas herself, only her features were stronger and more clearly defined, and her hair was darker. It was the same picture, painted first by Raphaël, then by Rubens) (H IV 201). In this description, the same picture has been

---

[14] Carlo Ginzburg, 'Clues: Roots of an Evidential Paradigm', in *Clues, Myths, and the Historical Method*, trans. by John and Anne C. Tedesechi (Baltimore, MD: Johns Hopkins University Press, 1989), pp. 87–113, p. 101.

painted by two different masters. Traugott's experience of Dorina is, in essence, the experience of *similarity*, of an uncanny closeness to an original that cannot exist both as ideal and as a reality in Traugott's real life.

The effect is repeated when Dorina's father is shown not to be Berklinger, as Traugott had originally expected and desired, but another distorted version of Berklinger:

> Traugott sah nun wohl, daß die Höhe des Gerüstes in der Kirche, auf dem der Alte stand, ihn sehr getäuscht hatte. Statt des kräftigen Berklinger war dieser alte Maler ein kleinlicher, magerer, furchtsamer, von Armut gedrückter Mann. Ein trügerischer Schlagschatten hatte in der Kirche seinem glatten Kinn Berklingers schwarzen krausen Bart gegeben. (H IV 201–2)

> Traugott could now see that the height of the scaffold on which the old man had been standing in the church had deceived him. The aged painter was, unlike the robust Berklinger, a diminutive, lean, humble man, stricken by poverty. In the church, a deceptive shadow had seemed to bestow upon his smooth chin Berklinger's curly black beard.

As the scaffolding distorts the scale of the image, the deceptive shadow throws the appearance of Berklinger's beard onto his face, as a para-physiognomic projection; a legible layer not etched into or emerging from the face, but pitched onto it. Dorina's father, proportionally distorted, takes on a momentarily skewed appearance which, like Berthold's perspectival guidelines, is only the result of accidental light and shadow. Dorina and her father – images cast in the likeness of Berklinger and Felizitas – are, in their momentary similarity to those originals, resonant in appearance with everything they are not. Like painted figures, they are the result of the distorting apparatus of representation, of copying, of mimesis. They are the products only of similitude, and they are equally 'the real thing', flesh and blood, living and tangible. We are left with the familiar scene of Hoffmann's archetypal young artist caught between idealised and real images: 'Felizitas stand ihm wieder lebhaft vor Augen, und doch war es ihm, als könne er Dorina nicht lassen' (Felizitas appeared vividly before his eyes, yet it seemed to him he could not desert Dorina). Whereas the 'lebhaft', lifelike image remains a projection, a 'geistig Bild' (an image in his mind), Dorina is characterised by the erotic affect inspired by a real body: 'süße Schauer' (sweet trembling) and 'sanfte Glut' (gentle heat) (H IV 202). Finally, both Christina and Felizitas end up as bourgeois wives, both swapping one fiancé for another in the kind of mercantile exchange that transforms the otherworldly *Artushof* gallery back into the *Börse*.

In committing his art to paper, Traugott signs away the possibility of possessing his ideal. This is a compromise he is forced to repeatedly acknowledge. The repeated moment of his acknowledgement takes the form of the 'Schnörkel' or the 'Umriss': the contour, the figure's potentially deceptive edge, the physiognomic outlines that fuzz and blur features into indistinction. Such outlines, as figures that trace the passage between 'seeing' and *schauen*, like the inky lines of Hoffmann's physiognomic *Brustbild*, are also ironic figures that lead Traugott astray. The irony is intensified by Felizitas's marriage to Hofrath Mathesius, a move that has led Claudia Liebrand to call the whole work a 'Komödienschema' (comedy scheme), operating in 'trivialer Lustspielmanier' (the fashion of a popular comedy) by pitting the literal against the figurative in a 'Doppelspiel' (double play) of meanings.[15] Liebrand connects the tale's comedic quality to its original publication in the popular *Taschenalmanach* (pocket almanac) *Urania, Taschenbuch für Damen auf das Jahr 1817*. But the version that found its way into the *Serapionsbrüder* gives expression to a significant attentiveness to copies and imitations, in a recycled series of visual layers, which thus inevitably reflects on the collection of which it is a constituent piece. The artifice and brevity of its conclusion is part of the experience of an artwork that is contingent and that falls far from the ideal: one that reminds us of the Romantic narrative by virtue of a few salient traits and tropes, but that fails, or refuses, to deliver that experience in full, giving us instead only the feeling of similitude.

In *Der Sandmann*, the narrator begins with a flourish reminiscent of that of *Der Artushof*. Positing 'du' as his interlocutor, he describes the difficulty the writer has to find the words with which to begin his narrative and turns, by contrast, to the task of the painter:

> Hattest du aber, wie ein kecker Maler, erst mit einigen verwegenen Strichen, den Umriß deines inneren Bildes hingeworfen, so trugst du mit leichter Mühe immer glühender und glühender die Farben auf und das lebendige Gewühl mannigfacher Gestalten riß die Freunde fort und sie sahen, wie du, sich selbst mitten im Bilde, das aus deinem Gemüt hervorgegangen! (H III 26)

---

[15] Claudia Liebrand, *Aporie des Kunstmythos: Die Texte E. T. A. Hoffmanns* (Freiburg: Rombach, 1996), p. 146.

But if, like a bold painter, you had first sketched in a few audacious strokes the outline of the picture you had in your soul, you would then easily have been able to deepen and intensify the colours one after the other, until the varied throng of living figures carried your friends away and they, like you, saw themselves in the midst of the scene that had proceeded from your own soul.

Again the compulsive 'keck' announces a shift into the rhetoric of the painter. The narrator goes on to describe the series of letters with which he began the story as 'den Umriß des Gebildes, in das ich nun erzählend immer mehr und mehr Farbe hineinzutragen mich bemühen werde' (the outline of the picture, into which I will endeavour to introduce more and more colour as I proceed with my narrative), hoping to complete his figures 'wie ein guter Portraitmaler' (like a good portrait painter). Again, it is the outline that is made central – the figure that calls for completion, here in the addition of colour. The narrator concludes with his hope 'dass du es ähnlich findest, ohne das Original zu kennen' (that you will find it a good likeness, without knowing the original) (H III 27). He thus describes his method quite candidly as the production of a sense of similitude and similarity. If we are to take seriously what Hoffmann's narrators call the 'duplexity' of the human condition, then we cannot deal in originals or authentic experiences when we are dealing with artworks. Mimesis is directed instead towards the dispersal and disruption of the ideal, which is experienced, if not as a kind of madness, as it is in *Der Sandmann*, then as a kind of disillusionment, as in *Der Artushof*. And yet the act of reaching towards the ideal – the strains and contortions involved in doing so – is nevertheless, in Hoffmann's works, a justification for art in its own right.

Le Chef-d'œuvre inconnu (Conte fantastique)

On its first publication in *L'Artiste* in 1831, *Le Chef-d'œuvre inconnu*, like the initial draft of *La Peau de chagrin*, bore the parenthetic subtitle '(Conte fantastique)', an epithet that disappeared after its extensive rewriting in 1836–7. This perplexing pretext might seem, at least to the reader of the 'standard' Furne version of the text, more a provocation than a descriptive label. Certainly it stands as testament to the eagerness with which the term was applied in the early 1830s. Less obviously a 'conte fantastique' than *La Peau de chagrin*, the primary fantastic quality of *Le Chef-d'œuvre inconnu*, as I will show through particular reference to the original version, lies not in magical objects or inexplicable events but in the study of a singular fantasy driven to demonic obsession: in the fatal, Faustian – and, in Hoffmann's term, Serapiontic – mistake of the artist who equates life with art.

That vexing Hoffmannesque pretext is both insistent and resistant, placed in a paratextual zone in the Genettian sense: a 'zone between text and off-text, a zone not only of transition but also of transaction: a privileged place of a pragmatics and a strategy'.[16] Its appearance between parentheses pushes it further 'off' or outside the sanctioned textual space even before it disappears altogether. It is, as Genette suggests, a pragmatic, strategic, transactional element: first, because Balzac was advertising his tale in the fashionable literary terminology of the time, and second, because it sets up the stakes of our reading. Its function is less one of cataloguing or labelling than it is of inscription, for the 1831 version of *Le Chef-d'œuvre inconnu* contains a definition of the fantastic within itself, a definition that is slowly – but not completely – eroded in subsequent revisions. The pretext persists, despite its disappearance, as 'one of many veils or *parerga* that distort our reading', like one of the many layers of paint that complicate the representation of Frenhofer's model.[17]

The tale begins with a typically Balzacian touch of melodrama, as the tremulous young Nicolas Poussin pauses on the threshold of great art:

> Quand il parvint en haut de la vis, il demeura pendant un moment sur le palier, incertain s'il prendrait le heurtoir grotesque qui ornait la porte de l'atelier [. . .]. Le jeune homme éprouvait cette sensation profonde qui a dû faire vibrer le cœur des grands artistes, quand, au fort de la jeunesse et de leur amour pour l'art, ils ont abordé un homme de génie ou quelque chef-d'œuvre. (B X 413–14)

> When he arrived at the top, he lingered for a moment on the landing, hesitating to lift the grotesque door-knocker which embellished the door of the studio [. . .]. The young man was experiencing that profound sensation which has stirred the hearts of all great artists when, in the prime of their youth and their love for art, they encounter a man of genius or a masterpiece.

---

[16] Gérard Genette, *Paratexts: Thresholds of Interpretation*, trans. by Jane E. Lewin (Cambridge: Cambridge University Press, 1997), p. 2.

[17] Marie Lathers, 'Modesty and the Artist's Model in *Le Chef-d'œuvre inconnu*', *Symposium*, 46.1 (1992), 49–71 (p. 52).

Another hopeful hero in the cut of Anselmus, Raphaël and Traugott, Poussin is introduced to us in the moment of his encounter with the bounding lines of an artistic world sealed off from the uninitiated. By coincidence, the renowned painter Frenhofer also appears on the scene. Porbus lets them both in, and all three enter the studio to examine his masterpiece, the *Marie égyptienne*. Frenhofer declares that the painting, although good, is not yet complete, for 'elle ne vit pas' (she does not live) (B X 416), and proceeds at length to expound his theories on art. Poussin, under the scrutiny of his elders, quickly dashes out a copy to prove his own artistic potential. On his return home, Poussin begs his uncommonly beautiful lover Gillette to pose for Frenhofer as a model, so that Frenhofer, in turn, will reveal to them his own masterpiece, Catherine. Gillette agrees, knowing that in some vital way she has been sacrificed in the name of art. In the second part of the tale, some three months later, after Frenhofer has expressed doubts about exposing his treasured masterpiece to the eyes of others, the transaction is carried out and Gillette poses nude for Frenhofer in a sealed room. Porbus and Poussin, who have been speculating about what might be going on in the room, are finally permitted a glimpse of Frenhofer's *chef-d'œuvre*. They see nothing but a canvas covered in erratic lines and pools of colour, with the exception of a single, exquisitely rendered foot. When the dismayed Poussin declares out loud what he sees – 'il n'y a rien sur sa toile' (there is nothing on his canvas) (B X 437) – Frenhofer angrily banishes them from his studio. He is found dead in his studio amongst the ruins of his burned paintings the next day. Frenhofer's delusion – which stems at least in part from the fact that he believes himself to be a kind of Pygmalion figure, capable of creating not just lifelike art but life itself – is mirrored by Poussin's willingness to exchange his lover and model Gillette for a glimpse of Frenhofer's painting. In that sense, like *La Peau de chagrin*, the tale is structured by a doubleness which, on this occasion, is centred on the naked female body, serving both as model and as representation – and as bartering tool between men.

Whilst *Le Chef-d'œuvre inconnu* has been hailed as an unwitting manifesto for modernist and non-representational art by such figures as Cezanne, Picasso and De Kooning, it is, I argue, more illuminating to consider the tale within its own aesthetic context of the 1830s: the years of a burgeoning realism, in which the stakes and strategies of that category were taking shape. Critical evaluations are almost as contested as they could be on this point. For Alexandra Wettlaufer, the tale documents 'a final refusal of the

"realism" of the painted image and a stark illustration of the futil-
ity of trying to instill art, or confuse art, with life'.[18] Sandy Petrey,
taking a slightly different stance, emphasises Frenhofer's curiously
and stubbornly mimetic understanding of his own work, despite
having produced an abstract artwork himself.[19] Frenhofer has utter
faith, that is, that what he has produced is like reality; so very like
reality, indeed, that its viewers will find themselves not in the presence of a 'tableau' but of a 'femme'. He believes that he has achieved
a realism to rival the illusion of Zeuxis's painted grapes, so perfectly
rendered that birds snap at them. In the first version of the story, as
Petrey points out, Frenhofer remains absorbed in his own illusion: it
is not until the revised version of 1836–7 that Balzac changes heart
and has Frenhofer burn his painting and kill himself – though it is
still arguably not clear, from Frenhofer's pronouncements, to what
extent he recognises that he has produced little more than a scribble.
This change of heart in itself must suggest to us that there is more to
Frenhofer's painting than too much paint.

Models

The fantasy explored by the tale is of a representational mode that
is not bound to any consensus imitative syntax. When Frenhofer
exclaims that 'La mission de l'art n'est pas de copier la nature, mais
de l'exprimer!' (the objective of art is not to copy nature, but to
express it!) (B X 418) he is not exhorting the abandonment of nature
in favour of abstraction, nor indeed the prioritising of internal vision
over the careful study of reality. Frenhofer wants to paint a woman,
after all: he seeks a model because he needs to find a point in the
world on which to rest his Archimedean lever, as it were, and he is
prepared to travel far and wide to find it – 'Je me décide à voyager et
vais aller en Turquie, en Grèce, en Asie pour y chercher un modèle
et comparer mon tableau à diverses natures' (I've made up my
mind to travel – I will go to Greece, Turkey, even Asia to look for a
model; I want to compare my picture to various beauties in nature).
Crucially, here, he does not pursue a singular woman so much as the
status or essence of woman-ness, in its diverse and serial forms, in a
long-repeated process of comparison and retouching.

---

[18] Alexandra Wettlaufer, *Pen vs Paintbrush: Girodet, Balzac, and the Myth of Pygmalion
in Post-Revolutionary France* (New York, NY: Palgrave, 2001), p. 248.
[19] Sandy Petrey, *In the Court of the Pear King: French Culture and the Rise of Realism*
(Ithaca, NY: Cornell University Press, 2005), p. 40.

Frenhofer's pronouncements sound remarkably close to some of those more expansive understandings of mimesis that were outlined in Chapter 2: descriptions of mimesis not as the careful copying of natural forms (which Frenhofer scornfully compares to the act of making a cast of an object) but as the revelation of nature's essential structures. 'Art,' as Petrey points out, 'does not get any more realist': nor, Auerbach might interject, can it get much more Romantic. Petrey goes on to conclude that the tale 'complicates mimetic views of art at least as impressively as it foreshadows nonmimetic views'.[20] By explicitly peeling mimesis away from the act of painting what you see at one particular moment, the tale taps into a reading of mimesis more at home within Romantic theories of art-making as a quest for a rendering of overarching natural structures towards which the finished artwork claims only to gesture.[21]

Whilst René Guise and Sigbrit Swahn have cautioned against the positing of earlier works as 'models' for Balzac's text, I want to suggest an intertextual relationship of modelling between Hoffmann and Balzac that is characterised less by the mastery of the artist's gaze over his model than by a power struggle effected across a scene of looking and representation on the one hand, and revealing and resistance on the other.[22] Foundational to this thinking is previous criticism on *Le Chef d'œuvre inconnu* that has emphasised the agency of the tale's real model, Gillette, unsettling her from her status as passive referent into an active participant both in the artwork and, in turn, in the written text.[23] 'Model', we recall on a perusal of the *OED*, refers both to the original entity on the basis of which a representation is formed – to 'a person, or a work, that is proposed or adopted for imitation' – and to the representation itself, to the 'person or thing that is the likeness of another'.[24] Copy and original collide in the modelling. Whilst René Guise warns, then, of Balzac's relationship to Hoffmann, that there is 'un monde entre la réminiscence et le recours conscient à un modèle' (a world between a reminiscence and conscious recourse to a model), we might point out that recourse to a model need not always be fully conscious or active,

[20] Ibid., pp. 40–1.

[21] See Patrizio Collini, 'Iconolâtrie et iconoclastie: "Le Chef-d'œuvre inconnu" et le romantisme allemand', *L'Année balzacienne*, 1.5 (2004), 75–85.

[22] Sigbrit Swahn, 'Le Chef d'œuvre inconnu, récit hoffmannesque de Balzac', *Studia Neophilologica* 76.2 (2004), 206–14, pp. 206–7.

[23] See Lathers, 'Modesty and the Artist's Model'; Knight, *Balzac and the Model of Painting*.

[24] 'model, n. and adj.', *OED Online*, Oxford University Press <www.oed.com> [accessed 10 October 2022].

nor fully unconscious or passive – that modelling might instead resemble an interplay between two participants who switch between more active and more passive modalities.[25]

It should be stated at this point that the Hoffmannesque link, in this case, is unquestioned.[26] René Guise goes so far as to call *Le Chef-d'œuvre inconnu* a 'pastiche' of Hoffmann.[27] In 1828, *Le Gymnase* – a journal printed on Balzac's press – had published the first translation of Hoffmann's *Der Baron von B.*, under the title *L'Archet du baron de B.*[28] It was translated for a second time by Loève-Veimars as 'La leçon du violon' in *L'Artiste* only a few months before the first instalment of the first version of *Le Chef-d'œuvre inconnu* was published in the same journal. Critics have repeatedly made note of the remarkable similarities between Hoffmann's musical tale and Balzac's 'conte fantastique'.[29] In *Der Baron von B.*, a young student, encouraged by his mentor, takes music lessons from the renowned Baron of B., and in doing so a triangular constellation of masters and pupils forms around the artwork (though here it is a musical performance, not a painting). Yet when the student sees the musician perform for the first time, his illusions are shattered:

> Dicht am Stege rutschte er mit dem zitternden Bogen hinauf, schnarrend, pfeifend, quäkend, miauend – der Ton war dem zu vergleichen, wenn ein altes Weib, die Brille auf der Nase, sich abquält, den Ton irgend eines Liedes zu fassen. (H IV 904)

> He slid the quivering bow tightly up the strings, rasping, whistling, squawking, yowling – the tone was comparable with the struggling of an old bespectacled woman trying to catch the tune of a song.

---

[25] René Guise, 'Balzac et l'étranger', *L'Année balzacienne* (1970), 3–19, p. 13.

[26] See, for example, Gabriele Brandstetter, 'Kritzeln, Schaben, Übermalen: Bild-Löschung als narratives Verfahren bei Hoffmann, Balzac, Keller und Hofmannsthal', in *Homo Pictor*, ed. G. Böhm and Stephan Hauser (Munich: De Gruyter, 2001), pp. 353–72; Marianne Kesting, 'Das imaginierte Kunstwerk: E. T. A. Hoffmann und Balzacs *Chef d'œuvre inconnu*, mit einem Ausblick auf die gegenwärtige Situation'; Max Andréoli, 'Sublime et parodie dans les *Contes Artistes* de Balzac', *L'Année balzacienne* (1994), p. 19; Pierre Laubriet, *Un catéchisme esthétique: Le Chef d'œuvre inconnu de Balzac* (Paris: Didier, 1961), pp. 31–40.

[27] René Guise, 'Introduction' [*Chef d'œuvre inconnu*], B X, pp. 393–412 (p. 410).

[28] Wayne Connor, 'Reviewed Work(s): Balzac's Frenhofer', *Modern Language Notes*, 69.5 (1954), 335–8 (p. 337).

[29] William Paulson, 'Pour une analyse dynamique de la variation textuelle: Le Chef-d'œuvre trop *connu*', *Nineteenth-Century French Studies*, 19.3 (1991), 404–16 (p. 406); Swahn, 'Le Chef-d'œuvre inconnu', p. 212; Guise, 'Notes et Variantes' [*Chef-d'œuvre inconnu*], B X, pp. 1410–28; Fernand Baldensperger, *Orientations étrangères chez Honoré de Balzac* (Paris: Champion, 1927), pp. 108–9.

In this distinctly unerotic formulation, Hoffmann subverts the image of the female muse associated with the production of art as the performance opens up a scene not of transcendence but of bathos, a fall into ugly reality. Like Frenhofer, the Baron is a convincing theorist of his art, as well as a renowned practitioner, but in the context of the narrative produces only chaos and noise; and, like Frenhofer, he is unaware that what he has produced fails to convince.

The similarities between Frenhofer and Berklinger of *Der Artushof* are yet more striking: both are old and knowledgeable but eccentric men who seem to have stepped out of a painting themselves and who are found raving in startlingly precise terms about the representational content of paintings they claim to have completed on canvases which are, in Berklinger's case, blank, and in Frenhofer's, so overdone as to be undone. If Frenhofer is a character of 'direct Hoffmannesque descent', his forbears include both the Baron of B. and Berklinger.[30] By the point of writing his tale Balzac had also most likely read Loève-Veimars's first volume of translations, which included *Die Brautwahl*, *Die Jesuiterkirche in G.* and *Der Artushof*, each of which will have a further role to play in the argument in what follows: that Balzac's reflection on (and of) the male Romantic artist, and his equation of life and art, is mobilised as a way of reflecting on realist premises.

Critical to this argument is the fact that Balzac incorporated into the 1831 version of the tale a definition of *le fantastique* that he sees to be embodied in the character of Frenhofer, and that serves as proof of his close engagement with Hoffmann's works at this time:

> Le mépris que ce vieil homme affectait d'exprimer pour les plus belles tentatives de l'art, sa richesse, ses manières, les déférences de Porbus pour lui, cette œuvre tenue si long-temps secrète, œuvre de patience, œuvre de génie, sans doute, s'il fallait en croire la tête de vierge que le jeune Poussin avait si franchement admirée et qui était là, belle encore près de l'Adam de Mabuse; pour toutes ces singularités, l'idiome moderne n'a qu'un mot: *c'était indéfinissable!* . . . Admirable expression! elle résume la littérature fantastique; elle dit tout ce qui échappe aux perceptions bornées de notre esprit; et, quand vous l'avez placée sous les yeux d'un lecteur, il est lancé dans l'espace imaginaire; alors, le fantastique se trouve tout germé, il pointe comme une herbe verte au sein de l'incompréhensible et de l'impuissance. . .

---

[30] Sotirios Paraschas, *The Realist Author and the Sympathetic Imagination* (Oxford: Legenda, 2013), p. 83.

Donc ce vieillard, maître Frenhofer paraissait indéfinissable, incompréhensible, et, tout ce que la riche imagination de Nicolas Poussin put saisir de claire et de perceptible, en voyant cet être surnaturel (surnaturel est encore une belle expression !), c'est qu'il était le type le plus complet de la nature artiste [. . .].[31]

The scorn which the old man affected to express for the most beautiful artistic endeavours, his wealth, his mannerisms, Porbus's deference towards him, and that work of art that he had kept secret for so long – that work of patience and doubtless of genius, judging by the head of the virgin that Poussin had so candidly admired, and which was still beautiful even next to Mabuse's 'Adam'; for all these peculiarities our modern language has only one word: *it was indefinable!* . . . A fine expression! It sums up the literature of the fantastic; it means everything that escapes the mind's limited faculties of perception; and, when placed before a reader's eyes, the reader is launched into an imaginary realm; thus, the fantastic is found budding, emerging like a blade of grass from within the incomprehensible and the impotent . . .

So this old man, master Frenhofer, appeared indefinable, unknowable, and the most clear and distinct thing that Nicolas Poussin's rich imagination could seize upon when he looked at this supernatural being (supernatural is another fine expression!) was that he was the most complete type of the artistic nature [. . .]

Balzac's narrator defines 'le fantastique' in epistemological terms, channelling it through the fashionable term 'indéfinissable'.[32] The fantastic is that which indicates a movement beyond the limits of the categories laid out by human perception and understanding, thus stimulating the imagination of the reader. It is found budding in what we do not understand, 'l'incompréhensible', and indicates what we cannot name, 'l'indéfinissable'. It is the unknowable or unknown: the 'inconnu'. As Francesca Brittan has noted, the reviews that introduced Hoffmann into the French journals made use of that word 'inconnu', as in Saint-Marc Girardin's description of Hoffmann's ability to transport his readers into a 'monde inconnu'

---

[31] Honoré de Balzac, 'Le Chef-d'œuvre inconnu', *L'Artiste: Journal de la littérature et des beaux-arts*: pt 1, 'Maître Frenhofer', 1 (31 July 1831), 319–23; pt. 2, 'Catherine Lescaut', 2 (4 August 1831), 7–10. Here pt. 1, pp. 321–2.

[32] José-Luis Diaz, in a contrasting reading to mine here, argues for the ironic tone of this section as part of a wider project of 'démystifier' (demystifying) the fantastic genre by showing up its reliance on so many voguish terms. José-Luis Diaz, 'Ce que Balzac fait au fantastique', *L'Année balzacienne* 13 (2012), 61–83.

(unknown world).[33] Perhaps, then, that first version of *Le Chef-d'œuvre inconnu*, with its incorporated theory of 'le fantastique', derives its title in part from a particular modern idiom that bore a strong association with Hoffmann. The Hoffmannesque fantastic, Balzac suggests, sets up a conflict within what Kathryn Hume calls 'consensus reality' (though it does not, as she suggests of fantastic literature, actually depart from it), but it does so from *within* reality's own terms, becoming a kind of falling out or off or in between categories of knowledge, aptly caught by such terms as 'indéfinissable' and 'inconnu'.[34]

Line

Frenhofer's theory of art is of indubitably Serapiontic heritage: art is an expression and not merely a copy of life, he declares, and his resounding call that 'la mission de l'art n'est pas de copier la nature, mais de l'exprimer!' (The mission of art is not to copy nature, but to express it!) is reminiscent both in structure and in sense of Berklinger's claim that 'mein Bild soll nicht bedeuten, sondern sein!' (my image should not signify, but be!). For an artwork to express nature but not to copy it, or, in Hoffmann's version, for it to be and not to signify: as we have seen, this correction of the imitation principle had been formulated not as an alternative to, but from *within* mimetic thought, taken up by Romanticism from neoclassicism. For Frenhofer, to reproduce a subject's anatomical outlines, her 'figure' and not her 'forme', is to fail in this task: 'vous croyez avoir tout fait lorsque vous avez dessiné correctement une figure et mis chaque chose à sa place d'après les lois de l'anatomie!' (you think you have done it all once you have correctly drawn a figure and put everything in its place according to anatomical law!) (B X 416). To (merely) adhere to received artistic conventions or schemata, he suggests, can result only in flattened or shadow-like versions of images, 'figures', which do not truly live: 'Vos figures sont alors de pâles fantômes coloriés que vous nous promenez devant les yeux, et vous appelez cela de la peinture et de l'art' (your figures are pale coloured phantoms that you walk about in front of our eyes, and you call that painting and art) (B X 419).

---

[33] Francesca Brittan, *Music and Fantasy in the Age of Berlioz* (Cambridge: Cambridge University Press, 2017), p. 109, n38; Saint-Marc Girardin, 'Contes fantastiques d'Hoffmann, traduction d'un extrait du *Pot d'or*', *Revue de Paris*, II (1829), 67–130, p. 67.

[34] Kathryn Hume, *Fantasy and Mimesis: Responses to Reality in Western Literature* (New York, NY: Methuen, 1984), p. 20.

It is on this basis that Frenhofer condemns the painted line, thereby inscribing himself into a debate around the prioritisation of colour versus line drawing that had been active since the Renaissance, when the Venetians (colour) were pitted against Raphael (line), and that had been reincarnated in the debates between the Rubénistes (colour) and the Poussinistes (line), and again in the nineteenth century in the rivalry between Delacroix (colour), and Ingres (line). Frenhofer, who belongs to the school of colour, praises 'l'ardeur éblouissante, l'heureuse abondance des peintres italiens' (the dazzling ardour, the cheerful abundance of Italian paintings) over the 'flegme minutieux, la raideur précise' (meticulous composure and strict resolve) of Dutch and German painters (B X 417). Frenhofer sees the line as an artificial intervention in painting that does not exist in nature: 'la ligne est le moyen par lequel l'homme se rend compte de l'effet de la lumière sur les objets; mais il n'y a pas de lignes dans la nature où tout est plein' (the line is the means by which man perceives the effect of light upon objects; but there are no lines in nature, where everything is solid) (B X 424–5). The line deadens the artwork, he argues, by marking only its incommensurability with life.

The task, as Frenhofer sees it, is to reproduce reality without attempting to copy it through those conventions that have traditionally structured how artists both see and represent reality – that is, to do away with convention and to get at the world in some more essential way. This is a task that a number of Hoffmann's artist figures grapple with. Indeed, for all of the varied pronouncements on art made by Hoffmann's characters, the notion of a representation of nature that surpasses the mere imitation of nature is one of his most abiding interests. The young Edmund Lehsen of *Die Brautwahl*, for example, is busily painting a landscape when he is interrupted by the goldsmith Leonard. Edmund explains his technique in the following:

> Ist es Ihnen nicht auch so, wenn Sie sich in der Natur ganz Ihrem sehnsüchtigen Gefühl überlassen, als schauten durch die Bäume, durch das Gebüsch, allerlei wunderbare Gestalten Sie mit holden Augen an? – Das war es, was ich in dieser Zeichnung recht versinnlichen wollte, und ich merke, es ist mir gelungen. (H IV 655)

> Does it not also seem to you, when you abandon yourself wholly to your desires and longings in the natural landscape, as if all kinds of wondrous figures were gazing at you with loving eyes through the trees and the undergrowth? That is what I wanted to give expression to in this drawing, and it appears I have succeeded.

From Edmund's remarks, it is not clear whether or not he has actually added to his landscape painting elements that are not, in fact, present in the scene before him. What he admits to is to 'versinnlichen', that is, to bringing out the *sense* of the 'wondrous figures' that he sees there in a particular longing mood, and not necessarily to painting the figures themselves. In those uncertain words, he is able to open up an interstitial space between his internal vision and his fidelity to nature: this is the space of the world as it is filtered and distorted by the self. The innocent-sounding question he poses to the goldsmith Leonard, his interlocutor – 'Does it not also seem to you . . . ?' – cements the sceptical problem that Stanley Cavell picks out elsewhere in Hoffmann's work: the entirely 'ordinary' fact that we cannot properly know the existence of other minds. For Cavell, it is precisely the ongoing threat of scepticism that generates the uncanny effects of *Der Sandmann* as embodied in the very real risk that one might fall in love with an automaton.[35] Good resemblances are uncanny, threatening to dethrone the real, but so too are bad resemblances that nonetheless seem to convince. The affect generated by the Baron von B.'s dismal musical production in his audience (though not an attempt at representation) is that of 'ein *unheimlicher* Spuk' (an *uncanny*, spooky feeling) (H IV 905, my emphasis). The sensation of the uncanny, here, is generated by our inability to know how the world appears to somebody else. That ignorance opens up inlets in our everyday experiences through which a feeling of unfamiliarity may momentarily surge.

If we turn to *Die Jesuiterkirche in G.* – in some ways a companion piece to *Der Artushof* – we encounter once again the doctrine of a representation that surpasses copying, given this time in the advice of an old Maltese artist, one of two tutors in the tale, to the young artist Berthold:

> Auffassung der Natur in der tiefsten Bedeutung des höhern Sinns, der alle Wesen zum höheren Leben entzündet, das ist der heilige Zweck aller Kunst. Kann denn das bloße genaue Abschreiben der Natur jemals dahin führen? – Wie ärmlich, wie steif und gezwungen sieht die nachgemalte Handschrift in einer fremden Sprache aus, die der Abschreiber nicht verstand und daher den Sinn der Züge, die er mühsam abschnörkelte, nicht zu deuten wußte. So sind die

---

[35] Stanley Cavell, 'The Uncanniness of the Ordinary', in *In Quest of the Ordinary: Lines of Skepticism and Romanticism* (Chicago, IL: University of Chicago Press, 1988), pp. 153–80.

Landschaften deines Meisters korrekte Abschriften eines in ihm fremder Sprache geschriebenen Originals. (H III 129–30)

The apprehension of nature in the deepest import of that higher sense, which kindles all beings to a higher life, that is the sacred end of all art. Can the mere precise copying of nature lead to this? How poor, how stiff and forced, is the appearance of a manuscript copied from another in some foreign language, which the copyist does not understand, and is, therefore, unable to give the strokes, which he has laboriously imitated, their proper significance. Thus your master's landscapes are correct copies of an original author in a language which is strange to him.

The Maltese artist is introduced as an alternative art tutor to Hackert, the German painter who teaches Berthold how to paint competent, if hackneyed, landscapes. The Maltese artist, by contrast, is a proponent of enthusiastic Romantic painting – who does not reject mimesis per se, who indeed exhorts the 'Auffassung der Natur' through learning nature's hidden language – but who rejects mimesis *as copying*. Once Berthold, having decided to follow the Malteser's teachings, comes to possess his ideal in reality, in the figure of Fürstin Angiola von T., he finds that he is no longer able to represent her without both his pictures and the woman herself seeming to him ugly and distorted. Whether or not Balzac had read any or all of these tales, these artist figures offer themselves up as prefigurings of Frenhofer, whose artistic ideal proves so fatally incompatible with reality. The scene featuring the blank grey canvas in *Der Artushof* is, as mentioned, a fleeting, dreamlike scene, as if only half-enunciated, scarcely held up for examination. It can best be understood as part of a repeated patterning of absent artworks across Hoffmann's works: it is echoed, for instance, in *Die Elixiere des Teufels*, when a painter sits alone in his room 'und starrte Tagelang eine große aufgespannte Leinwand an, indem er versicherte, wie er eben jetzt an ganz herrlichen Gemälden arbeite' (staring all day long at a great canvas, declaring that he was working on great paintings) (H II.2 177). By transforming Berklinger's absent picture into a kind of surplus, Balzac refines Hoffmann's model by intensifying the uncertainty about what is actually present on Frenhofer's canvas. The 'conte fantastique' expresses a problem which undergirded the Romantic response to artistic production and with which Hoffmann had grappled again and again: there is no common basis for judgements of reality, and therefore for representations, that is not filtered through the mists of the self. What Balzac draws out of that situation is a tale in which the ideal is not reconcilable with reality except to the extent that the artist is able to convey his *experience* of the ideal on the canvas. If what Frenhofer produces is only colour and line, sheer form itself (and that perplexingly perfect foot), and this is apparently the culmination of his relationship with his art – the decade he has spent working on, and living with, the artwork he thinks of as a woman – then in a very real way he has succeeded in his task, for the artwork *remains* the consummate expression (or perhaps reflection) of that relationship in Frenhofer's eyes:

> 'Où est l'art? perdu, disparu! Voilà les formes mêmes d'une jeune fille. [. . .] Mais elle a respiré, je crois! Ce sein, voyez? Ah! qui ne voudrait l'adorer à genoux? Les chairs palpitent. Elle va se lever, attendez' (B X 435).

> 'Where is the art? Gone, vanished! Here are the true forms of a young girl. [. . .] But, I do believe she has taken a breath! You see that chest? Ah! Who could fail to worship her on his knees? The flesh trembles. She's about to get up, wait a moment.'

In so many minute ways, what Frenhofer says is correct: the recognisable 'artwork' as such has disappeared and something else has emerged on his canvas. As with Serapion himself, a degree of ambiguity lingers over whether Frenhofer is a failure or in some sense still a genius. Representation as such, realist or otherwise, as Gombrich reminds us, is a result not of translating concrete reality but of working with inherited conventions in combination with our sensory experience. If we do away with those conventions and simply paint what we see, the sceptics will tell us that nobody can judge that painting on the basis of its likeness. It is for this reason that ambiguity reigns over whether Berklinger and Frenhofer are failures or misunderstood geniuses. Balzac has made a dialogic contribution to Hoffmann's Serapiontic scheme by offering up a new chapter into the Serapiontic series that, like Hoffmann's own tales, both echoes and distorts its predecessors, at the same time as it attempts a definition of 'le fantastique'.

Study

Published in six versions over sixteen years, *Le Chef-d'œuvre inconnu* is mobile and unfixed, and therefore in a certain sense as indefinite and strange as Frenhofer's masterpiece, straining at the confines of the 'finished' work and offering up different forms under different lights (where Porbus sees 'une femme là-dessous', Poussin sees 'rien') (B X 436–7). George Edgar Slusser suggests that the text is less a product than a 'process' – one that, he argues, draws closer to the fulfilment of the Hoffmannesque performer figure that Balzac would finally complete in *Gambara*.[36] Whether or not this teleological approach is helpful, it certainly holds that the text, as one of the *Études philosophiques*, resembles a study or 'étude' in the true painterly sense: as a preparatory set of experiments or sketches seeking to tackle a problem in representation, composition, etc. In this case, as I have shown, the study takes on a problem that is best understood to be rooted in a set of questions that Hoffmann had grouped under the label 'Serapiontic'. It might in that sense be given another subtitle: 'a study in Hoffmann'.

Balzac's most significant alterations to the text were those made in the version of 1836/7, in which he expanded Frenhofer's art theory considerably and changed the ending to have Frenhofer burn his masterpiece and commit suicide. This new ending aligns Frenhofer with the character Horace de Saint-Aubin, the pseudonym adopted by Balzac for several of his unsuccessful commercial novels written between 1822 and 1825, and who was the subject of a biography, *Vie et malheurs de Horace de Saint-Aubin*, in 1836. This biography, ostensibly authored by Balzac's young assistant Jules Sandeau, had been commissioned by Balzac, if not partially written by him.[37] Saint-Aubin's fate is to burn his works after meeting a certain thinly disguised 'jeune homme qui achevait les *Scènes de la vie privée* et la *Physiologie du marriage*' (young man who had written *Scenes of Private Life* and the *Physiology of Marriage*).[38] In this sense, Balzac's edits to *Le Chef-d'œuvre inconnu* at around the same time give Frenhofer a particular autobiographical aspect – one that is heightened further by the deletion of the label 'conte fantastique' and by the insertion of the dedication 'À un Lord . . .' – Lord R'Hoone being another of the young Balzac's literary pseudonyms. In this light it is tempting to read *Le Chef-d'œuvre* as a renunciation of youthful Romantic aspirations by a Balzac whose project *La Comédie*

[36] Serge Zenkine, 'Le chef-d'œuvre et son modèle. Balzac et ses continuateurs', *The Balzac Review/Revue Balzac*, 2 (2019), 167–207, p. 168. George Edgar Slusser, 'Rameau's Nephew and his Progeny: The Artist as Performer in E. T. A. Hoffmann and Balzac' (unpublished doctoral thesis, Harvard University, 1974), p. 164.

[37] See Thierry Bodin, 'Les métamorphoses d'Horace ou quelques avatars romanesques de Jules Sandeau', *L'Année balzacienne*, 5 (1984), 15–36 (pp. 20–1).

[38] Jules Sandeau, *Vie et malheurs de Horace de Saint-Aubin* (Paris: Pressédition, 1948), p. 99.

humaine, with its more precisely sociological intentions, was well underway, marked by the publication of the first instalment of *Illusions perdues* in 1837. But any reader of Hoffmann will recognise that Frenhofer's suicide in fact brings him closer to Hoffmann's artists, for whom the ideal is so fatally incompatible with life that they often die in extraordinary or suspicious circumstances, as do both Berklinger of *Der Artushof* and Berthold of *Die Jesuiterkirche in G.* What might appear as a performed strangulation of the Romantic impulse is then, simultaneously, proof of a continued entanglement with Hoffmann, one that itself – as *étude* – remains equivocal, if not incomplete. As critics since Elizabeth Teichmann have suggested, the year 1836 had inaugurated a renewed engagement with Hoffmann's works occasioned by the publication of Henry Egmont's new translations and efforts to rehabilitate his image.[39]

William Paulson has argued that Balzac's major intervention after the 1831 version was the erasure of a number of rhetorical flourishes that signal to the reader 'qu'il lisait un récit fait de signes' (that he was reading a tale constructed of signs), in a strategy that apparently mirrors Frenhofer's own attempt to do away with convention as such: that which 'rappelle au spectateur qu'il regarde un tableau, et non la vie même' (reminds the viewer that he is looking at a painting, and not at life itself).[40] It is true that a surprising amount of the later, 'standard' version of the text is taken up by dialogue without narrative commentary. What Paulson does not note is that where those rhetorical flourishes *do* persist, they are made almost entirely in reference to Frenhofer. Rather than a parallel between narrator and artist, then, I see a striking tension: for where Frenhofer claims to want to do away with such interventions as the painted line, the tale's narrator, precisely in his descriptions of Frenhofer, employs a heavy-handed pictorialist rhetoric that draws attention to the tropes that sustain the representation:

> Imaginez un front chauvé, bombé, proéminent, retombant en saillie sur un petit nez écrasé, retroussé du bout comme celui de Rabelais ou de Socrate; une bouche rieuse et ridée, un menton court, fièrement relevé, garni d'une barbe grise taillée en pointe [. . .]. Mettez cette tête sur un corps fluet et débile, entourez-la d'une dentelle étincelante de blancheur et travaillée comme une truelle à poisson, jetez sur le pourpoint noir du vieillard une lourde chaîne d'or, et vous aurez une image imparfaite de ce personnage auquel le jour faible de l'escalier

[39] Elizabeth Teichmann, *La fortune d'Hoffmann en France* (Geneva: Droz, 1961), p. 232.
[40] Paulson, 'Pour une analyse dynamique', p. 411.

prêtait encore une couleur fantastique. Vous eussiez dit une toile de Rembrandt marchant silencieusement et sans cadre dans la noire atmosphère que s'est appropriée ce grand peintre. (B X 414–15)

Imagine a bulging forehead sloping down to a tiny squashed turned-up nose like Rabelais's or Socrates'; smiling wrinkled lips, a short chin held high and adorned with a grey beard trimmed to a point; [. . .]. Set such a head upon a weak and puny body, swathe it in extravagant curlicues of immaculate lace, drape a heavy gold chain over the black doublet beneath, and you will have an imperfect image of this personage to whom the dim light of the staircase lent a further tinge of the fantastic. It was as if a canvas by Rembrandt were walking, silent and unframed, through the tenebrous atmosphere that great painter has made his own.

Yvette Went-Daoust calls this a sequence of 'écriture picturale' (pictorial writing): comprising a *tableau*, as she notes, through engaging a 'métalangage de la peinture' (metalanguage of painting) allowing the character to take shape 'comme s'il oeuvrait sur une toile' (as if unfolding on a canvas).[41] It is a style that mobilises literature's own pictorial conventions, tapping into realism's assumption that how we read is fundamentally conditioned by how we see, and by how we might imagine or describe what we see. The chain of imperatives – 'imaginez', 'mettez', 'entourez-la', 'vous eussiez dit' – suggests the interrupting staccato movements of the artist's brush (like Frenhofer's 'paf, paf, paf' and 'Pon! pon! pon!'), hovering somewhere between narrator and reader, and casts the narrator as the fourth artist of the tale, to widen up the homosocial circle of Poussin, Porbus and Frenhofer. By participating in this inter-reflecting series of scenes of scribbling, drawing, painting and watching, the narrator is explicitly identified with the figure of the artist.

Wettlaufer singles out the 'imperfect' nature of the image that arises and notes of this self-reflexive passage that 'an image is an *image* and, whether painted or described, will always be imperfect, falling short of the reality of lived experience'.[42] This is key: if Frenhofer is not in fact, like Berklinger, a living portrait who has somehow wandered beyond the frames of his canvas, he is nonetheless, if we are to take the narrator's description seriously, another kind of living portrait. Frenhofer has become the subject of the

---

[41] Yvette Yvonne Marie Went-Daoust, 'Le Chef-d'œuvre inconnu de Balzac ou l'écriture picturale', in *Description-Écriture-Peinture*, ed. by Yvette Yvonne Marie Went-Daoust (Groningen: CRIN, 1987), pp. 48–64 (pp. 49, 53).

[42] Wettlaufer, *Pen vs Paintbrush*, p. 221.

artwork, the portrait at its heart. In that sense the tale is something like the fable of a reverse Pygmalion, in which the artist himself has become the spectacle through his own erotic investment in his artwork. As in *Der Artushof*, what we are left with is an 'image imparfaite' or 'flüchtige Umrisse': the figure and not the form, to use Frenhofer's terms. These tales of failed image-making are both mediated by a narrator who admits, in turn, to being able to achieve only the compromise of the shadowy *Ebenbild* or semblance. The seeming paradox of representation as it is expressed so pertinently in Hoffmann's tales, not least in *Der Artushof*, is that no matter how successfully the artist does his job, all that can emerge on the manuscript or the canvas is a kind of compromise. A representation is characterised as much by its absences and gaps as by its contents. Balzac pushes at that idea through his 'study' of a Hoffmannesque artist. As the tale is altered in subsequent revisions, Balzac's realist strategy shows itself to be grounded in the tropes and rhetorical categories that we recognise as participants in the structuring of our experience, *even as* those tropes and categories define something as un-real, as fiction. The fantastic, as the mode of the un-real in Balzac's definition, in this tale once defined as a '(conte fantastique)', will always be realism's interlocutor: it exists, as he speculates in the first version of the story, in the in-between spaces, such as prefaces and other paratexts, and in the 'inconnu'.

* * *

In *Dreaming in Books*, Andrew Piper draws a connection between the strain made by Porbus and Poussin to study Frenhofer's portrait – 'en se mettant à droite, à gauche, de face, en se baissant et se levant tour à tour' (moving first to the right, then to the left, then head-on, lowering and raising themselves by turns) (B X 66) – and the logic of anamorphosis, which demands a processual visual strain, requiring 'the reader-viewer to move one's eye and body to make something legible'.[43] E. T. A. Hoffmann describes his interest in anamorphic images in an entry in his notebook from 1821:

> Ein sehr schönes Bild ist von den sogenannten deformierten Gemählden herzunehmen. – Es sind z.B. auf einer Tapete verschiedene Theile, Züge eines Bildes verstreut, so daß man nichts deutliches wahrnimmt, aber ein besonders dazu geschliffnes Glas

[43] Andrew Piper, *Dreaming in Books: The Making of the Bibliographic Imagination in the Romantic Age* (Chicago, IL: University of Chicago Press, 2009), p. 217.

vereinigt die verstreuten Züge, und durch dasselbe schauend erblickt man das Bild.[44]

A very beautiful image can be extracted from the so-called deformed paintings. – For example, various parts and strokes [Züge] of an image are scattered across a carpet, so that one perceives nothing clearly, but a glass polished especially for that purpose brings together the scattered traits, and through that glass one sees the image.

The oblique dispersal of 'Züge', which gather in formation to suggest a projected form, is resonant of the contours in *Der Artushof*, the constituent lines of either an ideal form or a duplicitous *Trugbild*. Every scene of reading or of ekphrasis, in image or text, occasions a particular internal doubling, where the reader's site of reading encounters the narrator's or fictional character's site of reading, or indeed of painting. Traugott and Poussin, as apprentice painters and observers, become the sites of such doubling. The result is not an intensification of feeling so much as it is a fracturing or splintering: such that the result is the sense of having not the whole thing, but only the figure, an 'image imparfaite'. Perhaps what we have here is the prefiguration of an impressionist aesthetic in which the filtering of an individual's embodied experience is made part of the picture.

Works of realism later in the nineteenth century would continue to be interested in skewed and unfinished images, as well as in unfinished scribbles and doodles. In Gottfried Keller's *Der grüne Heinrich* (1854–5/1879–80) Heinrich Lee's formation as a writer arrives through the event of making a non-representational work of art. As he tests his pen on the paper, the strokes come together to form an unexpected, living abstract work:

So versank ich in eine tiefe Zerstreuung und strichelte gedankenlos daneben, wie wenn man die Feder probiert. An diese Kritzelei setzte sich nach und nach ein unendliches Gewebe von Federstrichen, welches ich jeden Tag in verlorenen Hinbrüten weiterspann, sooft ich zur Arbeit anheben wollte, bis das Unwesen wie ein ungeheueres graues Spinnennetz den größten Teil der Fläche bedeckte.[45]

---

[44] Cited in Günter Oesterle, 'Die folgenreiche und strittige Konuktur des Umrisses', in *Bild und Schrift in der Romantik*, ed. by Günter Oesterle and Gerhard Neumann (Würzburg: Königshausen & Neumann, 1999), pp. 27–58 (p. 124).

[45] Gottfried Keller, *Gesammelte Werke*, vol. 2, *Der grüne Heinrich*. Zweite Fassung, ed. Walter Morgenthaler (Zurich: Büchergilde Gutenberg, 1960), p. 511.

I became lost in a deep preoccupation and went on making strokes unthinkingly, as one does in testing a pen. Close to this scrawl there gradually came to be an unending web of pen-strokes which I spun out further every day, sitting in fruitless brooding, as often I tried to begin work, until the monster, like a vast grey cobweb, covered the greater part of the surface.

Here, further into the heart of realism in the latter half of the nine-teenth century, the scandal of abstraction has been muted. Whilst Keller's *Kritzelei* has unsurprisingly been heralded as a prefiguring of modernist art, the scrawl might equally be understood as a further example of a realism slowly tangling and untangling itself. Gabriele Brandstetter, Barbara Naumann and Andrea Meyertholen have offered compelling readings of this scene, moving beyond the sugges-tion that it might foreshadow non-representational art, or represent some kind of psychological mindmap of Heinrich, to focus on the *Kritzelei* itself as medium.[46] As a web of marks that has no commer-cial value according to the demands of the market, nor any aesthetic value according to contemporary standards, Heinrich's activity in the *Kritzelei* is nonetheless described as a kind of 'work'. But the piece, completed in what seems to be a trance-like state, refuses to reach a point at which it might be described as a finished work. It is a web of lines and strokes that shuttle between word and image, between production, overproduction and non-significance, between work and distraction, raising the question about whether such mark-making is a doing, a non-doing, or an undoing (if Hoffmann's was a non-doing, Balzac's an undoing, Keller's surely oscillates between both). The strain depicted in the act of making, and viewing, a non-representational image, is here reconceived as a pleasure. The non-representational art form, here, is taken more seriously as work: as the squiggle or doodle moves further towards the centre stage, the work of doodling lies, almost paradoxically, in the pleasures of mark-making.

---

[46] Brandstetter, 'Kritzeln, Schaben, Übermalen'; Andrea Meyertholen, 'It's Not Easy Being Green: The Failure of Absrtact Art in Gottfried Keller's *Der grüne Heinrich*', *German Studies Review*, 39.2 (2016), 241–58; Barbara Naumann, 'Körperbild und Seelenschrift: Eine Szene in Gottfried Kellers "Der grüne Heinrich"', in *Verkörperungen*, ed. by André Blum and others (Berlin: Oldenbourg Akademieverlag, 2012), 217–22.

Chapter 5

Cross: *Die Elixiere des Teufels* and *L'Élixir de longue vie*

The self-generating and interlocking arabesques and scribbles of the previous chapters have indicated thus far that the narrative line as motif is rarely singular, nor meaningful on its own terms, but rather marks a place of encounter between self and work, as a moment of inscription or as gestural flourish. This becomes all the more apparent when the line is twisted into the figure of the cross, which will work as the guiding motif for the studies in this chapter.

The cross, an intersection, denotes a crossroads, an opening of ways, but also a crossfire or exchange of blows. To be 'crossed', in another context, means to be afflicted or marked. We might be reminded of Anselmus of *Der goldne Topf*, who laments 'Wahr ist es doch, ich bin zu allem möglichen Kreuz und Elend geboren!' (In truth, I am born to all possible crosses and misery!) (H II.1 231). Before it came to denote the intersection of two lines, the word 'cross' referred to the Christian crucifix and to the effigies made in its shape.[1] The verb to 'cross', accordingly, meant 'to make the sign of the cross' long before it came to mean 'to intersect'. *Die Elixiere des Teufels* and *L'Élixir de longue vie* both feature images of Christian crosses in the context of a playful Gothic anticlericalism. But the cross also plays a formal role, as an explicit confusion or contradiction of plot lines. For Medardus of *Die Elixiere des Teufels*, hounded by his double, lines of genealogy and inheritance proliferate, as if deliberately set against one another, culminating in a moment at which a particular cross-shaped scar on his neck fails to do its identificatory work, and

---

[1] The first entry for 'cross' in the *Oxford English Dictionary* is 'The instrument of crucifixion with its representations and *fig.* applications. A kind of gibbet used by the ancients (and in later times by some non-Christian nations); a stake, generally with a transverse bar, on which they put to a cruel and ignominious death certain criminals, who were nailed or otherwise fastened to it by their extremities.' 'Cross, n.', *OED Online*, Oxford University Press <www.oed.com> [accessed 18 January 2017].

his second self is permitted to live on as an impostor. In *L'Élixir de longue vie*, a single line of inheritance – a bloodline – is confounded by a Faustian attempt to prolong life indefinitely in an endeavour that ends in gruesome misadventure.

The relationship between the two texts is characterised by contradiction, in the precise sense of a 'talking against'. *L'Élixir de longue vie* is the only one of Balzac's narratives to acknowledge Hoffmann explicitly as an influence – in a preface that was added to the tale on its incorporation into *La Comédie humaine*, sixteen years after its first publication in *La Revue de Paris* in 1830. And yet, as critics have discussed at length, the intertextual allusion has little bearing on the narrative itself, which is a retelling of a story by Richard Steele. Another fantastic Balzacian *conte*, *Sarrasine*, published in the issue directly preceding this one, had borne the epigraph: 'Croyez-vous que l'Allemagne ait seule le privilège d'être absurde et fantastique?' (Do you believe Germany alone has the prerogative of being absurd and fantastic?) (B VI 1544) – an explicit response to the vogue for Hoffmann exploding across the Parisian literary reviews at that time. When *Sarrasine* was included in the *Scènes de la vie parisienne* in 1844, its epigraph was erased and replaced by a dedication to Charles de Bernard, who, as discussed in Chapter 3, had published a review of *La Peau de chagrin* in 1831 in which he claimed that work to be of explicitly Hoffmannesque descent. Where one Hoffmannesque preface was removed, another more veiled one was reinserted, and shortly afterwards *L'Élixir de longue vie* gained its own explicitly Hoffmannesque preface. The recognition of Hoffmann in these early works is thus characterised by the appearance and disappearance of attributions and prefaces. Hoffmann's presence and non-presence in these paratextual spaces makes him into something of a contradictory or obfuscatory pretext for Balzac. This is an idea that I will pursue in my conclusion.

Read alongside (or across) one another, the two narratives tell the story of what we might call a Gothic narrative extravagance. That vague term, 'Gothic', indicates not a homogeneous movement so much as the emergence of a set of literary trends, images and forms from a process of European 'cultural cross-fertilization' during the eighteenth and nineteenth centuries.[2] These two texts act out an example of one such intersection, in the sense that Hoffmann's novel experiences an unexpected afterlife

---

[2] Neil Cornwell, 'European Gothic', in *A New Companion to the Gothic*, ed. by David Punter (Oxford: Blackwell, 2012), pp. 64–76 (p. 68).

within Balzac's tale. As we will see, the figure of Hoffmann is of somebody remembered and recognised, but not quite, or not quite in full, as a spectral 'ami, mort depuis longtemps' (long-dead friend) (B XI 473), or a source text attributed to the wrong author, or a signature with an indistinct form. These variants – drawn, crossed out and compulsively redrawn – resemble the anonymous faces or the impossible shapes of intertextual resonance: of a troubled literary crossover.

Die Elixiere des Teufels
Elixirs

For the monk Medardus, for whom the text of *Die Elixiere des Teufels* serves as a kind of confessional autobiography, to have confessed – to have made a crossing into narrative – means to confront the narrative self in its wildest formulations. The novel takes the form of the written confession by Franz, alias Medardus, presented to the reader by an editor who claims to have found Medardus's near-illegible manuscript in the Capuchin monastery at 'B.'. In it we read how Medardus, as a young monk, tastes an antique wine kept in the reliquary believed to be the elixir with which the devil tempted St Anthony. Related to this, though perhaps not in a strictly causal sense, Medardus discovers within himself a particular passion for preaching at the pulpit. As his throngs of exalted spectators grow, so does his arrogance. He also learns the first temptations of the flesh, becoming consumed by desire for a young woman whom he identifies with the painting of St Rosalia hanging above the altar. Eventually Prior Leonardus, disconcerted by the young monk's behaviour, sends him on an errand to Rome. Armed with a bottle of the devil's wine, and already determined to go his own way, Medardus's journey has scarcely begun when he unwittingly causes a sleeping nobleman to fall from the edge of a ravine. Oblivious that the stranger, Count Viktorin, will rise, in near demonic state, from his fall, and that their lives are to run from now on in an abysmal 'Kreuzsymmetrie' (cross-symmetry), Medardus takes on the count's identity.[3] In a startling and often gruesome series of performances and switches of identity, he follows a path of murder, attempted

---

[3] Detlef Kremer, 'Gebrochene Identität mit Doppelgänger: *Die Elixiere des Teufels* (1815/16)', in *E. T. A. Hoffmann: Erzählungen und Romane* (Berlin: Erich Schmidt, 1999), pp. 40–63 (p. 54).

rape, repentance, self-chastisement and imprisonment – first in jail and then in an asylum – and is hounded throughout by a series of returning figures, including the painter and Viktorin himself, as Medardus's delirious *Doppelgänger*.

Medardus's grim narrative breaks off in the second part of the novel and crosses over into a set of others, including that of the old painter, whose genealogical account of Medardus's ancestry seems to explain the mysterious identities at play in his story. According to this account, Viktorin is his half-brother: both are the descendants of a line of sinful men, beginning with Francesko, the painter of the image of St Rosalia back in the chapel at B., who was seduced by a succubus-like woman in league with the devil. The implication is that Medardus/Franz is part of a line marked by generations of inherited wrongdoings: a line that will now, with his written confession, come to an end. When Medardus finally returns to his monastery, Prior Leonardus instructs him to write down his life story as penance for his sins. The intricately wrought novel that results from this task shows in no uncertain terms that a life may not be reduced to a single reading. Attention is drawn to this by means of the 'geheimer Faden' (secret thread) (H II.2, 12), a motif that is linked to the stem of the family tree and to the rapidly growing line of inherited sin, and which is taken up at several points in the narrative only to be abandoned or knotted into confusion. As a narrative that ostentatiously puts its own complexities on show – being near-impossible to follow – the thread of narrative logic is confounded by the paradoxical structure of the cross: the line cloned in a kind of cross-fertilisation and at odds with its own double.

The novel has served as a fertile testing ground for critical approaches, which have tended to orient themselves around their differing approaches to chaos and form. Whilst Manfred Momberger and Sarah Kofman read the novel as an exploration of the wild dispersal of a self deprived of any stable identity, other critics seek out its inherent patterns and orderings.[4] Ricarda Schmidt, for example, notes that the holes, breaks and inconsistencies picked out by Momberger are filled elsewhere in the novel through flash-backs and foreshadowings, making it, ultimately, a narrative of the 'Wiedergewinnung von psychischer Kohärenz' (restoration of

---

[4] Manfred Momberger, *Sonne und Punsch: Die Dissemination des romantischen Kunstbegriffs bei E. T. A. Hoffmann*; Sarah Kofman, 'Vautour rouge (Le double dans *les Élixirs du diable* d'Hoffmann)', in *Mimésis des articulations*, ed. by Sylviane Agacinski and others (Paris: Flammarion, 1975), pp. 95–163.

psychic coherence).[5] More recently, Yvonne Al-Taie has read the novel as two halves that reciprocally shed light on one another, one of which delivers Medardus's inexplicable sensational experiences, the other – the painter's manuscript – retroactively enforcing form.[6] Such structurally ordering accounts of the novel draw attention to the fact that Medardus scarcely deviates from the path set out for him by Leonardus.[7] Others anchor it within the context of German Romanticism, positioning it as an exemplar of Schlegel's 'gebildetes künstliches Chaos' (formulated artistic chaos), or relate it to literary-historical patterns, whether as *Bildungsroman*, Gothic novel (*Schauerroman*) or family novel (*Stammbaumroman*), diffuse identificatory labels that are a symptomatic response to a text that actively crosses between genres, as a kind of hybrid.[8]

My reading here responds to some of these questions raised around chaos and form through an investigation of what we might describe as the novel's representational excess – a particularly lurid or vivid, sensationalist quality that is engendered through its Gothic style and pictured in the figure of the doubled or serial self. This excessive quality, as I will show, takes on a distinct form. To this end, this chapter accounts for some of the more complex knots in the novel's narrative structure, taking seriously Momberger's claim that the central problem of the text is 'das Problem der Mimesis' (the problem of mimesis) and showing how that 'problem' is directed towards the self, in the context of a fictional autobiography concerned with the act of putting life into narrative. Moving beyond

---

[5] Ricarda Schmidt, 'Narrative Strukturen romantischer Subjektivität in E. T. A. Hoffmanns *Die Elixiere des Teufels* und *Der Sandmann*', *Germanisch-Romanische Monatsschrift*, 49 (1999), 143–60, p. 157.

[6] Yvonne Al-Taie, '"Des fremden Malers wunderbares Buch": Die doppelte Ordnung von Bild und Erzählung in E. T. A. Hoffmanns *Die Elixiere des Teufels* (1815/16)', in *Ding und Bild in der europäischen Romantik*, ed. Jakob C. Heller and others (Berlin: De Gruyter, 2021), pp. 265–81 (p. 266).

[7] Schmidt, 'Narrative Strukturen', p. 157.

[8] For Romantic irony, see Allienne R. Becker, '"Alice Doane's Appeal": A Literary Double of Hoffmann's *Die Elixiere des Teufels*', *Comparative Literature Studies*, 23.1 (1986), 1–11 (p. 3). For generic categorisations see, for example, Eric A. Blackall, who writes in *The Novels of the German Romantics* (Ithaca, NY: Cornell University Press, 1983) that 'the structure of *Die Elixiere* is clearly a geometrical progression. [. . .] It is a study of the surfacing of the subconscious' (p. 235). Sabine Kleine argues for a reading of *Elixiere* as a *Bildungsroman*, suggesting that it tracks 'the individuation of the protagonist in terms of his education and growth to maturity through contact with the world. The way into the world is identical with the way to the self.' In 'Elixiere des Teufels: Notes on E. T. A. Hoffmann's "Black Romanticism" and the Idealist Critical Response', *Journal of the Australasian Universities Language and Literature Association*, 91.1 (1999), 27–44 (p. 39).

Momberger's claim that 'die Unterscheidung zwischen Ebenbild und Trugbild, zwischen Kopie und Simulacrum [. . .] wird in diesem Roman fragwürdig' (the distinction between likeness and illusion, between copy and simulacrum [. . .] becomes uncertain in this novel), this chapter shows that mimesis is a phenomenological problem in this text, one that is experienced on the visual field but also registered in, and across, the body.[9] The novel reproduces an experience of the dislocations of writing about the self, such that the *Doppelgänger* motif emerges not just as a sign of psychic dislocation but also of narrative dislocation. It is, in that sense, a fitting interlocutor to Hoffmann's other major fractured novel, the fictional autobiography *Kater Murr*.

Elixiere plays with and reworks tropes typical of the Gothic novel, particularly of Matthew Lewis's *The Monk*, a text that occupies a crucial position within Hoffmann's, as the novel read by Aurelie, Medardus's half-sister and almost-lover (whom he attempts at various points to rape and kill). Indeed, *Elixiere* returns compulsively to the moment of crossover from one narrative into another, and with the shifting relationships of those narratives to one another. The preface of the editor, the inheritor of Medardus's papers, sets this chain of interlocking readings in motion:

> Entschließest du dich [. . .] mit dem Medardus, als seist du sein treuer Gefährte, durch finstre Kreuzgänge und Zellen – durch die bunte – bunteste Welt zu ziehen, und mit ihm das Schauerliche, Entsetzliche, Tolle, Possenhafte seines Lebens zu ertragen, so wirst du dich vielleicht an den mannigfachen Bildern der Camera obscura, die sich dir aufgetan, ergötzen. – Es kann auch kommen, daß das gestaltlossscheinende, so wie du schärfer es ins Auge fassest, sich dir bald deutlich und rund darstellt. Du erkennst den verborgenen Keim, den ein dunkles Verhängnis gebar, und der, zur üppiger Pflanze emporgeschossen, fort und fort wuchert in tausend Ranken, bis eine Blüte, zur Frucht reifend, allen Lebenssaft an sich zieht, und den Keim selbst tötet. (H II.2 12)

> Should you decide to accompany Medardus, as if you were his faithful companion, through dark cloisters and cells, through the bright, brightest world, and to bear with him the horror, fear, madness, ridiculousness of his life, then maybe you will derive some pleasure from those glimpses of a camera obscura which have been vouchsafed to you. It may even be that, as you take them into sharper focus, the seemingly shapeless forms become clearer and rounded

---

[9] Momberger, *Sonne und Punsch*, p. 156.

in form. You will recognise the hidden germ which, born of a secret union, grows into a luxuriant plant and spreads forth in a thousand tendrils, until a single blossom, swelling to maturity, absorbs all the life-sap and kills the seed itself.

The transformation of incontinent shapelessness into meaningful form in reading is a trope that we have encountered at several key moments already in this book. What the editor discusses specifically here is the process of bringing the events of Medardus's life into focus by means of the camera obscura, a visual technology used as a representational aid in achieving a sense of perspective. The therapeutic and spiritual redemption promised by the act of writing and reading – that is, of finding meaning within senselessness, or form within chaos – is thus given in starkly visual terms. Nicola Kaminski foregrounds the appearance of two optical media technologies, as what Friedrich Kittler has called 'Metapher der Lektüre' (metaphor of reading),[10] in a two-part model for the visual compulsions of the novel: first, the Enlightenment-rationalist optical tool mentioned here, the *camera obscura*, as a projection of external images into an interior as an aid for drawing; and second, the *laterna magica*, more readily associated with Romantic vision, as the 'Projektion höllischer Bilder' (projection of hellish images).[11] If the model of the *camera obscura* is associated with a realist or rationalist mode of visually reproducing the world, the narrator warns us in the short passage above that it too is involved in the production of illusions, being dependent on the viewer's willingness to process certain conventions of 'roundness' *as* three-dimensional, through a sensory or proprioceptive projection of the self. The process of perceiving the represented object as three-dimensional is precisely that: a *process*, in which the reader must actively take and hold ('fassen') the visual object in the ocular field, to bring it into focus.

In the fragmentary, near-cinematic image that we are subsequently given (as if through the projections of a magic lantern), the vegetal tendrils that grow from a seed into a plant transform the narrative line or 'Schnörkel' from an outline or filigree of ink into a three-dimensional Gothic figure, serpentine, living and recursive. This image marks the beginning of a complex network of deviant lines across the text: from the vegetal 'Faden', a sickened line of

[10] Friedrich Kittler, 'Die Laterna magica der Literatur: Schillers und Hoffmanns Medienstrategien', *Athenäum*, 4 (1994), 219–37, p. 221.

[11] Nicola Kaminski, *Kreuz-Gänge: Romanexperimente der deutschen Romantik* (Paderborn: Schöningh, 2001), p. 311.

inheritance (indebted to recent scientific discoveries and hypotheses about inherited illness) to the illegible handwriting of the painter's manuscript, to the reappearing motif of the cross.[12] The plant crosses back over itself and kills the thing from which it has grown, in a symbolic challenge to originality that will recur throughout the tale, and which will form the basis of its dark vision both of mimesis and of intertextuality: a vision oriented by the excesses of a Gothic representation that has grown wild.

The novel is a dizzying crossroads of other texts. Medardus's life-story, presented as a document salvaged from history, is critically linked to two other narratives: the legend of St Anthony, and the painter's manuscript given to Medardus by Prior Leonardus. The first of these texts, the legend of St Anthony, introduces the devil's elixirs into the novel. Potions, as a Gothic trope, are life-altering items, initiating a break or a turn in the course of a narrative on being consumed. Medardus's elixirs are brought into the text in a discussion between Medardus and Cyrillus regarding the supposed authenticity of religious relics. Medardus confesses his doubts regarding the provenance of these relics, pointing out that so many monasteries possess pieces of the Saviour's cross that 'unser Kloster ein ganzes Jahr hindurch damit geheizt werden könnte' (they would provide our monastery with firewood for a whole year). Cyrillus's objection is that the spiritual importance of such objects lies not in their actual origins but in the stories told about them, in their narrative identities: '*das*, wofür man sie ausgibt' (what they are claimed to be) as narrated in the documents that accompany them (H II.2 33). It is in the aftermath of these words that Medardus, back in the dark reliquary, succumbs to the elixirs:

> Glut strömte durch meine Adern und erfüllte mich mit dem Gefühl unbeschreiblichen Wohlseins – ich trank noch einmal, und die Lust eines neuen herrlichen Lebens ging mir auf! [...] Ein buntes Bild jug das andere bei dem, wie aus tiefem Schlaf ausgerüttelten Geiste vorüber. (H II.2 47)

> My veins glowed and I was filled with a feeling of indescribable satisfaction – I drank again, and there arose in me the desire for a new and splendid life! [...] One vivid impression after another passed through my mind, as if I had been shaken from a deep slumber.

---

[12] See Al-Taie, '"Des fremden Malers wunderbares Buch"', pp. 278–9.

The *Elixiere* may have no devilish powers at all. They smell suspiciously like Syracusan wine (H II.2 44). The 'current' they release – of alcohol and fumes but also Medardus's verbal 'Feuerstrom' (current of fire) (H II.1 49) at the pulpit – is only a doubled, if intensified, version of the first compulsive 'Strom der Rede' (current of words) (H II.2 41) that he delivered when preaching before. His preaching, as Friedrich Kittler points out, has already undergone a transmedial shift from written to spoken language: for when Medardus begins to preach, he need no longer think of his writing, '[denkt] nicht mehr an die Handschrift' (H II.2 38).[13] This shift, as I have begun to suggest, is crucial for a novel so concerned with acts of writing and inscribing, because it has to do with a fantasy of reading as a set of intermedial releases from the material constraints of script – shifts between touch, vision and sound – by which handwritten script gains life and body, akin to the processual visual experience of seeing a 'rounded' form. To drink the elixirs, for Medardus, is to enact one of these shifts but it is only a doubled version of what has already been. The elixirs, as the titular motif of the novel, are a figure for the confoundment of narrative lines in this work. If we are to read the text according to the logic of its elixirs, that is, the text takes on a particular form. The elixirs suggest that Medardus is, at least in part, being played by the devil, as an object controlled by unknown forces. This is the narrative that Medardus himself assumes when explaining himself to the Pope: 'wie ein von giftigen Dünsten geschwängertes Wasser gab er Kraft dem bösen Keim, der in mir ruhete, daß er fortzuwuchern vermochte!' (H II.2 300) (Like water impregnated with foul odours, it gave strength to the seed of evil latent within me, so that it could grow rampant!). According to the conversation between Medardus and Cyrillus, this may be a fiction – the elixirs might be nothing but wine, and Medardus was preaching before he ever opened the bottle – but it need not be discounted entirely. Not every proclaimed splinter of the cross is what we presume it to be, but the doubt in its authenticity is not enough to cut those narratives short. Its copied or repeated versions are permitted to live out their narrative lives such that those copies cross back into the space of the original.

Hoffmann's deftness in *Elixiere* consists in creating multiple, distinct narrative trajectories that allow for discordant, if not exactly contradictory, interpretations of Medardus's predicament. Victoria Dutchman-Smith has given a lucid account of the role of the devil's

---

[13] Kittler, 'Die Laterna magica der Literatur', p. 234.

wine, suggesting that it unfolds a set of symbols and structures that embrace a 'conscious fluidity and doubling of narratives'.[14] The major doubling of the narrative occurs in the novel's inclusion of the old painter's manuscript. Once again, the editor's promise that messy images will cohere into intelligibility seems to hold – almost word for word this time, for, fittingly, Leonardus describes how what had previously resembled 'verworrenes Gekritzel' (confused scribblings) in the manuscript 'nur dann erst erkennbar und lesbar wurde, als du, mein lieber Bruder Medardus! mir gebeichtet hattest' (did not become recognisable and intelligible to me until you, my dear brother Medardus, had made your confession to me) (H II.2 274). The two narratives – Medardus's life and the painter's document – become intelligible only when they are brought into conversation with one another. For Medardus finds the life narrated in the painter's manuscript to be recognisable as his own:

> Das, was der Maler auf den letzten Seiten des Buchs in kleiner, kaum lesbarer bunt gefärbter Schrift zusammen getragen hatte, waren meine Träume, meine Ahnungen, nur deutlich, bestimmt in scharfen Zügen dargestellt, wie ich es niemals zu tun vermochte. (H II.2 275)

> The barely legible writing in brightly coloured ink on the final pages described all my dreams and forebodings, but with such clear, sharply defined outlines as I could never have achieved.

The painter's script is 'kaum lesbar' (barely legible) and yet delineates the features of Medardus's predicament more clearly and distinctly, we are told, than Medardus might have managed himself. The manuscript that follows seemingly puts into focus a set of otherwise indistinct images or episodes – Medardus's life – by purporting to set out, in near diagrammatic terms, the course of history that has led to its emergence. Yet the painter's story is so strange and complicated that it is almost impossible to visualise, not simply because of the sheer number of characters and events he draws out, but also because the painter has the habit of referring to characters by their epithets rather than by their names, and because some characters, such as Medardus's mother, remain unnamed. There has nonetheless been a tendency in scholarship to reproduce images of Medardus's family tree. Critics including C. G. von Maasen, Walter Harich, Kurt Willimczik, Kenneth G. Negus and Hartmut Steinecke devote

---

[14] Victoria Dutchman-Smith, *E. T. A. Hoffmann and Alcohol: Biography, Reception, and Art* (Leeds: Maney Publishing, 2009), p. 155.

articles to working out Medardus's genealogy or contrive family trees to map the complex connections and interactions between characters.[15] The novel's own obsession with sources and with its literary genealogy is thus mirrored outwards by its readers' desire to recast it in supplementary documentation that might give it shape, to make the 'vast chaos [. . .] formed and meaningful'.[16]

Other critics cast doubt on the validity of the painter's manuscript as a model for reading. Freud, in a humorous moment of his essay 'Das Unheimliche', writes that: 'Zu Ende des Buches, wenn die dem Leser bisher vorenthaltenen Voraussetzungen der Handlung nachgetragen werden, ist das Ergebnis nicht die Aufklärung des Lesers, sondern eine volle Verwirrung desselben' (Towards the end of the book, when the reader is told the facts, hitherto concealed from him, from which the action springs, the result is not that he is at last enlightened, but that he falls into a state of complete bewilderment).[17] For Manfred Momberger, the painter's manuscript is fragmentary and disjointed, such that Medardus can conclude only one thing from his reading: 'daß seine Lebensgeschichte die eines Anderen ist' (that his life story is that of another).[18] For Jeremy Tambling, the understanding Medardus draws from the manuscript – that his *Doppelgänger* is in fact his half-brother Viktorin – 'would resolve nothing. The text denies any way of knowing, which makes more ironic Leonardus's demand to Medardus that he write his autobiography [. . .] Medardus cannot know his own life.'[19] Medardus's narrative has a more complicated relationship to his life than we might have tacitly assumed in reading it.

At a crucial juncture on his path, Medardus discovers the importance of such documentary narratives to authenticate identity when a village judge in an unnamed town demands of him: 'Den Paß oder in den Turm!' (Your papers, or into the tower!) (H II.2 100). Medardus's choice is to make himself intelligible, in society's terms,

[15] E. T. A. Hoffmann, *Hoffmanns Sämtliche Werke*, ed. by Carl Georg von Maassen, 9 vols (Munich, Leipzig: Müller, 1908–28), II, p. 375; Walter Harich, *E. T. A. Hoffmann: Das Leben eines Künstlers*, 2 vols (Berlin: Reiß, 1920), I, p. 282; Kurt Willimczik, *E. T. A. Hoffmann: Die drei Reiche seiner Gestaltenwelt* (Berlin, 1939), p. 123; Kenneth G. Negus, 'The Family Tree in E. T. A. Hoffmann's *Die Elixiere des Teufels*', PMLA, 73.5 (1958), 516–20 (p. 519); Hartmut Steinecke in H II.2, p. 592.

[16] Negus, 'The Family Tree', p. 520.

[17] Sigmund Freud, 'Das Unheimliche', in *Gesammelte Werke*, ed. Anna Freud and others, 18 vols (London: Imago, 1940–68) XII, pp. 229–68 (p. 246).

[18] Momberger, *Sonne und Punsch*, p. 155.

[19] Jeremy Tambling, 'Hoffmann's *Die Elixiere des Teufels*: The Double, the Death Drive, and the Apotropaic', *Forum for Modern Language Studies*, 51.4 (2015), 379–93 (pp. 391–2).

by flattening himself out into a socially legitimised narrative, or to be lost to the life of the criminal or madman, the nobody or the nameless. Recognition demands due payment. That Medardus is able to short-circuit the system by bribing the judge, thus feeding money back into the demand for a narrative, intensifies the sense of contrivance by which our validated social identities are given credence. Like Balzac's Colonel Chabert, who returns from war to find himself dead – legally, officially, on paper – Medardus is drawn into a line of characters who come to understand the fatal implications of having come apart from the self's documentary supplement.

Cross

The figure of the cross, not unlike the elixirs themselves, inscribes the tale into a literary genre, particularly as allusion to Lewis's *The Monk*, in which the cross is an extravagantly Gothic distortion of a religious symbol, emblazoned on the forehead of the Wandering Jew. Crosses, as noted, are always reproductions of an original model. And the figure of the cross appears again and again in acts of visual representation: one of Medardus's earliest memories is of a young child under whose hands the figure of the cross, like a natural hieroglyph or a face in the landscape, seems to draw itself of its own accord:

> Ich schenkte ihm alle meine bunten Steine und er wußte damit allerlei Figuren auf dem Erdboden zu ordnen, aber immer bildete sich daraus zuletzt die Gestalt des Kreuzes. (H II.2 16–17)

> I gave him all of my coloured stones and he laid them out on the earth in all sorts of shapes, but in the end they always came together in the form of a cross.

To draw a cross is to draw two lines that intersect: it is to draw something twice, and is in that sense an act of doubling as much as it is an act of erasure, in the sense of crossing out. It thus describes the contradiction of the *Doppelgänger*: the second self both confirms the original by reproducing it, and threatens to displace it; as in Freud's 'Das Unheimliche' when he notes the *Doppelgänger*'s contradictory role as both a ward against death and a harbinger of death. *Die Elixiere* is full of multiply drawn figures, the central of which is St Rosalia, who is painted twice by Francesco. In his article on *Die Elixiere des Teufels* Charles Passage cites an anecdotal episode of Hoffmann's life in which, in the autumn of 1809, he drew a picture of his young music student Julia Marc alongside her two siblings; Passage reports that 'he easily completed the figures of the sister and brother but that he reworked the face of Julia ten times'.[20] Whilst the biographical sketch remains vague and anecdotal, it stages a seductive fantasy in which compulsion, copy and desire are played out over the face, as each successive copy fails in its task to stand in for the original.

The most vivid cross in the narrative is the cross-shaped scar on Medardus's throat, which is seared there in a childhood scene in which Medardus is embraced by the abbess:

> Da rief die Fürstin mit der tiefsten Wehmut: Franziskus! Und hob mich auf und drückte mich heftig an sich, aber in dem Augenblick preßte mir ein jäher Schmerz, den ich am Halse fühlte, einen starken Schrei aus, so daß die Fürstin erschrocken mich los ließ [. . .]; es fand sich, daß das diamantne Kreuz, welches die Fürstin auf der Brust trug, mich, indem sie heftig mich an sich drückte, am Halse so stark beschädigt hatte, daß die Stelle ganz rot und mit Blut unterlaufen war. (H II.2 18)

> The abbess cried in tones of deep emotion: 'Franciscus!' And she lifted me up and pressed me tightly to herself. At that moment a sudden pain in my neck caused me to cry out, at which the frightened abbess let me go [. . .]; the diamond crucifix she wore on her breast had so hurt my neck when she clasped me to her that the place was red and bruised.

In a later episode, the auspicious cross-shaped mark becomes a node of recognition that ultimately fails, allowing Medardus to live on as his own impersonator and so, by means of his double, to part ways with his self. This recognition scene comes in a chapter significantly named 'Der Wendepunkt' (The Turning Point), when Medardus has been condemned to prison under suspicion of the murders of Hermogen and Euphemie (of which he is, by his own account, guilty). The court case is an exercise in narrative invention as Medardus fleshes out a fictional Romantic identity for himself as a Polish count under the name of Leonard, and convinces himself of it entirely, if not his listeners: 'indem ich Alles befriedigend beantwortete, ründete sich das Bild davon so in meinem Innern, daß ich selbst daran glaubte' (by giving satisfactory answers to all the questions asked of me, I rounded off the image in my own mind

---

[20] Charles Passage, 'E. T. A. Hoffmann's "The Devil's Elixirs": A Flawed Masterpiece', *Journal of English and Germanic Philology*, 75.4 (1976), 531–45 (p. 540).

so that I really believed in it myself) (H II.2 199). Then, before the judge, and even when the attempt seems completely lost in the face of their scepticism: 'aufzuschreiben beschloß ich daher den Roman, der mich retten sollte! [. . .] Alles formte sich wie eine geründete Dichtung, und fester und fester spann sich das Gewebe endloser Lügen' (I decided to make a record of the romantic story which would clear my name! [. . .] The whole thing took on the shape of a rounded work of poetry, and the tissue of endless lies grew more and more closely woven) (H II.2 208–9). The repeated use of 'ründete' and 'geründet' (rounded) echoes the *Herausgeber*'s initial promise that the substance of the novel will become 'deutlich und rund' (clear and rounded) in reading, recalling the three-dimensional figures projected by a camera obscura. The figure is rounded by means of particular (narrative) conventions and is shared by the viewer, who must in turn process those conventions in order to see the rounded figure *as* round.

Medardus, like any criminal, must be identified before the law, and the task of identification falls to Brother Cyrillus. Medardus's cross-shaped scar, an unmistakable mark of his identity 'die die Zeit nicht vertilgen konnte' (which time could not eradicate), threatens to give him away. Cyrillus, knowing this, cries out on seeing it – 'Heilige Mutter Gottes, es ist es, es ist das rote Kreuzzeichen!' (By the Holy Virgin! That is it! That is the red cross-shaped mark!) (H II.2 205). Thus, Medardus is recognised, and on being recognised he is condemned. It is, so far, a classic scene of anagnorisis, one that triggers the reader's own recognition of such scenes: above all, the recognition of Odysseus by his servant Euryclea by means of an old hunting scar on his thigh. Unlike Odysseus's scar, which spells his reintegration into society, Medardus's spells his extermination. But after one delirious night in his cell, the trope of anagnorisis is scandalised in a strange anticlimax, when Medardus is declared to be innocent after all and is acquitted. The body's signature turns out to be no sufficient guarantee of identity against the presence of his *Doppelgänger*, who has appeared in the town, resembling 'jener abscheuliche Mönch' (that odious monk) (H II.2 218) and confessing to the crimes that Medardus has committed. For the scar, which is submerged under the discussion of the 'ganz genaue Ähnlichkeit' (complete and exact resemblance) between the two, is, as with Medardus's other features, perfectly replicated on the person of his double. The indexical sign, supposedly guaranteeing the singularity of the human body, is dethroned of its semiotic power and proven to wield no more identificatory power than the more arbitrary and forgeable signs of clothes or documents. As Andrew Webber notes: 'the security of anagnorisis, as ensured by the canny forces of criminal law and mental order, is confounded by the *Doppelgänger* mystery, and the scar remains a resistant mark of unsolved crimes and untreated trauma.'[21] With the exception of one further cursory mention in a vision, the scar then disappears from the novel altogether (H II.2 313).

For Auerbach in *Mimesis*, the episode of Odysseus's scar in the *Odyssey* works as an exemplary moment in the classical separation of styles. The scar provides the impetus for a narrative digression: not to build suspense, but as a seam tracing the segue into the following narrative episode and marking the parity of the temporally disconnected episodes it stitches together. Terence Cave takes up the same scene in *Recognitions* as he constructs a counter-account to Auerbach's *Mimesis*. 'Recognition', Cave writes, 'works against mimesis in Auerbach's sense of the word.' The scar is, for both, the point of entry into a second narrative. But where for Auerbach the crossing is smooth, for Cave it marks a rupture, and is 'a sign that the story, like the wound, may always be reopened'.[22] Recognition, Cave explains through the cases of Martin Guerre and Odysseus, 'unmasks a crisis' because at moments of recognition, gaps in our knowledge are opened up and the 'most fundamental of the ordering structures of life – the difference between individuals – is at least temporarily shaken'.[23] In the famous recognition plot of Martin Guerre, a man disappeared from his community near Toulouse. Eight years later, a man claiming to be Martin Guerre returned, and was accepted back by the community and by his wife. A few years later, a second Martin Guerre returned, and the first one was declared an impostor and hanged. On at least one of these occasions, an impostor succeeds in displacing an original. Anagnorisis, Cave argues, 'makes the world (and the text) intelligible. Yet it is also a shift *into* the implausible.'[24] Recognition plots bring to the fore what he calls the 'scandal' inherent in mimetic narrative, which is described by Auerbach, he argues, in terms far too 'reassuring'.[25] Hoffmann, we might say, amplifies the scandal of the recognition plot, exposing the unsettledness of

---

[21] Andrew Webber, *The Doppelgänger: Double Visions in German Literature* (Oxford: Clarendon Press, 1996), p. 189.

[22] Terence Cave, *Recognitions: A Study in Poetics* (Oxford: Oxford University Press, 1990), p. 11, p. 24.

[23] Ibid., pp. 14–15, 13.

[24] Ibid., p. 1.

[25] Ibid., p. 22.

mimetic fiction diagnosed by Cave by having the recognition scene function and malfunction at once, splitting an identity into two.

Medardus, having traipsed through his own odyssey of dubious encounters, falsely assumed personae and wrongdoings followed by bouts of guilt and repentance, emerges before an authority finally bent on pinning him down, and at that moment again he can only break in two. Medardus's figurative path, which leads him into hedonism and sin, is, after all, geographically contemporaneous to, but set at spiritual loggerheads with, the path of redemption set out for him by Leonardus. This gives rise to the feeling of compromise and of paradox that I have suggested to be engendered by the figure of the cross. It is a sign, too, that the individual's actions are already decided upon by the actions of his predecessors or spiritual betters: that Medardus is the plaything of powerful forces.

In Rome, and beginning his penance in earnest, under the gaze of his onlookers Medardus feels himself explicitly to be a character in his own life-story, 'Held[en] irgend eines frommen Märchens' (hero of some religious tale) (H II.2 298). The strange events in Rome – events that bring the body violently into play – will close my reading of *Elixiere* as an exploration of mimesis as it works upon the body. The first of these events is the puppet play, which Medardus stumbles upon after his meeting with the Pope. Medardus is amused to recognise the diminutive Belcampo, the peculiar, capering hair-dresser character who has surfaced, and intervened, at various fortuitous points in Medardus's narrative, always in the doubled role of both 'puppet and puppeteer', as Lucia Ruprecht notes, and here playing the part of Goliath – or rather of Goliath's head (H II.2 303).[26] As Belcampo's head plays amongst the puppets, the living body is transformed into an artwork. The metamorphosis of life into narrative is a grotesque reflection of what Medardus has done all along, particularly in the Baron's castle, where in a parallel case of life mimicking performance he plays the role of Viktorin playing at being a monk. The sinister abbot who approaches Medardus seems to acknowledge this as he warns him: 'spiele deine Rolle – ausgespielt ist bald, was munter und lustig begann' (Go on playing your role – what begins happily will soon be played out) (H II.2 304). The appearance of the living head given over to the story performed on stage is then gruesomely repeated in the following scene by the rolling head of Cyrillus, who is decapitated by the Dominican monks

---

[26] Lucia Ruprecht, *Dances of the Self in Heinrich von Kleist, E. T. A. Hoffmann and Heinrich Heine* (Aldershot: Ashgate, 2006), p. 72.

before Medardus's eyes. The act is repeated for a final time, in a distorted variation, when the Dominicans attempt to poison Medardus, who deftly pours the liquid down his sleeve rather than his throat. In place of his head, he loses his arm – the organ most closely linked to writing – as once again a part of the body is given over to the vicissitudes of plot and play.

He retraces his steps from Rome, in pieces, back to the Capuchin monastery. On the way he is made to feel, again, in visceral terms, the person, or character, he has become. This comes first in the form of Reinhold's terror, on being told as Medardus nears that he is being approached by a monk: 'Der Alte nahm alle Kraft zusammen, die ihm geblieben, um vor mir zu fliehen, wie vor dem reißenden Tier' (the old man summoned his remaining strength to flee from me as from a beast of prey); and Medardus's reaction is likewise to flee – 'fort von dem Schauplatz meiner höchsten Frevel' (away from the scene of my most dreadful crimes) (H II.2 318). He then finds himself at the *Teufelssitz*, the fearful spot from which the sleeping Viktorin had earlier tumbled to his death. In fact, Medardus wakes up there, having been approached by a peasant keen to tell him of the mad Capuchin monk who once haunted that very area. It seems that he has fallen asleep in the very same place that Viktorin once had: a place that is now, significantly, marked with a cross. His final penance, once back at the Capuchin monastery, is to write down his life story. 'Die Fantasie', Leonardus declares, 'wird dich wirklich in die Welt zurückführen, du wirst alles [. . .] noch einmal fühlen' (The fantasy will lead you back to the world, you will [. . .] feel everything once again) (H II.2 349). The punishment, then, is to feel – or rather, is to feel again – the self, in the double formation that the narrative provides. It is to feel oneself at once as narrative object and narrative subject.

Jeremy Tambling argues that 'Hoffmann departs earlier, and more decisively [. . .] from any realist mode, as we see in *Die Elixiere des Teufels*.'[27] In this he writes against critics who have seen *Elixiere* as a precursor to the realist novel, such as Christiane Zehl Romero, who suggests that Hoffmann, in bringing together the genre of the Gothic novel with an interest in the psyche, 'puts the lesson of Romanticism to "realistic" use, for a deeply questioning look at man and his precarious hold upon the world'. Hoffmann paves the way for writers such as Balzac, Zehl Romero goes on, by having 'rescued the gothic from its remote and merely sensational associations to bring it to

---

[27] Tambling, 'Hoffmann's *Die Elixiere*', p. 379.

contemporary life and new artistic vitality'.[28] He brings a Gothic register to the representation of the mind's tenuous hold on the self.

Whether or not *Elixiere* acts either as antagonist to or as precursor of the realist novel, it prepares the way – and in a manner that is particular for Hoffmann because of its form as a novel – for writers such as Balzac. This is, for one thing, a question of literary inheritance. Works that inscribe themselves in the Gothic tradition consciously account for their own literary genealogy. But more importantly, *Elixiere* articulates its narrative subject through his encounters with a world shown to be infinitely reproducible in its appearance. The cross, as I have shown, comes to resemble the ultimately reproducible image or sign, as an identificatory mark whose identificatory work is undone by its being reproduced, redrawn, crossed out and mirrored on the physiognomy of the *Doppelgänger*. And if Hoffmann here looks forward to Balzac, the gaze is obliquely returned in a prefatory note to one of Balzac's most Gothic tales.

L'Élixir de longue vie

L'Élixir de longue vie is singular amongst Balzac's early tales in being prefaced, in its revised version of 1846, by an *avis au lecteur* (notice to the reader). In no other prefatory note of *La Comédie humaine* is the reader called upon so unmistakably as in this narrative conceit.[29] The short note begins with an overt reference to Hoffmann:

> Au début de la vie littéraire de l'auteur, un ami, mort depuis longtemps, lui donna le sujet de cette Étude, que plus tard il trouva dans un recueil publié vers le commencement de ce siècle; et, selon ses conjectures, c'est une fantaisie due à Hoffmann de Berlin, publiée dans quelque almanach d'Allemagne, et oubliée dans ses œuvres par les éditeurs. *La Comédie humaine* est assez riche en inventions pour que l'auteur avoue un innocent emprunt; comme le bon La Fontaine, il aura traité d'ailleurs à sa manière, et sans le savoir, un fait déjà conté. (B XI 473)

---

[28] Christiane Zehl Romero, 'M. C. Lewis' *The Monk* and E. T. A. Hoffmann's *Die Elixiere des Teufels*: Two versions of the Gothic', *Neophilologus*, 63 (1979), 574–82 (p. 581).

[29] See Aude Deruelle, 'Les adresses au lecteur chez Balzac', *Cahiers de Narratologie*, 11 (2004), 2–11. Deruelle opens by tracking the sparsity with which the word 'lecteur' is used as a narrative appeal, noting that *L'Élixir de longue vie* is the only work with a dedication titled 'Au Lecteur' (p. 3).

At the outset of the writer's literary career, a friend, long since dead, gave him the subject of this Study, which he then found in a collection published at around the beginning of the century; and which, to the best of his belief, is a fantasy that comes from Hoffmann of Berlin, published in some German almanac and omitted by the editors of his collected works. *La Comédie humaine* is rich enough in inventions that its author might admit to an instance of having innocently borrowed his material; like the worthy La Fontaine, he will have treated in his own way – and without knowing it – a tale already told.

We are dealing here with the only one of Balzac's narratives to be marked from the very outset, in an extra-diegetic feint, with the stamp of the Hoffmannesque. Balzac is in essence updating the 'found manuscript' trope of Gothic fiction (mobilised by Hoffmann himself in various forms, not least in *Elixiere des Teufels*) for a new literary landscape: one in which the figure of Hoffmann assumes the place of an obscure origin story. Hoffmann is the pretext – that is, both introduction and justification – for Balzac's narrative work. And although he leaves his source text unnamed, his reader is deliberately invited to think of *Die Elixiere des Teufels*: first in the unmistakable echo of its title, and second in the clue he gives us that this particular source material was a narrative that had been omitted from his collected works. For *Die Elixiere des Teufels* was indeed left out of Loève-Veimars's edition of Hoffmann's work: the novel had been translated into French by Jean Cohen in 1829 but was falsely attributed to Carl Spindler.[30] Yet the statement of origins is garbled by the vagueness of memory and by the mediating role of that faceless third party who is said to have provided Balzac with his original. The ambiguous phrasing hints that the friend himself might be a ghostly figure. The spectral reputation of Hoffmann's character and works at this time, and the Gothic trope of the found manuscript, would not rule out such a reading of the 'long-dead friend'. This acknowledgement of Hoffmann is thus troubled: he is not drawn out in full, but only intimated, as if in silhouette or in outline – and then only retroactively, sixteen years after the tale's original publication. His features are blurred by the dreamlike quality of the anecdote. As simultaneously unclear and suggestive as the arabesque of *La Peau de chagrin*, the paratextual contrivance of this *avis au lecteur* narrates the reading of

---

[30] See René Guise, 'Balzac, lecteur des Élixirs du diable', *L'Année balzacienne*, 10 (1970), 57–67 (p. 60). The French translation of *Elixiere* was Carl Spindler [E. T. A. Hoffmann], *L'Élixir du diable, histoire tirée des papiers de frère Médard, Capucin*, trans. by Jean Cohen, 4 vols (Paris: Mame et Delaunay-Vallée, 1829).

a fiction that it refuses to name: less a confession of inheritance or of imitation than of a haunting.

Criticism on *L'Élixir de longue vie* has been devoted in large part to unravelling the claims of its preface and to constructing an alternative line of inheritance considered to be more plausible, a search for the tale's 'real' origin story, as it were. In the 1950s and '60s, Pierre-Georges Castex, Elizabeth Teichmann and Bruce Tolley published articles working to figure out the true source of *L'Élixir*.[31] This was identified as a story by Richard Steele in the *Spectator*, one that Steele claims to have taken himself from an original text by Adam Olearius, and which had been abridged and adapted anonymously as *L'Élixir de l'immortalité* in *L'Almanach des prosateurs* in 1805. Since we know that Balzac borrowed this volume from the library in 1829, Steele's story is taken to be, in Tolley's words, 'without doubt the direct source of *L'Élixir*'.[32] In October 1830, weeks after the publication of *L'Élixir,* an article appeared in *Mercure de France au dix-neuvième siècle* under the name of Paul Pry (a pseudonym of Amédée Pichot, director of *La Revue de Paris*) which summarised Steele's original story as 'Les aventures de trois Valentins'. The article implicitly accuses Balzac of plagiarism, soberly insisting on the primacy of the original version: 'on relira toujours avec plaisir le conte original du *Spectateur*' (we will always return, with pleasure, to read the original story of the *Spectator*).[33] Balzac's preface takes its place, in this account, as a characteristically defensive (and belated) apology for having 'innocently borrowed' his material – but, strangely enough, acknowledges the wrong source. Castex, Teichmann and Tolley all agree, moreover, that *Die Elixiere des Teufels* and *L'Élixir de longue vie* offer little, by way of their narrative content, to invite a comparative reading.

Critics since have lingered longer over the apparent misattribution of Balzac's paratext. Given Balzac's intense if sporadic engagement with Hoffmann's works, to claim that his presence in this tale is a mere error of memory would be to underestimate the force of this engagement and, potentially, to underestimate the playfulness

[31] Pierre-Georges Castex, *Le Conte fantastique en France de Nodier à Maupassant* (Paris: José Corti, 1987), pp. 194–5; Elizabeth Teichmann, 'Une source inconnue de l'*Élixir de longue vie*', *Revue de littérature comparée*, 24 (1955), 536–8; Bruce Tolley, 'The Source of Balzac's l'*Élixir de longue vie*', *Revue de littérature comparée*, 37 (1963), 91–7.

[32] Tolley, 'The Source', p. 93.

[33] Paul Pry, 'L'Élixir de vie', *Le Mercure de France au dix-neuvième siècle*, 3 (1830), 227–9 (pp. 227–8).

of Balzac's gesture. The intertextual network of *L'Élixir de longue vie* is extensive indeed, encompassing not just Hoffmann's novel and Steele's tale, but also the legend of Don Juan, *Faust*, and Maturin's *Melmoth*, which Balzac would come to work with more closely in *Melmoth reconcilié*. As a meeting point of several inter-texts, acknowledged and accounted for in different ways, the tale is in more ways than one the story of a strange, hybrid inheritance. After acknowledging the alternative origin story put forward by Teichmann and others, René Guise asks why Balzac might have been tempted to attribute the 'paternity' of the tale to Hoffmann rather than to Steele, and Edgar Pankow probes further, asking: 'was hätte es dann zu besagen, daß Balzac sich gerade *in dieser Weise und in bezug auf Hoffmann* getäuscht haben sollte?' (what does it mean that Balzac was mistaken *in this way and in relation to Hoffmann*?).[34] It is in response to these very compelling questions that I offer my reading of Balzac's tale, with its spurious claim to a Hoffmannesque inherit-ance, by engaging the false origin story in a productive criss-crossing between original and copy, text and pretext. In doing so I will show that Balzac's narrative, when read alongside Hoffmann's, is able not just to generate but also, in fact, to think about a particular Gothic affect, one that has to do with picturing intertextual transfer as the reanimation of dead flesh.

Edgar Pankow, who has offered the fullest close reading of this pair of texts to date, examines them through an explicitly Bloomian framework of anxiety-riddled influence in which the Balzacian narrator desires to overcome his forefather by displac-ing him.[35] The literary crossover, in this reading, is defined as 'ein Konflikt zwischen Autopoiesis und literarischer Filiation, zwischen textueller Selbstbestimmnug und Abhängigkeit von intertextuellen Vernetzungen' (a conflict between autopoeisis and literary filiation, between a text's self-determination and its dependence on intertex-tual networks).[36] In 1830, Pankow reminds us, Balzac was first fash-ioning himself as author, having only recently begun to sign his texts as 'de Balzac'. The part played by Hoffmann in this authorial self-staging is, accordingly, a contradictory one, as he is both engaged as pretext and then displaced via the obfuscatory strategies of the *avis au lecteur*. Moving away from Pankow's paradigm of influence,

---

[34] Guise, 'Balzac, lecteur', p. 57. Edgar Pankow, 'Literatur – Geschichte: Honoré de Balzac und E. T. A. Hoffmann und die Genese von Traditionen im *Élixir de longue vie*', *Arcadia*, 39 (2004), 27–54 (p. 34).

[35] Pankow, 'Literatur – Geschichte', p. 29.

[36] Ibid., p. 32.

I intend instead to trace, across these two texts, a particular representational transgression or excess that is signalled by a garbled story of origins. The Gothic representation, that is, is shown to transgress some more rational, contained notion of 'lifelikeness'.

In *Die Elixiere des Teufels*, we remember, the relationship between Christian relics and their origins is explicitly troubled. Something of that relationship is pictured in the cinematic serpentine stem of the *Vorwort* that turns back over itself to devour its own roots. In turn, the form of the tale, as confession, can be read as an attempt to overcome an individual story of origins through writing. It is, critically, not a project of destabilising origins, and thus of dethroning mimesis entirely, but rather of the kind of mimesis that produces something that, through the sort of excess that Walter Scott found so offensive to taste (the lurid or grotesque; what he called 'supernatural' or indeed, in those drastic capitals 'the FANTASTIC') seems to threaten to overrun or outdo its point of reference. In Balzac's tale – which first invokes Hoffmann as pretext, then offers up a tale that has little to do with it – and in the narrative itself, in which fathers and sons vie to outlive one another, that dynamic is imitated and then drawn out to an extreme. As such it builds a theory of Gothic affect or *Schauer*, which may stimulate and overwhelm the reader's senses not through the kind of measured lifelikeness we might expect of mimetic fiction in a more recognisably realist mode, but through a particular representational excess – as in, for example, the life imbued to an undead body.

Nicole Sütterlin has recently traced, through the figure of Hoffmann's vampire, a 'poetics of the undead' in which the vampire 'stands for a poetological principle that inverts the traditional doctrine of *energeia* or *evidentia*, the classical rhetorical technique of vivid representation into a notion of the artwork as undead, rather than vivid'.[37] In the Serapion brethren's discussions surrounding the tale *Vampyrismus*, they theorise the 'dark side of Romanticism's "Lebendigkeit", the perverse proximity of poetic animation and vampirism'.[38] In this chapter, I suggest that the idea of a mimesis characterised not by rational, measured lifelikeness or vividness, but by an uncanny excess (what we might call luridness, ghastliness, sensationalism), as in the reanimation of dead flesh, also has particular

---

[37] Nicole Sütterlin, 'Transgressions: On the (De-)Figuration of the Vampire in E. T. A. Hoffmann's "Vampyrismus"', trans. by Christopher R. Clason and Alexander Lambrow, in *Transgressive Romanticism*, ed. by Christopher R. Clason (Liverpool: Liverpool University Press, 2018), pp. 114–32 (p. 115).

[38] Ibid., p. 119.

relevance for *L'Élixir de longue vie*, and can help to draw out an otherwise hidden strand of Balzac's Hoffmannesque style. Dorothy Kelly has recently examined Balzac's ongoing fascination with the trope of the living dead as a metaphor for historical persistence in modern France. This, however, is a tale that concerns the 'real' living dead.[39] Its narrative energy is engendered through death: both in its garbled origin story, in which a dead friend (perhaps even a dead Hoffmann) is made into pretext for the text proper. Second, the narrative itself follows the actual reanimation of corpses, in which fathers assume a vampiric role by attempting to live beyond their allotted lifespan – in order to *inversely* make a point about the figuratively vampiric inheritance customs of France, in which sons live off the deaths of their fathers. Balzac ends his text with an appropriately gruesome climactic flourish that can be better understood when we pay attention to its inheritance, for the Gothic flourish or affect – as in German *Schauer* – is a product of the text's rhetorical acknowledgement of that inheritance. I will therefore take seriously what Olivier Besuchet neatly calls Balzac's 'fausse piste hoffmannienne'[40] (the Hoffmannesque wrong way), allowing the reading to emerge from a confusion of paths. The apparent falseness of the paratextual claim, the cross-inheritance, will come, appropriately, to mark my reading of these two tales of heredity, sin, and of the fictional life or body both animated and compromised by mimesis.

Elixir

The story is divided into two sections, which trace the life and death of a father and his son respectively (in its original 1830 version, these halves were clearly separated under the titles of 'Festin' and 'Fin'). It opens onto a lavish party hosted by Don Juan Belvidéro at his palace in Ferrare, whilst his ancient father Bartholoméo lies dying. When the moment of death is imminent, Don Juan is called into his room. 'Jamais sur cette terre', the narrator explains, 'un père si commode et si indulgent ne s'était rencontré' (Never on this earth was there a father as helpful and indulgent). Don Juan Belvidéro, by turn, 'avait-il tous les défauts des enfants gâtés' (had all the faults of spoiled children) (B XI 477–8). The dying Bartholoméo instructs his

---

[39] Dorothy Kelly, *The Living Death of Modernity: Balzac, Baudelaire, Zola* (Oxford: Legenda, 2021).

[40] Olivier Besuchet, '"Rien de nouveau sous le soleil?" L'indice intertextuel dans *L'Élixir de longue vie* de Balzac', *A Contrario*, 20.1 (2014), 113–27 (p. 126).

son to apply to his skin, following the moment of his death, an elixir contained in a crystal glass, intimating with his last words that it will bring him back to life. Don Juan tentatively dabs a little of the ointment onto one of his father's eyes and the eye unmistakably comes to life. After some deliberation, and averting his own gaze, Don Juan squashes it and pockets the elixir. The second half of the tale follows his life after this fragmented version of a parricide, in the knowledge that he has the power to overcome death – but only on the condition that his own heir plays the part he refused to play himself. When his own deathbed scene arrives, Don Juan has manipulated the scene to be sure that his son Philippe will dutifully carry out what Don Juan did not. But, having anointed his father's head and arm, that arm, suddenly roused to life, grabs him around the neck, surprising him so much that he drops the vial and the remaining elixir evaporates. In a heavy-handed and grotesque conclusion, we see Don Juan – now in the form of a living arm and head attached to a dead body – declared a saint and brought to a mass before throngs of onlookers. Inside the church, his head detaches itself from his corpse and falls upon the head of the priest saying mass, who is killed between its teeth as it cries out 'Imbécile, dis donc qu'il y a un Dieu?' (Imbecile, say now that there is a God?) (B XI 495).

Balzac's text diverges from Hoffmann's in the newly central role it affords to the elixir. The elixir's transformative qualities in Balzac's *conte* are both more potent and more in keeping with its Gothic inheritance: it grants immortality to its user. Unlike Hoffmann's devilish wine, which may or may not possess magical powers, Balzac's is an ointment, and it works by being applied to the skin. On the other hand, alcohol plays a key role in the text, which opens onto a lavish party (as Michael Tilby notes, 'the origin of the Balzacian orgy as such is to be found in the tales of Hoffmann'[41]) and in a critical moment the elixir itself comes to resemble wine, when Don Juan studies the vial over the dead body of his father 'comme un buveur consulte sa bouteille à la fin d'un repas' (as a drinker consults his bottle at the end of a meal) (B XI 481). I showed in Chapter 3 that in the French translation of Hoffmann's *Don Juan*, an extra-diegetic warning about his alcoholism is issued to influence our own reading. Here, in Balzac's own take on *Don Juan*, a similar warning is issued:

---

[41] Michael Tilby, 'Balzac's Convivial Narrations: Intoxication and its Discourse in *La Comédie humaine*', in *Pleasure and Pain in Nineteenth-Century French Literature and Culture*, ed. by David Evans and Kate Griffiths (Amsterdam: Rodopi, 2008), pp. 53–72 (p. 60).

that the 'fantaisie due à Hoffmann' might be the product of that 'diseased' (à la Walter Scott) or intoxicated mind. In this sense Balzac's text might be said to be under the spell or indeed under the influence of Hoffmann's works.

Balzac's text takes from Hoffmann's not just the elixir as titular motif, but also its fantasy of a peculiar male-gendered kinship. Proposed twice over in Balzac's tale is a family structure in which the father would outlive his son and thus inherit his own inheritance. As much as this is a story about the inheritance of wealth, it is a story about a son who copies his father: a structure of doubling that plays out the contradiction (talking *against*) or 'double talk' engendered by the narrative break between the *avis au lecteur* and the narrative proper. Both fathers, Bartholoméo and Don Juan, want to upturn the laws of inheritance – the keystone of the *Code Civil* – by defying death and keeping their wealth instead of passing it on. Engaging the ironies of a comedy parenting manual, Balzac's tale shows the failure of this project in two episodes: first, in the rebellion of the spoiled Don Juan, who decides in a crucial moment of reflection that he wants his father's inheritance for himself; and second, when the obedient son Philippe falters. This two-pronged failure reinstates the inevitable forward thrust of inheritance practices. Kelly thus reads the tale in the terms of a 'failed revolt against the marriage/inheritance system', representing 'the strength of that system as well as the inevitable [. . .] transmission of social codes'.[42] As both she and Pankow have noted, the link between the inheritance system in which Balzac is interested, and to which the elixir would be the cure, and the literary inheritance between Hoffmann and Balzac proposed in the preface, is not an arbitrary one. Balzac's preface, after its false acknowledgement of Hoffmann, moves directly into an explicit polemic on the self-serving greed inspired by the inheritance system, which blatantly encourages sons to wish for the death of their forefathers, such that 'on vit de la mort' (one lives from death) and that 'Dieu seul sait le nombre des parricides qui se commettent par la pensée!' (God knows how many parricides are committed in thought!) (B XI 473–4). The elixir proposes an alternative narrative strategy. In a family whose inheritor-son is replaced by the father, in a neat Oedipal inversion, the logic of heterosexual reproduction is preemptively cut short. A line of genealogy is replaced by the inheritance system of the double or the clone and the father becomes the

---

[42] Dorothy Kelly, 'The Marriage of Don Juan: Balzac and the Inheritance of Culture', *Dix-Neuf: Journal of the Society of Dix-Neuviémistes*, 11 (2008), 49–58 (pp. 55, 49).

recipient of his own legacy. This might suggest an extreme vision of the kind of queer family narrative that Michael Lucey considers in *The Misfit of the Family*:

> The concept of *héritier* lies at the center of a complex legal, histori-cal, cultural, and psychological web that could be thought of as the French epistemology of the family. This epistemological web is *felt* as well as *known*. How it is felt and known in the 1820s, 1830s, and 1840s, both by those woven into it and by those woven out of it, was one of the primary theoretical concerns of Honoré de Balzac.[43]

L'Élixir de longue vie offers an extreme demonstration of how that web is 'felt' – felt, that is, in its insistent presence, reflected through the face of a nightmare alternative. This potential family narrative calls back to Medardus's cursed male familial line, knotted through with incestuous and illegitimate relationships and haunted by another father who will not die, in the figure of the old painter. As Christine Lehleiter has shown, *Die Elixiere des Teufels* is a patrilinear text, governed by an obsessive logic of fraternity – from the institution of the monastery to Medardus's forefather, the artist Francesko who has intercourse with the figure of his painting, a product of his own making.[44] This patrilinear order is refracted through the queer figure of Belcampo, the hairdresser and Medardus's devoted and eccentric companion, who is explicitly unbound by family ties and whom Seán Williams describes as being 'free of the burden of inheritance'.[45] *L'Élixir de longue vie* also plays with acts of doubling, as the son copies his father in the project of reanimation. The potential of a queer reproduction is transformed into the vision of another kind of Pygmalionesque (or Frankenstein) monster.

Flesh

Bartholoméo and Don Juan aim to circumvent reproduction through a process of magical reanimation and uncanny return. This project has consequences for the discursive status of the artwork in the text, which finds itself at the centre of a set of tensions between the seduction of transient pleasures and the desire for longevity.

---

[43] Michael Lucey, *The Misfit of the Family: Balzac and the Social Forms of Sexuality* (Durham, NC: Duke University Press, 2003), p. 4.

[44] Christine Lehleiter, *Romanticism, Origins, and the History of Heredity* (Lewisburg, PA: Bucknell University Press, 2014), pp. 187–201.

[45] Seán Williams, 'E. T. A. Hoffmann and the Hairdresser around 1800', *Publications of the English Goethe Society*, 85.1 (2016), 54–66 (pp. 57, 59).

The opening scene of the party combines hedonistic intoxication with the ekphrastic rhetoric of a still life: it is described as a 'merveilleux spectacle' (wondrous spectacle) registered via the physical appearances of the female guests who are presented as living works of art and decoration: 'vêtues de satin, étincelantes d'or et charges de pierreries qui brillaient moins que leurs yeux' (dressed in satin, sparkling with gold and covered in jewels that shimmered less than their eyes) (B XI 474). The women, significantly, do not talk but *seem* to talk – that is, they are 'read' by an anonymous onlooker – following the repeated formula 'l'une semblait dire' (one of them seemed to say) – and what each of them seems to say are variations on the willing sacrifice of longevity (and virtue) for their momentary pleasures. In this way, the text opens up a scene of explicitly visual decadence, shortly before introducing an alternative in the character of Don Juan's father, the ascetic Bartholoméo:

> Si ce volontaire anachorète allait et venait dans le palais ou par les rues de Ferrare, il semblait chercher une chose qui lui manquait; il marchait tout rêveur, indécis, préoccupé comme un homme en guerre avec une idée ou avec un souvenir. Pendant que le jeune homme donnait des fêtes somptueuses [. . .], Bartholoméo mangeait sept onces de pain par jour et buvait de l'eau. S'il lui fallait un peu de volaille, c'était pour en donner les os à un barbet noir, son compagnon fidèle. (B XI 477)

> If this voluntary hermit came or went in the palace or in the streets of Ferrara, he seemed to be looking for something that he had misplaced: he walked as if in a dream, undecided about something, preoccupied like a man at war with an idea or a memory. Whilst the young man hosted sumptuous banquets [. . .], Bartholoméo ate seven ounces of bread a day and drank water. If he took a bit of poultry, it was so that his faithful companion, a black poodle, might have the bones.

Bartholoméo resembles the repentant Raphaël at the end of *La Peau de chagrin* or the repentant Medardus at the end of *Die Elixiere des Teufels*, both of whom, having given in to the pleasures of the senses, must finally stifle their desires in order to prolong their lives. The black poodle that accompanies him is a note that we are treading close to a specifically Faustian pact, emphasised by the pointedly named guest 'Brambilla' – a direct reference to Hoffmann's *Prinzessin Brambilla* – who asks the company 'avez-vous remarqué le chien noir?' (Have you noticed the black dog?) (B XI 482). This mixing together of elements from the German literary tradition, with its somewhat misplaced nod to Hoffmann (who nonetheless proves his own interest in the Faustian pact, channelled through its Schlemihlian adaptation, in *Abenteuer der Silvester-Nacht*), is paradigmatic for the tale's entangled literary inheritance. In this way, Balzac's text inscribes itself into a discussion about the kind of life that is worth living – pleasurable at the expense of its length, or long at the expense of pleasure – which is the same tussle that plays out in *La Peau de chagrin*. Besuchet, in fact, calls those two works 'deux pans d'une même méditation sur la durée de la vie et les sacrifices à faire pour la prolonger' (two facets of a singular meditation on the duration of life and on the sacrifices we might make to prolong it).[46] If *La Peau de chagrin* is devoted to the exploration of desire and its sapping effects on life, *L'Élixir de longue vie* casts a glance towards a life that is long for length's own sake, opening up an image of life that is reduced, finally, to mere animation.

The reanimation of flesh occurs first in the fleshy, vulnerable site of the eye. Having embalmed his dead father's eye in the liquid, Don Juan looks on in horror as the scene unfolds in a dizzy spectacle of looking and returning glances.

> 'Ah! ah!' dit don Juan en pressant le flacon dans sa main comme nous serrons en rêvant la branche à laquelle nous sommes suspendus au-dessus d'un précipice.
>
> Il voyait un œil plein de vie, un œil d'enfant dans une tête de mort, la lumière y tremblait au milieu d'un jeune fluide; et, pro-tégée par de beaux cils noirs, elle scintillait pareille à ces lueurs uniques que le voyageur aperçoit dans une campagne déserte, par les soirs d'hiver [. . .]. Il éclatait tant de vie dans ce fragment de vie, que don Juan épouvanté recula, il se promena par la chambre, sans oser regarder cet œil, qu'il revoyait sur les planchers, sur les tapisseries. La chambre était parsemée de pointes pleines de feu, de vie, d'intelligence. Partout brillaient des yeux qui aboyaient après lui! (B XI 483–4)

> 'Aha!' said Don Juan. He gripped the flask tightly, as we clutch in dreams the branch from which we hang suspended over a precipice. For the eye was full of life. It was a young child's eye set in a death's head; the light quivered in the depths of its youthful liquid bright-ness. Shaded by long dark lashes, it sparkled like the strange lights that travellers see in lonely places in winter nights. [. . .] Life was so dilated in this fragment of life that Don Juan shrank back; he walked up and down the room, he dared not meet that gaze, but he saw

---

[46] Besuchet, '"Rien de nouveau sous le soleil?"', p. 124.

nothing else. The ceiling and the hangings, the whole room was sown with living points of fire and intelligence. Everywhere those gleaming eyes haunted him.

A singular chiasm emerges in this unsettling scene, in which a tussle over life is pictured as a tussle over the power of vision: the father's life is distilled within a single glittering eye, following which a whole swarm of eyes seems to blink at Don Juan from the room. The eye becomes the symbolic nodal point of a struggle over life. The platitudinous promise Don Juan had made to his dying father before understanding his project, after all, was made in terms of images: 'votre image sera sans cesse dans mon cœur' (your image will forever remain in my heart).

For Pankow, the eye is also a motif for literary creation. Pankow has pointed out the significance of the multiplying eyes as a trope inherited from Hoffmann, most obviously from *Der Sandmann*, although, as I have suggested earlier in this chapter, the embodied and processual nature of vision is also a key motif in *Elixiere*.[47] The eye is the organ by which the perceiving subject takes on the world: the point at which that world is distilled into images, and a point of the body's greatest vulnerability. In a brief collision or crossover between vision and touch, the parricide can be carried out only in blindness as Don Juan averts his own eyes and the father's eye is crushed beneath the (covered) skin of the son: 'il écrasa l'œil, en le foulant avec un linge, mais sans le regarder' (he extinguished the eye, pressing it with the linen cloth, his gaze averted) (B XI 484–5).

That the tussle between the two men is a tussle of power over sight is then clinched by the statue Don Juan erects in the name and memory of his father, which, in its ironically religious posture, is turned into a visual spectacle of his parricide:

> Il éleva un monument de marbre blanc sur la tombe de son père, et en confia l'exécution des figures aux plus célèbres artistes du temps. Il ne fut parfaitement tranquille que le jour où la statue paternelle, agenouillée devant la Religion, imposa son poids énorme sur cette fosse, au fond de laquelle il enterra le seul remords qui ait effleuré son cœur dans les moments de lassitude physique. (B XI 485)

> He erected a monument of white marble on his father's tomb, and employed the greatest sculptors of the time on it. He did not recover perfect ease of mind until the day when the paternal statue, kneeling before Religion, imposed its enormous weight upon the grave into

---

[47] Pankow, 'Literatur – Geschichte', p. 51.

which he had buried the one feeling of remorse that had touched his heart in moments of physical weakness.

The statue whose white marble reflects back the white of Bartholoméo's dying eye is a picture of the duplicitousness of images; a monument to what has been lost in order for appearances to remain as they are. For the son's secret is not just that he has killed his father, but that he will make exactly the same attempt against the laws of life, death and inheritance as Bartholoméo did. The destiny he prepares for himself is to copy his father – and when this destiny plays out, it is copy, in the form of brute repetition, that ruins him. For if what stops Bartholoméo's plans is the most violent iteration of touch, what stops Don Juan's, when Philippe falters, is a disastrous movement of his body explicable only as mechanical reflex: 'Quand il eut mouillé le bras droit, il se sentit fortement étreindre le cou par un bras jeune et vigoureux, le bras de son père!' (When he had moistened the right arm, he felt himself grabbed by the throat, a young and strong arm held him in a tight grip, it was the arm of his father!) (B XI 492). Despite having mastered the scene so as to take control of it entirely, by keeping the room in darkness and by manipulating the behaviour of his son to make him obedient, his body gets in the way of what he wants. And so the final image of Don Juan is that of the copy driven to its most hideous extreme as the 'œil d'enfant dans une tête de mort' is mirrored and horrifically amplified in the grotesque vision of a living head attached to a dead body: a partial and imperfect life, a biological rather than spiritual life. The discourse of images is bundled together with the brute materiality of flesh. The tale draws out a provocative reading of the artwork not as vivification, as lifelikeness, but as something that lasts for the sake of lasting, excessive and thus paradoxically emptied out: living and despiritualised flesh.

Balzac's living-dead father is, in that sense, along with such contemporary creatures as Frankenstein's monster, a forerunner of the magical being that most famously embodies living-dead flesh, the zombie, whose 'essence', according to Peter Dendle, 'is supplanted, stolen, or effaced consciousness; it casts allegorically the appropriation of one person's will by another'.[48] Not only is Balzac's undead creature a result of successive appropriation of wills (in the double sense of 'will' – the father's project for immortality but also his

---

[48] Peter Dendle, 'The Zombie as Barometer of Cultural Anxiety', in *Monsters and the Monstrous: Myths and Metaphors of Enduring Evil*, ed. by Niall Scott (Amsterdam: Rodopi, 2007), pp. 45–57 (p. 47).

financial will, his inheritance) but it is also, as I have shown, a symbol of intertextual persistence. At one point in the middle of the tale, Don Juan, whose insights into society's hidden forces make him a master dissembler, is pictured as 'Maître des illusions de la vie' (Master of life's illusions) (B XI 486). Like the addict or the alcoholic, the master of illusions is also subject to his illusions: this, as I have shown, resonates with the image of Hoffmann circulating in France at that time. Don Juan is, finally, no more than a literary copy:

> Il fut en effet le type du Don Juan de Molière, du Faust de Goethe, du Manfred de Byron et du Melmoth de Maturin. Grandes images tracées par les plus grands génies de l'Europe [. . .]! Images terribles que le principe du Mal, existant chez l'homme, éternise, et dont quelques copies se retrouvent de siècle en siècle. (B XI 486–7)

> He was, in fact, Molière's Don Juan, Goethe's Faust, Byron's Manfred, Mathurin's Melmoth. Great allegorical figures traced by the greatest men of genius in Europe [. . .]! Terrible allegorical figures that are made eternal by the principle of evil that exists at the heart of man, and which reappear copied from century to century.

To this list may be added Hoffmann's Medardus, himself already a composite image, a point on a long line of Faustian wrongdoers. The elixir, as the twice-drawn motif copied from *Elixiere* into *L'Élixir*, is the motif of a tale about the life-diminishing risks that are run in mimetic reproduction. Balzac's narrative offers a kind of commentary on this compulsive mimetic or imitative desire, one that expresses itself in the terms of a conflictual imitation. We are left, with the 'cross' that highlights the reproducibility of motifs from one tale to another, with the embodied experience of a tale's inscription into a literary tradition, as it theorises its place within a criss-crossing, perhaps partially plagiarised, Gothic tradition.

* * *

The errant son's body in *L'Élixir* is left deformed or crossed by a wager made against inheritance. The body lives on only in parts, a grotesque composition of fragmented limbs. Balzac's tale of literary and social inheritance foregrounds the living arm and head, uncannily persistent forms of life as the legacy of Hoffmann's *Die Elixiere des Teufels*.

In this chapter I have argued that mimetic narratives involve a compromise, as an impersonator threatens to usurp its original; as life folds into writing and writing into life. This I have traced through figurings of the cross. Following Medardus's cross-shaped scar, the proof of his impossible double identity, Balzac's *élixir* is another literary device that plays out across the subject's skin. The son anoints the flesh of the father in the name of extending his life and escaping the laws of inheritance. In *La Peau de chagrin*, Raphaël's scrap of skin marks out the loss of life in the name of fulfilling his desires. These three texts thus feed into a troubled chain of literary inheritance. *L'Élixir de longue vie* both calls back to Hoffmann's *Die Elixiere des Teufels* as its predecessor and looks forward to *La Peau de chagrin*. The triad of Gothic or fantastic skins – in which the skin marks the sensuous edge between the subject and his world, a middling layer between subject- and object-life – might resemble strange visions of the act of writing or inscription, always calling to how that act might feel or work upon the body. What makes *L'Élixir* and *Elixiere* unexpected forefathers of *La Peau de chagrin*, a novel that so singularly bridges 'le fantastique' and 'le réalisme', is that they suggest how an experience of 'le fantastique', even in its most awful or most garbled forms, might come to usurp or to confound a reality shown to be composed of reproducible images. This experience in Balzac's early work is insistently marked, as we have seen, by the figure of Hoffmann.

The Gothic body in European nineteenth-century literature is one of the non-human or the not-quite-human, figured in hideous lifelikeness by the monster of Mary Shelley's *Frankenstein*, the ultimate animated compendium of body parts. The Gothic inheritance of Hoffmann appears in the form of another impossible body: the double. For Neil Cornwell, Hoffmann's influence on the Gothic genre is such that without him, 'many subsequent works in the Gothic mode (by Nerval or Gogol, Poe or Dostoevsky, and indeed many others) would seem inconceivable'.[49] The league of nineteenth-century doubles and clones that follows him includes the figures of Stevenson's *Strange Case of Dr Jekyll and Mr Hyde*, Poe's *William Wilson* and Maupassant's *Le Horla*. Hoffmann's work resonates, too, in the robotic fantasies of the fin de siècle, such as Villiers de l'Isle Adam's *L'Ève future*, which recalls both Hoffmann's automata tales and the impossible predicament of the *Doppelgänger* or the clone, as a kind of object-self. The Gothic also carries a bodily charge into nineteenth-century realism. In the British context, a 'Victorian Gothic' has been theorised in which the Gothic remains a primarily 'affective form', persisting in linguistic and imagistic formulations

---

[49] Cornwell, 'European Gothic', p. 70.

in the works of writers such as Wilkie Collins and the Brontës.[50] For Balzac, the Gothic flourishes of his early career, most evident in texts such as this and *Melmoth réconcilié*, a retelling of Maturin's *Melmoth the Wanderer*, feed into the realism of his later works. *La Comédie humaine* teems with devilish figures and infernal pacts, making, as one critic notes, 'Gothic diabolism credible in a realistic setting, in the banks and theatres of Paris'.[51] As the diabolical Vautrin wagers in *Le Père Goriot*: 'Je vous défie de faire deux pas dans Paris sans rencontrer des manigances infernales' (I defy you to walk a couple of yards anywhere in Paris without stumbling upon some infernal contrivance) (B III 140).

The fascination for and fear evoked by the spectacle of the Gothic body, and its strange variations on human life, culminates here in an image of Balzac's text feeding from the dead body of Hoffmann's, in its own extravagant Gothic flourish as reference to its literary predecessor. 'Toute la civilisation européene', in the words of his preface, 'repose sur l'HÉRÉDITÉ comme sur un pivot' (the whole civilisation of Europe turns upon the principle of hereditary succession as upon a pivot) (B XI 474). And as the elixirs reproduce themselves and one pact begets another, as the living arm replaces the withered arm and one decapitation follows the last, the production of new textual life self-consciously evokes, and draws energy from, the dead words of another writer. To come 'under the influence' of Hoffmann's bloody text, finally, suggests another return to Chapter 3, and another way in which Balzac might incorporate Hoffmann, as in the image of the anonymous narrator of *Der goldne Topf*, who consumes the figure of one of his own characters in a glass of punch.

---

[50] Ruth Robbins and Julian Wolfreys (eds), *Victorian Gothic: Literary and Cultural Manifestations in the Nineteenth Century* (Basingstoke: Palgrave, 2000).
[51] Hope Crampton, 'Melmoth in "La Comédie Humaine"', *Modern Language Review*, 61.1 (1966), 42–50 (p. 48).

Conclusion: Fiction's Pretexts

'It occurred to me that the novel, though fictional, isn't uniformly fictional. Endings are fake, because nothing in real life ever ends; characters are composites, because real people are either too close to you or too far. But the furniture and clothes: that stuff must almost all be real. There's no way Balzac invented all that furniture. All those soaring ambitions and human destinies are just a pretext for telling the truth about the sofas and the clocks.'
—Elif Batuman, 'Elif Batuman's Diary: Pamuk's Museum'[1]

A mimetic view of literature insists on the relationship between a text and a pretext. In practice, a pretext is a slippery thing, folding its opposite into itself by referring both to the text that comes before the text and to what *else* comes before the text. For a thinker such as Derrida, this difficulty is elided because there is nothing outside text: every text is itself already a pretext, folding into and conditioning an endless chain of further texts. For Genette, a pretext, like other paratextual forms, is situated both inside the work and beyond it – as a threshold, 'a transitional zone between text and beyond-text'.[2] It is true that text is also a significant part of the pretextual – the world at large – not least in the sense that the world is full of text, and that we understand the world through those texts. But mimetic texts insist on something pretextual precisely in the sense of the non-textual (whether as world or as affect, body, thing, self). The pretext is their condition for being. My readings here, accordingly, have been drawn to the material stakes of the text, insistent that our encounter with

---

[1] Elif Batuman, 'Elif Batuman's Diary: Pamuk's Museum', *London Review of Books*, 43.11 (7 June 2012), pp. 38–9.
[2] Gérard Genette, *Paratexts: Thresholds of Interpretation*, trans. by Jane E. Lewin (Cambridge: Cambridge University Press, 1997), p. 407.

a narrative matters: how it feels, what it looks like on the page, the journals and translations we find it in.

In its more commonplace usage, a pretext is an excuse or a pretended reason for something. Reality is a pretext for realism in this sense, too: a point made in Elif Batuman's witty reversal of logic, cited above, when she claims of Balzac that 'all those soaring ambitions and human destinies are just a pretext for telling the truth about the sofas and the clocks'. Batuman – whose novels *The Idiot* and *Either/Or* take an interest in, and playfully style themselves upon, nineteenth-century realist narratives – is hinting at the opposite received truth. Talking about clocks is a way of talking about something beyond clocks, as in Lukács's notion that realist details gesture metonymically towards a more totalising structure of meaning.[3] But Batuman's statement also defamiliarises a more commonplace truth: that the artifice of narrative form, its manufactured endings and its composite characters, is a vehicle for exploring the details of real lived experience. In both senses, the real and the artifice meet, cross over, and occasionally fuzz into indistinction.

We can get on board with the project of nineteenth-century realism more easily, I think, when we understand it less as a project of signifying an inert reality than as a project of supplementing a reality already understood to be finite, dynamic and shifting. The notion of pretext, split into the paradoxical pair of meanings noted above – text and non-text – reflects the Merleau-Pontian chiasm that relates and separates self and other, and reminds us that mimesis is a destabilising, disordering notion that tends to conflate insides and outsides, copies and originals, self and other, whilst simultaneously holding them apart from one another. The lines of Chapter 2, which incorporate both text and non-text into a single image, are consummate examples of this intricate confusion. Those lines, not unlike signatures, represent idiosyncratic traces of the writing self. As fragmentary figures, they gesture towards something more complete – the text they supposedly mimic.

There is a provisional and playful sense to the texts by Balzac that I have discussed in this book, as an early realist narrative voice gropes around for self-justification, for something to model itself on. Nineteenth-century realism's commitment to a pretextual world is registered, on a metadiscursive level, in a series of rhetorical allusions

---

[3] Georg Lukács, 'Narrate or Describe? A Preliminary Discussion of Naturalism and Formalism', in *Writer & Critic and other Essays*, ed. and trans. Arthur D. Kahn (New York, NY: Merlin, 1970), 110–48.

to other models of representation, the most common of which are its deferential references to the visual arts, from sketching to painting and, later in the century, to photography. But sometimes those pretexts are intertexts, and this leads me to the first major point of my conclusion: that Balzac engages Hoffmann and his tales as a kind of pretext that, not unlike the flourish of pictorial language, positions, pivots and in some sense justifies his own work. These references are not to be understood as incidental decoration, nor as broad-brushstroke taxonomising or cataloguing, but rather as urgent inscription. As Dirk Göttsche and Nicholas Saul argue in the context of German realism, 'the internal contradictions of Realist theory effectively place (references to) Romanticism at the very heart of Realist poetics'.[4] Whilst there are several writers who turn up repeatedly in Balzac's works by name, and some of them far more frequently than Hoffmann – Scott, Rabelais, Diderot, Shakespeare – Hoffmann's place in *La Comédie humaine* is characterised by the energy of a particular kind of frustrated ambivalence: by the force with which Balzac occasionally dismisses or disavows him, and by the alternation of that disavowal with approbation, whether explicit or grudging. This may give us a sense that Hoffmann's place in *La Comédie humaine* plays a role in Balzac's own self-definition as writer and as realist.

It is also a strange fact that the two authors continued to be paired together across the course of the nineteenth century. Fyodor Dostoevsky – a writer who has himself been associated with the term 'Romantic realism', as the author of works that range in style from *The Double* to *The Brothers Karamazov*[5] – names Hoffmann and Balzac alongside one another in a letter in a reading list of 1838.[6] Jules Champfleury, in the preface to his 1856 translation of Hoffmann, *Contes posthumes d'Hoffmann* (Hoffmann's Posthumous

---

[4] Dirk Göttsche and Nicholas Saul, 'Introduction', in *Realism and Romanticism in German Literature. Realismus und Romantik in der deutschsprachigen Literatur* (Bielefeld: Aisthesis, 2013), pp. 9–30 (p. 16).

[5] Donald Fanger, *Dostoevsky and Romantic Realism: A Study of Dostoevsky in relation to Balzac, Dickens, and Gogol* (Cambridge, MA: Harvard University Press, 1965).

[6] 'You plume yourself on the number of books you have read. . . . But don't please imagine that I envy you that. At Peterhof I read at least as many as you have. The whole of Hoffmann in Russian and German (that is, "Kater Murr", which hasn't yet been translated), and nearly all Balzac. (Balzac is great! His characters are the creations of an all-embracing intelligence. Not the spirit of the age, but whole millenniums, with all their strivings, have worked towards such development and liberation in the soul of man)' Dostoevsky, letter to his brother dated 9 August 1838. *Letters of Fyodor Michailovitch Dostoevsky to his Family and Friends*, trans. by Ethel Golburn Mayne, ed. by Alexander Eliasberg (London: Chatto & Windus, 1914), p. 4.

Tales), confesses 'Aussi ne renierais-je jamais l'influence qu'ont exercé sur moi Diderot, Balzac et Hoffmann plus particulièrement' (And I would never deny the influence exercised on me, in particular by Diderot, Balzac and Hoffmann).[7] Baudelaire writes, in an article on Poe originally published in *La Revue de Paris* in 1852: 'Que ne fit pas Hoffmann pour désarmer la destinée? Que n'entreprit pas Balzac pour conjurer la fortune?' (What did Hoffmann not do to disarm destiny? What did Balzac not undertake to make his fortune?).[8] A peculiar tension is engendered by the symptomatic juxtaposition of two writers whose representational practices are canonically seen as oppositional.

Hoffmann, as I have shown in this book, is committed to the pretextual reality predicated by a mimetic view of art, in the specific sense that he develops a narrative method that seeks to probe beyond the given or the immediately perceptible, to include experiences of dreams, visions, intoxication, déjà vu, the powers exerted by artworks over human minds, uncanny encounters, and the many other strangenesses that form part of the texture of 'real' human life. His methods can be helpfully understood via a realist interpretation of anamorphosis and caricature as modes that use distortive or de-realising techniques as part of a representational practice. Hoffmann is adept at incorporating complicated parts of the self within the work of art. He also elucidates specific models to demonstrate how his narratives work: in the Jacques Callot essay and associated pictorial flourishes, and in the shifting relationship of Serapiontic texts and discussions, which build on one another to develop an accumulative critical attitude. These meta-narrative excursions do not diverge from the fictions but occur within or alongside them, making complicated use of framing techniques such that the sliding relationship between text and pretext is able to mirror something of the complexity in the relationship between text and world.

The figure of Hoffmann appears frequently in Balzac's own framing devices. This is the obvious way in which Hoffmann is a kind of pretext for Balzac: he is drawn on in Balzac's prefaces, paratexts and early draft versions of his early works: in subtitles and epithets such as 'conte fantastique' in *Le Chef-d'œuvre inconnu* and *Sarrasine*, in the 'avis au lecteur' of *L'Élixir de longue vie*, in journalistic material relating to and early draft versions of *La Peau*

---

[7] Jules Champfleury, *Contes posthumes d'Hoffmann* (Paris: Michel Lévy, 1856), p. 1.

[8] Charles Baudelaire, 'Edgar Allan Poe. Sa vie et ses ouvrages', in *Œuvres complètes*, II, pp. 249–88 (p. 249).

de chagrin, and in that novel's pictorial epigraph, which evokes Sterne but also unwittingly marks a significant common interest with Hoffmann. A key part of Balzac's paratextual allusions to Hoffmann – as border-work or model – is, as I have noted at several points in this book, an advertising strategy aligning Balzac's early works with the fashionable genre of 'le fantastique' of the early 1830s. Whilst there is good evidence that Balzac was an enthusiastic reader of Hoffmann throughout the 1830s at least, this reading takes place within particular limited conditions: in French translations, and amidst the media-discursive framework of the Parisian journals. Ambivalences are produced when Balzac chooses to erase some of them in later editions. In Balzac's explicit citations of his name, 'Hoffmann' becomes a shorthand for the inventive capacities of Romanticism, evoked as a foil to realism's claimed methods – assemblage, documentation, reproduction – and in that sense they might form a neat case study into realism's rhetorical dismissals of Romanticism in articulating its own new project. Hence, Hoffmann is the 'chantre de l'impossible' (bard of the impossible) (B VII 956), introducing us to a 'monde inconnu'[9] (unknown world) where realism thinks itself committed to the possible – to the workings of chance, as Balzac puts it in his *Avant-propos*. The 'Hoffmannesque' label, we might then argue, is used as a way of disguising the realist writer's own reliance on his imagination.[10] The pretext, after all, is etymologically a textured veil hung *over* the text it precedes, being related to *praetexere*, 'to disguise', as well as to *praetextus*, 'a display'.[11] With its ambivalences, its disavowals and repressions, the pretext is also a particular identificatory strategy – a showy declaration of what realism is not (imaginative invention), in order to profess what it is (serious observation). Invoking a pretext always involves some measure of self-displacement.

But when we examine the texts themselves, and in particular those texts of the early 1830s that most readily summon up Hoffmannesque intertexts, a closer engagement with Hoffmann's own anamorphic mimetic attitude is on show. In *La Peau de chagrin*, Balzac orients

[9] Saint-Marc Girardin, 'Contes fantastiques d'Hofmann, traduction d'un extrait du *Pot d'or*', *Revue de Paris*, II (1829), 67–130, p. 67.
[10] Lilian Furst's argument, similar to my suggestion here, is that the realists 'conceal *poeisis*' by means of 'a pretense of mimesis', though I diverge from Furst in the sense that she insists on a definition of mimesis as copying. *All Is True: The Claims and Strategies of Realist Fiction* (Durham, NC: Duke University Press, 1995), pp. 189–90.
[11] Marie Lathers, 'Modesty and the Artist's Model in *Le Chef-d'œuvre inconnu*', *Symposium*, 46.1 (1992), 49–71, p. 52.

his narrative around the model of hallucination and the figure of the *Doppelgänger*. The novel, as an exploration of youthful male desire, opens up a self that is found to be cracked in two: into the writing, experiencing subject and the literary object of the writer's experiences, writer and character in one. This novel is perhaps Balzac's most Hoffmannesque text, generating a fantastic plot fully grounded within a realist mode, and open above all to the ambivalences of the self as refracted through writing. In *Le Chef-d'œuvre inconnu*, Balzac investigates a question that Hoffmann first opens up in the Serapiontic series, about an obsessive approach to representation and the quest to create life through art. That representation, in both texts, turns out to be crucially limited by the edges and borders of the perceiving self. Representation, as it turns out – and as the impressionists would insist – is dependent on the filtering of individual experience, and requires a processual, strenuous work of the body to be properly viewed. In *L'Élixir de longue vie*, mimesis as intertextuality – the claimed imitation of Hoffmann – ends up calling the relationship between copy and original into disarray, and the crossover engenders a kind of living death, in terms of both motif and Gothic style.

In these early works of *La Comédie humaine*, we see a shifting positioning and repositioning of text with regard to the world in Balzac's experiments with fantastic and Gothic modes and with the narrative possibilities of a non-representational artwork. Explicitly 'Hoffmannesque' characters (Frenhofer), motifs (a magic skin, a pair of disfigurative opera glasses) and plots (a frenzied quest for immortality) are mobilised as part of Balzac's systematising approach to the representation of French society. In that sense, Hoffmann is not just an arbitrary point of reference for Balzac, a fashionable cultural coordinate, but a pretextual model in almost the same sense as those more standardly realist allusions to the act of painting.

***

By 1836, the year of publication of the first instalments of *Illusions perdues*, the French vogue for Hoffmann was already on the wane. Jules Janin, who had been accused of jumping on the Hoffmann bandwagon only three years earlier, declared that his day was over: 'Hoffmann descendit de son trône de nuages, sans un éclair pour lui tracer sa route' (Hoffmann descended from his throne of clouds, with not a single light to illuminate his route).[12] And whilst from

---

[12] He is accused in the anonymous article '*Contes fantastiques*, par M. Jules Janin', *L'Artiste*, 13.4 (28 October 1832), p. 148.

this point onwards, into the more canonical portions of *La Comédie humaine*, Balzac's flourishes of the fantastic are less evident, they do not disappear so much as they are driven underground, recurring in, say, aspects of the appearance of the arch-criminal Jacques Collin, alias Vautrin, and in other undertones that Auerbach would describe as 'demonic'. My suggestion – the second major strand of this conclusion – is that across *La Comédie humaine*, if not for the very first time then perhaps in the most concrete way, that style that we call the 'Hoffmannesque' (summoning up an atmosphere of unease, strangeness, alienation) occurs. It occurs not as imitation or homage, as in the sense of Jules Janin or Théophile Gautier, but as the reflection of, or gesture towards, a distinct style. If Balzac 'created' the nineteenth century, as Oscar Wilde's Vivian has it, then he also 'created' the Hoffmannesque. The 'esque' is key here. As a suffix denoting likeness, the 'esque' signals, as Jane Bennett argues, a relationship less of imitation than of playful improvisation – no less committed to mimesis but more careful to delimit the self as an entity distinct *from*, even if tangled up within, the (pretextual) other.[13] The 'esque', as in the 'arabesque', is itself eminently pretextual, as much as it is both manneristic and, in a certain sense, extravagant or even camp – and it is an indication towards something else or something other, as in Corporal Trim's playful gesture or in other stylistic or decorative flourishes. Balzac's ambivalent, conflicted, ongoing interest in Hoffmann's works runs parallel to the canonisation of the 'Hoffmannesque' as mode across *La Comédie humaine*.

Two passages from later works by Balzac serve as a useful illustration of this point. The first comes from the introduction to *Le Cabinet des Antiques* (The Cabinet of Antiquities) (1838), in which Émile Blondet remembers peering in at the window of the decrepit aristocrats of the Hôtel d'Esgrignon as a child:

> Enfin ni Maturin ni Hoffmann, les deux plus sinistres imaginations de ce temps, ne m'ont causé l'épouvante que me causèrent les mouvements automatiques de ces corps busqués. (B IV 976)

> Neither Maturin nor Hoffmann, the two most sinister imaginations of our time, ever gave me such a thrill of terror as I used to feel when I watched the automatic movements of those bodies sheathed in whalebone.

---

[13] Jane Bennett, 'Mimesis: Paradox or Encounter', *MLN*, 132.5 (2017), 1186–1200 (p. 1192).

The second example comes from *Une fille d'Ève* (A Daughter of Eve) (1838–9), from the introductory description of the German music teacher Schmucke:

> Enfin, son vieux corps, mal assis sur ses vieilles jambes nouées et qui démontrait jusqu'à quel point l'homme peut en faire l'accessoire de son âme, appartenait à ces étranges créations qui n'ont été bien dépeintes que par un Allemand, par Hoffmann, le poète de ce qui n'a pas l'air d'exister et qui néanmoins a vie. (B II 278)

> Finally, his old body, badly perched upon its knotted old legs, proving to what extent man can make it the mere accessory of his soul, belonged to those strange creations which have been properly depicted only by a German, by Hoffmann, the poet of that which does not seem to exist and yet lives.

Both of these passages give a clear sense of how a Gothic or fantastic register seeps into and enlivens the realism of Balzac's later works. In both passages, Hoffmann's name is invoked to mark uncanny moments when living bodies appear momentarily dead or robotic: that is, where life appears briefly as semblance. In these moments – in his gestures towards the Hoffmannesque – Balzac touches upon a particular quality of experience in which real things momentarily attain a fictional or artificial character. Hoffmann's name presides over moments when life itself seems fictional, and when the normal order of things is briefly confused. As pretextual supplement, Hoffmann himself becomes a fiction, another kind of character, and is reified into the quality of his own works as he comes to embody the slippage between art and life.

* * *

One of Balzac's most devoted readers, Oscar Wilde, offers a wilfully contradictory, unexpected and witty commentary on mimesis – in the guise of a defence of an apparently anti-mimetic view of art – in a fictional dialogue named 'The Decay of Lying', first published in 1889 and heavily edited in 1891. A discussion of Oscar Wilde may seem out of place in the conclusion of a study of a German and a French writer from the first half of the nineteenth century. But Wilde, who is often glossed as an ardent defender of an 'anti-mimetic' approach to art, is for that reason well placed to comment on the fate of mimesis over the course of the nineteenth century and to emphasise its contradictory, chiasmic and subversive energies.[14] 'The Decay of Lying'

---

[14] Nidesh Lawtoo has examined Wilde's contradictory approach to mimesis in 'The Critic as Mime: Wilde's Theatrical Performance', *Symploke* 26 (2018), 307–28.

is presented as a diatribe against mimesis and realism by its spokes-person Vivian, who, in the course of a discussion with Cyril, praises art's unique capacity to lie and invent, its commitment to the 'telling of beautiful untrue things', and the strange and unique propensity of Nature to imitate it.[15] The dialogue reveals a complex debt to mimesis that Vivian's oppositional statements acknowledge even as they push at the edges of received wisdom. Despite mounting a scath-ing critique of realism, the essay also serves as a place of expression for Wilde's great enthusiasm for the works of Balzac.

Vivian does not deny the existence of a powerful and pervasive imitative faculty. On the contrary, he insists upon it, though he attri-butes that faculty to 'Life' rather than to 'Art'. He reverses received ideas and conventions involved in debates about mimesis that have been rehearsed over the course of the nineteenth century, and in doing so he underlines their status as convention. Thus, for example, Vivian declares that 'life imitates art far more than Art imitates life'; that 'a great artist invents a type, and Life tries to copy it, to repro-duce it in a popular form, like an enterprising publisher'.[16] Holbein, Van Dyck, Balzac and others, he declares, have created the characters that populate nineteenth-century reality; impressionist artists have 'invented' London's 'brown fogs' and 'lovely silver mists'.[17] Vivian's proposition is both extravagant witty and deeply serious. And yet the point is not just to invert, to wilfully remind us of the opposite commonplace – the doctrine that art imitates life – but to continue the game of mirrorings and inversions seemingly indefinitely, by pointing out, as well, that artifice too has a stake in reality; indeed that (as I have suggested across this book, not least with regard to the logic of caricature) fiction can be more real than the real world; and the real, in turn, more hackneyed and artificial than works of art. The impressionists have 'invented' London's fogs in the impor-tant sense that they have conditioned us how to see them: 'people see fogs, not because they are fogs, but because poets and painters have taught them the mysterious loveliness of such effects'.[18] This proposi-tion is not anti-mimetic so much as it is a challenge to the traditional ways we might have of ordering or positioning realism and mimesis in relation to each other, a challenge that insists on finding space for the subject's own imitative impulses within a mimetic framework.

---

[15] Oscar Wilde, 'The Decay of Lying', in *The Complete Works of Oscar Wilde* (London: HarperCollins, 2003), pp. 1071–92 (p. 1091).

[16] Ibid., p. 1083.

[17] Ibid., p. 1086.

[18] Ibid., p. 1086.

If Vivian seems to define mimesis, a term he does not use, as the more encompassing 'imitation', we should note that Wilde himself is avowedly, unapologetically imitative – even plagiaristic – in his works. His signature style is characterised by the use of aphoristic, epigrammatic forms that recycle received wisdom (taken, for example, from writings by Walter Pater and others), usually inverting its logic in the form of witty snippets that flurry and swarm in contagious-seeming proliferative patterns. As Colin Burrow remarks, 'the problem with Wilde is not just that he and every character he created always sound like they're quoting Oscar Wilde, but that after him quotations that didn't sound at least a little bit like Oscar Wilde were unlikely to be quoted, because they didn't sound like quotations.'[19] Wilde's appreciation of Lucien de Rubempré – a character raised up, here and in others of Wilde's essays, as one of Balzac's finest creations – is understandable from this angle. In learning to write as a journalist in *Illusions perdues*, Lucien learns the necessity of changing his opinions to profit from them in order, ultimately, to survive. The lesson he must learn in Paris, delivered by Lousteau – and which ultimately destroys him – is that 'un journaliste est un acrobate' (a journalist is an acrobat) (B V 355) who must opportunistically empty out his self of static truths or opinions to write, instead, from a lithe and changeable standpoint, with the purpose of making alliances and money: for 'the journalistic word has ceased to have any connection with the reality that it is supposed to represent. It has become a kind of empty signifier that can be made to say anything, to mean anything.'[20] Wilde's own games with language might be described in the terms of a kind of acrobatics as he swings between oppositional statements, taking especial delight in paradox and its many forms. As he declares in 'The Truth of Masks': 'a truth in art is that whose contradictory is also true'.[21] These language games expose both the fantasy and the anxiety of an unboundaried self that might at any moment come undone in a swarm of fashionable flourishes or witty repartees. In this sense, contradiction and paradox are mobilised in pursuit of representing a fundamentally incoherent identity. The channelling of opinions through the mask of a fictional character (many of which are identifiable as Wilde's, having been echoed in other journalistic works) is a good example of this. Wilde would

---

[19] Colin Burrow, 'Think Outside the Bun', *London Review of Books*, 44.17 (8 September 2022).

[20] Peter Brooks, *Honoré de Balzac* (Oxford: Oxford University Press, 2022), p. 26.

[21] Oscar Wilde, 'The Truth of Masks', in *The Complete Works of Oscar Wilde*, pp. 1156–73 (p. 1173).

have understood the irony of engaging the consummately mimetic form of a staged dialogue to rage against mimesis (Plato, of course, had committed the same contradiction), and he deliberately leaves indistinct the boundary lines between his own opinions and those of his character Vivian. The challenge of distinguishing between author and character, life and fictional representation, would inspire the material of the preface to *Dorian Gray*, where those boundaries were blurred for more vital and life-affirming ends: to shatter claims of sexual immorality.

Balzac is Vivian's prime example of the writer of an art that is truer than life:

> The nineteenth century, as we know it, is largely an invention of Balzac. Our Luciens de Rubempré, our Rastignacs, and De Marsays made their first appearance on the stage of the *Comédie Humaine*. We are merely carrying out, with footnotes and unnecessary additions, the whim or fancy or creative vision of a great novelist.

Vivian/Wilde does not think of Balzac as a realist per se: he associates that term more with Zola, whose 'unimaginative realism' (or what we might call naturalism) he contrasts unfavourably to Balzac's 'imaginative reality'. Vivian goes on:

> A steady course of Balzac reduces our living friends to shadows, and our acquaintances to the shadows of shades. His characters have a kind of fervent fiery-coloured existence. They dominate us, and defy scepticism. One of the greatest tragedies of my life is the death of Lucien de Rubempré. It is a grief from which I have never been able to completely rid myself. It haunts me in my moments of pleasure. I remember it when I laugh. But Balzac is no more a realist than Holbein was. He created life, he did not copy it.[22]

A 'course' of Balzac's medicine plunges us back into a kind of sickness in which reality suddenly appears dulled and wanting against the vividness of fiction. If Wilde does, in the way outlined above, identify with Lucien and his performative, porous being, then the tragedy of Lucien's death is the tragedy that Balzac does not (or cannot) *allow* him to survive: it is in that sense the tragedy of fiction, of its separation from reality, of mimesis – which, as chiasm, joins the two but will not conflate them. When Vivian announces that Lucien's suicide represents 'one of the greatest tragedies' of his life, Wilde marks a foundational moment in Balzacian readership, and

---

[22] Wilde, 'The Decay of Lying', p. 1077.

in Balzac scholarship, that will run and recur in varying imitative formulations across Balzac's eternal readership.[23] In the course of a heated discussion with Richard Ellmann across the pages of the *New York Review of Books*, Susan Sontag acknowledges herself as 'one of the countless readers of Balzac brought to tears by the suicides of Esther Gobseck and Lucien de Rubempré'.[24] A. S. Byatt, in an article from 2005, admits to having found 'tears rising to my eyes' at Lucien's death.[25] Lucien opens up a channel through which Balzac's writing spills into real life. These readers emphasise what they feel in response to his death, whose response comes in what might appear as an excessive flourish, marked by a 'spirit of extravagance' that Sontag describes elsewhere as camp: the documentation of their tears.[26] The demand that literature makes of us as readers is made upon our emotional lives and our embodied selves. Mimesis again shifts the border and seems to happen at an affective crossover, in what the reader gives of him- or herself in response to the text. Then, of course, these tears are worked back into writing (if they were not fictional in the first place), to re-enter the world of text.

Having begun this book with David Koreff's journey from Berlin to Paris, as Hoffmann's tales seemed to intrude into real-life France, I am tempted now to end with these Balzacian figures who trip likewise from fiction into the real. It is a foundational commonplace of (non-academic) literary discourse to see 'reality' or 'realism' as the measure of good fiction. We continue to be seduced by the promise 'based on a true story'. On the other hand – and here the gendering impulses of mimesis come into play – at the time of writing this conclusion, Elif Batuman's *Either/Or* has been faced with the inevitable charges of sticking *too closely* to the contours of life. Batuman's realism is viewed in the terms of a kind of stasis – an accusation that is almost exclusively reserved for female writers.[27] It would be redundant to note that a writer like Balzac, who claimed precisely to stick

[23] Ibid, p. 1077.

[24] Richard Ellmann, 'A Late Victorian Love Affair', *New York Review of Books* (4 August 1977); Susan Sontag, 'Vautrin's Cigar', *New York Review of Books* (27 October 1977).

[25] A. S. Byatt, 'The Death of Lucien de Rubempré', *Kenyon Review*, 27.1 (2005), 42–64 (p. 42).

[26] Susan Sontag, 'Notes on "Camp"', in *Camp: Queer Aesthetics and the Performing Subject: A Reader*, ed. by Fabio Cleto (Edinburgh: Edinburgh University Press, 1999), pp. 53–65, p. 59.

[27] As one recent reviewer points out: 'Across three books, Batuman [. . .] has written about herself, or something very close to herself, in incremental, almost diaristic form, like an oyster secreting its shell.' Dwight Garner, 'In Elif Batuman's "Either/Or", a Witty and Perceptive Young Woman Returns', *New York Times*, 9 May 2022.

to the contours of life, could never have been accused of the same kind of laziness, or to speculate on where the boundary-line of 'sufficient' invention might lie. This is only further evidence that mimesis has historically been the property of men.

Undeniably, fiction loops back and forth, into and out of life, with varying degrees of grace and intensity. Mimesis, as a structure to describe that relationship, serves to acknowledge something of this messiness. 'Realism' and 'Romanticism', in their turn, are unreliable terms in this light, though they are interesting and often very helpful ones, being as labels no more than approximations of what they want to suggest. As Auerbach notes in the Epilegomena to *Mimesis*, the value of such terms lies in their capacity to arouse in hearers or readers a set of ideas that facilitate our understanding of what is meant in a particular context. He adds: 'exakt sind sie nicht' (they are not exact).[28] The readings of this book, accordingly, have aimed to unfold some of the more interesting and peculiar areas of their inexactness. Hoffmann, Balzac's 'chantre de l'impossible' (B VII 956), turns out to provide Balzac with new ways of metabolising real life into his fiction, paying testament to the fact that the life-giving or life-interfering capacity of literature does not necessarily lie in its capacity to reflect.

Mimesis, when divested of its servitude to the mirror or the lamp, and when brought to bear on a phenomenological, embodied experience of narrative, denotes a vital set of exchanges in literary production. As a wrangling or grasping, it gets at the meeting point of life with art, the point at which the one crosses over into the other, and crosses back again. For there is nothing, as Hoffmann's own fictional writers all agree, as 'toll und wunderlich' (strange and surprising) – as fictional-seeming – as life itself.

---

[28] Erich Auerbach, 'Epilegomena zu Mimesis', *Romanische Forschungen*, 65.1/2 (1953), 1–18, p. 16.

Bibliography

Abrams, M. H., *The Mirror and the Lamp: Romantic Theory and the Critical Tradition* (Oxford: Oxford University Press, 1976)

Al-Taie, Yvonne, '"Des fremden Malers wunderbares Buch": Die doppelte Ordnung von Bild und Erzählung in E. T. A. Hoffmanns *Die Elixiere des Teufels* (1815/16)', in *Ding und Bild in der europäischen Romantik*, ed. by Jakob C. Heller and others (Berlin: De Gruyter, 2021), pp. 265–81

Alter, Robert, *Partial Magic: The Novel as a Self-Conscious Genre* (Berkeley, CA: University of California Press, 1975)

Andréoli, Max, 'Sublime et parodie dans les *Contes Artistes* de Balzac', *L'Année balzacienne* (1994), 7–38

Aristotle, *Poetics*, trans. by Malcolm Heath (London: Penguin, 1996)

Auerbach, Erich, 'Epilegomena zu Mimesis', *Romanische Forschungen*, 65.1/2 (1953), 1–18

—— 'Epilegomena to Mimesis', trans. by Jan M. Ziolowski, in *Mimesis*, trans. by Willard R. Trask (Princeton, NJ: Princeton University Press, 2003), pp. 559–74.

—— *Mimesis: Dargestellte Wirklichkeit in der abendländischen Literatur* (Tübingen: Francke Verlag, 2010)

—— *Mimesis: The Representation of Reality in Western Literature*, trans. by Willard R. Trask (Princeton, NJ: Princeton University Press, 2003)

—— 'Romanticism and Realism', in *Time, History, and Literature*, trans. by Jane O. Newman, ed. by James I. Porter (Princeton, NJ: Princeton University Press, 2014), pp. 144–56

—— 'Romantik und Realismus', in *Erich Auerbach: Geschichte und Aktualität eines europäischen Philologen*, ed. by Karlheinz Barck and Martin Treml (Berlin: Kadmos, 2007), pp. 426–38

—— 'Über die ernste Nachahmung des Alltäglichen', in *Erich Auerbach: Geschichte und Aktualität eines europäischen Philologen*, ed. by Karlheinz Barck and Martin Treml (Berlin: Kadmos, 2007), pp. 439–65.

Baldensperger, Fernand, *Orientations étrangères chez Honoré de Balzac* (Paris: Champion, 1927)

Balzac, Honoré de, 'Le Chef-d'œuvre inconnu', *L'Artiste: Journal de la littérature et des beaux-arts*, part 1, 'Maître Frenhofer', 1 (31 July 1831), 319–23; part 2, 'Catherine Lescaut', 2 (4 August 1831), 7–10

—— *Correspondance*, ed. by Roger Pierrot and H. Yon, 2 vols (Paris: Gallimard, 2006–)

—— *The Human Comedy*, trans. by Clara Bell and others, ed. by George Saintsbury, 40 vols (London: Dent, 1895–9)

—— *Lettres à Madame Hanska*, ed. by Roger Pierrot, 4 vols (Paris: Laffront, 1990)

—— *The Magic Skin*, trans. by Helen Constantine (Oxford: Oxford University Press, 2012)

—— (as Comte Alex de B—), 'Œuvres complètes de Ludwig Tieck', *Caricature*, 5 July 1832

—— *Œuvres diverses*, ed. by Pierre-Georges Castex and others, 2 vols (Paris: Gallimard, 1990–6)

—— *Pensées, Sujets, Fragments*, ed. by Jacques Crépet (Paris: Blaizot, 1910)

—— *The Unknown Masterpiece*, trans. by Richard Howard (New York: NYRB, 2000)

Barck, Karlheinz, '5 Briefe Erich Auerbachs an Walter Benjamin in Paris', *Zeitschrift für Germanistik*, 9.6 (1988), 688–94

—— and Anthony Reynolds, 'Walter Benjamin and Erich Auerbach: Fragments of a Correspondence', *Diacritics*, 22.3/4 (1992), 81–3

Bardèche, Maurice, *Balzac, Romancier* (Paris: Librairie Plon, 1940)

Barel-Moisan, Claire, and José Luis-Diaz (eds), *Balzac avant Balzac* (Paris: Christian Pirot, 2006)

Barnickel, Claudia, 'Serapiontisches Prinzip/"Prinzip der Duplizität"', in *E. T. A. Hoffmann Handbuch: Leben – Werk – Wirkung*, ed. by Christine Lubkoll and Harald Neumeyer (Stuttgart: Metzler, 2015), pp. 395–9

Barthes, Roland, *S/Z*, trans. by R. Miller (New York, NY: Hill and Wange, 1974)

Baudelaire, Charles, *Œuvres complètes*, ed. by Claude Pichois, 2 vols (Paris: Gallimard, 1975–6)

Beaumont, Matthew (ed.), *A Concise Companion to Realism* (Oxford: Wiley, 2010)

Becker, Allienne R., '"Alice Doane's Appeal": A Literary Double of Hoffmann's *Die Elixiere des Teufels*', *Comparative Literature Studies*, 23.1 (1986), 1–11

Begemann, Christian, '*Der Artushof* (1816)', *E. T. A. Hoffmann: Leben – Werk – Wirkung*, ed. by Detlef Kremer (Berlin: De Gruyter, 2009), pp. 93–6

Benjamin, Walter, *Gesammelte Schriften*, 7 vols, ed. by Theodor W. Adorno and Gershom Scholem with Rolf Tiedemann (Frankfurt am Main: Suhrkamp, 1972–99)

Bennett, Jane, 'Mimesis: Paradox or Encounter', *MLN*, 132.5 (2017), 1186–1200

Besuchet, Olivier, '"Rien de nouveau sous le soleil?" L'indice intertextuel dans *L'Élixir de longue vie* de Balzac', *A Contrario*, 20.1 (2014), 113–27

Blackall, Eric A., *The Novels of the German Romantics* (Ithaca, NY: Cornell University Press, 1983)

Blake, William, 'A Descriptive Catalogue of Pictures', in *The Complete Poetry and Prose of William Blake*, ed. by David V. Erdman (New York, NY: Anchor, 1988), pp. 529–51

Bodin, Thierry, 'Les métamorphoses d'Horace ou quelques avatars romanesques de Jules Sandeau', *L'Année balzacienne* (1984), 15–36

Bonard, Olivier, *La Peinture dans la création balzacienne: Invention et vision picturale de* La Maison du Chat-qui-pelote *au* Père Goriot (Geneva: Droz, 1969)

Borderie, Régine, 'Le Corps de la philosophie: *La Peau de chagrin*', *L'Année balzacienne*, 2 (2001), 199–219

Brandstetter, Gabriele, 'Kritzeln, Schaben, Übermalen: Bild-Löschung als narratives Verfahren bei Hoffmann, Balzac, Keller und Hofmannsthal', in *Homo Pictor*, ed. by G. Böhm and Stephan Hauser (Munich: De Gruyter, 2001), pp. 353–72

Bray, Patrick M., 'Balzac and the Chagrin of Theory', *L'Esprit Créateur*, 54.3 (2014), 66–77

Breuillac, Marcel, 'Hoffmann en France (Étude de littérature comparée)', *Revue d'histoire littéraire en France*, 13 (1906), 427–57, and 14 (1907), 74–105

Brittan, Francesca, *Music and Fantasy in the Age of Berlioz* (Cambridge: Cambridge University Press, 2017)

Brooks, Peter, *Body Work: Objects of Desire in Modern Narrative* (Cambridge, MA: Harvard University Press, 1993)

—— *Honoré de Balzac* (Oxford: Oxford University Press, 2022)

—— 'Narrative Transaction and Transference (Unburying "Le Colonel Chabert")', *NOVEL: A Forum on Fiction*, 15.2 (1982), 101–10

—— *Reading for the Plot: Design and Intention in Narrative* (Cambridge, MA: Harvard University Press, 1992)

Brown, Hilda Meldrum, *E. T. A. Hoffmann and the Serapiontic Principle: Critique and Creativity* (Rochester, NY: Camden House, 2006)

Brunel, Pierre, 'Notes', in Honoré de Balzac, Sarrasine – Gambara – Massimilla Doni, ed. by Pierre Brunel (Paris: Gallimard, 1995), pp. 8–32

—— 'La Tentation hoffmannesque chez Balzac', in *E. T. A. Hoffmann et la musique*, ed. by Alain Montandon (Bern: Peter Lang, 1987), pp. 315–24

Burrow, Colin, *Imitating Authors: Plato to Futurity* (Oxford: Oxford University Press, 2019)

—— 'Think Outside the Bun', *London Review of Books*, 44.17 (8 September 2022)

Burwick, Frederick, *Mimesis and its Romantic Reflections* (University Park, PA: Pennsylvania State University Press, 2001)

Byatt, A. S., 'The Death of Lucien de Rubempré', *Kenyon Review*, 27.1 (2005), 42–64

Caillois, Roger, 'Mimétisme et psychasthénie légendaire', *Minotaure*, 7 (1935), 4–10

—— 'Mimicry and Legendary Psychasthenia', trans. by John Shepley, *October*, 31 (1984), 12–32 (p. 28)

Castex, Pierre-George, *Le Conte fantastique en France de Nodier à Maupassant* (Paris: José Corti, 1987)

Cave, Terence, *Recognitions: A Study in Poetics* (Oxford: Oxford University Press, 1990)

Cavell, Stanley, 'The Uncanniness of the Ordinary', in *In Quest of the Ordinary: Lines of Skepticism and Romanticism* (Chicago, IL: University of Chicago Press, 1988), pp. 153–80

Champfleury, Jules, *Contes posthumes d'Hoffmann* (Paris: Michel Lévy, 1856)

Cheng, Joyce, 'Mask, Mimicry, Metamorphosis: Roger Caillois, Walter Benjamin and Surrealism in the 1930s', *Modernism/Modernity*, 16.1 (2009), 61–86

Cleary, Joe, Jed Esty and Colleen Lye (eds), *Peripheral Realisms* (= *Modern Language Quarterly*, 73.3 (2012))

Cohen-Vrignaud, Gerard, 'Capitalism's Wishful Thinking', *Modern Language Quarterly*, 76.2 (2015), 181–99

Collini, Patrizio, 'Iconolâtrie et iconoclastie: "Le Chef-d'œuvre inconnu" et le romantisme allemand', *L'Année balzacienne*, 5 (2004), 75–85

Connor, Wayne, 'Reviewed Work(s): Balzac's Frenhofer', *Modern Language Notes*, 69.5 (1954), 335–8

Cornwell, Neil, 'European Gothic', in *A New Companion to the Gothic*, ed. by David Punter (Oxford: Blackwell, 2012), pp. 64–76

Cozens, Alexander, 'A New Method of Assisting the Invention in Drawing Original Compositions of Landscape', in A. P. Oppé, *Alexander & John Robert Cozens* (London: Adam and Charles Black, 1952), pp. 165–87

Crampton, Hope, 'Melmoth in "La Comédie Humaine"', *Modern Language Review*, 61.1 (1966), 42–50

Curtius, Ernst Robert, *Balzac* (Bern: A. Francke, 1951)

Daemmrich, Horst, 'Wirklichkeit als Form: ein Aspekt Hoffmannscher Erzählkunst', *Colloquia Germanica*, 4 (1970), 36–45

Davies, Steffan, 'Exile and Reality in Erich Auerbach's *Mimesis*', in *From the Enlightenment to Modernism: Three Centuries of German Literature: Essays for Ritchie Robertson*, ed. by Carolin Düttlinger, Kevin Hilliard and Charlie Louth (Oxford: Legenda, 2022), pp. 333–46

De Lovenjoul, Charles Spoelberch, *Histoire des œuvres de H. de Balzac* (Geneva: Slatkine, 1968)

Dendle, Peter, 'The Zombie as Barometer of Cultural Anxiety', in *Monsters and the Monstrous: Myths and Metaphors of Enduring Evil*, ed. by Niall Scott (Amsterdam: Rodopi, 2007), pp. 45–57

Deruelle, Aude, 'Les adresses au lecteur chez Balzac', *Cahiers de Narratologie*, 11 (2004), 2–11

Diaz, José-Luis, 'Ce que Balzac fait au fantastique', *L'Année balzacienne*, 13 (2012), 61–83

Dostoevsky, Fyodor, *Letters of Fyodor Michailovitch Dostoevsky to his Family and Friends*, trans. by Ethel Golburn Mayne, ed. by Alexander Eliasberg (London: Chatto and Windus, 1914)

Downing, Eric, *Double Exposures: Repetition and Realism in Nineteenth-Century German Fiction* (Stanford, CA: Stanford University Press, 2002)

Dutchman-Smith, Victoria, *E. T. A. Hoffmann and Alcohol: Biography, Reception and Art* (Leeds: Maney Publishing, 2009)

Egmont, Henry (trans.), 'Notice sur la vie et les ouvrages d'Hoffmann', in *E. T. A. Hoffmann, Œuvres complètes de E. T. A. Hoffmann. Contes Fantastiques de E. T. A. Hoffmann, traduction nouvelle, précédée d'une notice sur la vie et les ouvrages de l'auteur par Henry Egmont*, trans. by Henry Egmont, 4 vols (Paris: Camuzeaux [vol. I] and Béthune & Plon [vols II–IV], 1836), I, pp. v–xxxi

Ellmann, Richard, 'A Late Victorian Love Affair', *New York Review of Books* (4 August 1977)

Elze, Jens (ed.), *Realism: Aesthetics, Experiments, Politics* (London: Bloomsbury, 2022)

Fanger, Donald, *Dostoevsky and Romantic Realism: A Study of Dostoevsky in Relation to Balzac, Dickens, and Gogol* (Cambridge, MA: Harvard University Press, 1965)

Fanning, Christopher, 'Small Particles of Eloquence: Sterne and the Scriblerian Text', *Modern Philology*, 100.3 (2003), 360–92

—— 'Sterne and Print Culture', in *The Cambridge Companion to Laurence Sterne*, ed. by Thomas Keymer (Cambridge: Cambridge University Press, 2010), pp. 125–41

Farrant, Tim, *Balzac's Shorter Fictions: Genesis and Genre* (Oxford: Oxford University Press, 2002)

Feuillebois, Victoire, 'Théophile Gautier's "Onuphrius" (1833) and the Critique of the Etiology of Pathological Reading', *Literature and Medicine*, 34.2 (2016), 370–88

Freud, Sigmund, 'The Uncanny', trans. by James Strachey, *Pelican Freud Library*, 15 vols (Harmondsworth: Penguin, 1973–86), XIV, pp. 339–76

—— 'Das Unheimliche', in *Gesammelte Werke*, ed. Anna Freud and others, 18 vols (London: Imago, 1940–68), XII, pp. 229–68

Fühmann, Franz, *Fräulein Veronika Paulmann aus der Pirnaer Vorstadt oder Etwas über das Schauerliche bei E. T. A. Hoffmann* (Munich: Deutscher Taschenbuch Verlag, 1984)

Furst, Lilian, *All Is True: The Claims and Strategies of Realist Fiction* (Durham, NC: Duke University Press, 1995)

Garner, Dwight, 'In Elif Batuman's "Either/Or", a Witty and Perceptive Young Woman Returns', *New York Times*, 9 May 2022

Gautier, Théophile, 'Les contes d'Hoffmann', in *Souvenirs de théâtre, d'art et de critique* (Paris: Charpentier 1883), pp. 43–50. Originally published in *Chronique de Paris*, 14 August 1836, pp. 133–5

—— *Histoire de l'art dramatique en France depuis vingt-cinq ans* (Paris: Édition Hetzel, Librairie Magin, Blanchard et Compagnie, 1859)

Gebauer, Gunter, and Christoph Wulf, *Mimesis: Kultur, Kunst, Gesellschaft* (Reinbek bei Hamburg: Rowohlt Taschenbuch Verlag, 1992)

Genette, Gérard, *Paratexts: Thresholds of Interpretation*, trans. by Jane E. Lewin (Cambridge: Cambridge University Press, 1997)

Gil-Curiel, Germán, *A Comparative Approach: The Early European Supernatural Tale. Five Variations on a Theme* (Frankfurt am Main: Peter Lang, 2011)

Gilpin, William, 'The Art of Sketching Landscape', in *Three Essays: On Picturesque Beauty; on Picturesque Travel; and on Sketching Landscape; to which is added a poem, on Landscape Painting* (London: Blamire, 1794), pp. 59–90

Ginzburg, Carlo, 'Clues: Roots of an Evidential Paradigm', in *Clues, Myths, and the Historical Method*, trans. by John and Anne C. Tedesechi (Baltimore: Johns Hopkins University Press, 1989), pp. 87–113

Girard, René, *Deceit, Desire, and the Novel: Self and Other in Literary Structure*, trans. by Yvonne Freccero (Baltimore, MD: Johns Hopkins University Press, 1965)

Girardin, Saint-Marc, 'Contes fantastiques d'Hofmann, traduction d'un extrait du *Pot d'or*', *Revue de Paris*, II (1829), 67–130

Goethe, Johann Wolfgang von, 'Einfache Nachahmung, Manier, Stil', in *Goethes Werke*, 13 vols, ed. by Erich Trunz and others (Hamburg: Christian Wegner Verlag, 1948–), vol. 12, pp. 30–4

Gombrich, E. H., *Art and Illusion: A Study in the Psychology of Pictorial Representation* (London: Phaidon, 1996)

—— and Ernst Kris, 'The Principles of Caricature', *British Journal of Medical Psychology*, 17 (1938), 319–42

Goodlad, Lauren M. E. (ed.), *Worlding Realisms Now*, (= *Novel: A Forum on Fiction*, 49.2 (2016))

Göttsche, Dirk, and Nicholas Saul (eds), *Realism and Romanticism in German Literature. Realismus und Romantik in der deutschsprachigen Literatur* (Bielefeld: Aisthesis, 2013)

Guise, René, 'Balzac et l'étranger', *L'Année balzacienne* (1970), 3–19

—— 'Balzac, lecteur des Élixirs du diable', *L'Année balzacienne* (1970), 57–67

Halliwell, Stephen, *The Aesthetics of Mimesis: Ancient Texts and Modern Problems* (Princeton, NJ: Princeton University Press, 2002)

—— *Aristotle's Poetics* (Chicago, IL: University of Chicago Press, 1998)

Hamilton, John T., 'Mi manca la voca: How Balzac Talks Music – or How Music Takes Place – in Balzac's *Massimilla Doni*', in *Speaking of Music: Addressing the Sonorous*, ed. by Keith Chapin and Andrew H. Clark (New York: Fordham University Press, 2013), pp. 120–37

Harich, Walter, *E. T. A. Hoffmann: Das Leben eines Künstlers*, 2 vols (Berlin: Reiß, 1920)

Heathcote, Owen, and Andrew Watts (eds), *The Cambridge Companion to Balzac* (Cambridge: Cambridge University Press, 2017)

Heffernan, James A. W., *Museum of Words: The Poetics of Ekphrasis from Homer to Ashbery* (Chicago, IL: University of Chicago Press, 1993)

Hildebrandt, Toni, 'Die tachistische Geste 1951–70', in *Bild und Geste: Figurationen des Denkens in Philosophie und Kunst*, ed. by Ulrich Richtmeyer, Fabian Goppelsröder and Toni Hindebrandt (Bielefeld: Transcript Verlag, 2014), pp. 45–64

Hoffmann, E. T. A. [attributed to Carl Spindler], *L'Élixir du diable, histoire tirée des papiers de frère Médard, Capucin*, trans. by Jean Cohen, 4 vols (Paris: Mame et Delaunay-Vallée, 1829)

—— *Hoffmanns Sämtliche Werke*, ed. by Carl Georg von Maassen, 9 vols (Munich: Müller, 1908–28)

—— *Œuvres complètes de E. T. A. Hoffmann. Contes Fantastiques de E. T. A. Hoffmann, traduction nouvelle, précédée d'une notice sur la vie et les ouvrages de l'auteur par Henry Egmont*, trans. by Henry Egmont, 4 vols (Paris: Camuzeaux [vol. I] and Béthune & Plon [vols II–IV], 1836)

—— *The Serapion Brethren*, 2 vols, trans. by Alex Ewing (London: George Bell and Sons, 1886–92)

Hogarth, William, *The Analysis of Beauty: Written with a View of Fixing the Fluctuating Ideas of Taste* (London: W. Strahan, 1772)

Holland, Jocelyn, *The Lever as Instrument of Reason: Technological Constructions of Knowledge around 1800* (London: Bloomsbury, 2019)

Hübener, Andrea, *Kreisler in Frankreich: E. T. A. Hoffmann und die französischen Romantiker* (Heidelberg: Winter, 2004)

Hume, Kathryn, *Fantasy and Mimesis: Responses to Reality in Western Literature* (New York, NY: Methuen, 1984)

Ingold, Tim, *Lines: A Brief History* (London: Routledge, 2007)

Jaffe, Audrey, 'Introduction: Realism in Retrospect', *Journal of Narrative Theory* (2006), 36.3, 309–13

James, Henry, *Literary Criticism: French Writers, Other European Writers, the Prefaces to the New York Edition*, ed. by Leon Edel and Mark Wilson (New York: Penguin, 1984)

Janin, Marie-France, 'Quelques emprunts possible de Balzac à Hoffmann', *L'Année balzacienne* (1970), 69–75

Jennings, Michael, *Dialectical Images: Walter Benjamin's Theory of Literary Criticism* (Ithaca, NY: Cornell University Press, 1987)

Jones, Charlotte, *Realism, Form, and Representation in the Edwardian Novel: Synthetic Realism* (Oxford: Oxford University Press, 2021)

Kaminski, Nicola, *Kreuz-Gänge: Romanexperimente der deutschen Romantik* (Paderborn: Schöningh, 2001)

Kanes, Martin, *Balzac's Comedy of Words* (Princeton, NJ: Princeton University Press, 1975)

Keller, Gottfried, *Gesammelte Werke*, II, *Der grüne Heinrich*. Zweite Fassung, ed. Walter Morgenthaler (Zurich: Büchergilde Gutenberg, 1960)

Kelly, Dorothy, *The Living Death of Modernity: Balzac, Baudelaire, Zola* (Oxford: Legenda, 2021)

—— 'The Marriage of Don Juan: Balzac and the Inheritance of Culture', *Dix-Neuf: Journal of the Society of Dix-Neuviémistes*, 11 (2008), 49–58

—— *Reconstructing Woman: From Fiction to Reality in the Nineteenth-Century Novel* (University Park, PA: Penn State University Press, 2007)

Kesting, Marianne, 'Das imaginierte Kunstwerk: E. T. A. Hoffmann und Balzacs *Chef d'œuvre inconnu*, mit einem Ausblick auf die gegenwärtige Situation', in *Romantik: eine lebenskräftige Krankheit: ihre literarischen Nachwirkungen in der Moderne*, ed. by Erika Tunner (Amsterdam: Rodopi, 1991), pp. 36–62

King, Jeri Debois, *Paratextuality in Balzac's* La Peau de chagrin: The Wild Ass's Skin (Lewiston, NY: Edwin Mellen, 1992)

Kittler, Friedrich, *Aufschreibesysteme 1800–1900* (Munich: Fink, 2003)

—— 'Die Laterna magica der Literatur. Schillers und Hoffmanns Medienstrategien', *Athenäum*, 4 (1994), 219–37

Kleine, Sabine, 'Elixiere des Teufels: Notes on E. T. A. Hoffmann's "Black Romanticism" and the Idealist Critical Response', *Journal of the Australasian Universities Language and Literature Association*, 91.1 (1999), 27–44

Knight, Diana, *Balzac and the Model of Painting: Artist Stories in 'La Comédie humaine'* (Oxford: Legenda, 2007)

Knox, Julian, 'Coleridge's "Cousin-German": *Blackwood's*, Alter-Egos, and the Making of a Man of Letters', *European Romantic Review*, 21.4 (2010), 425–46

Kofman, Sarah, 'Vautour rouge (Le double dans *les Élixirs du diable* d'Hoffmann)', in *Mimésis des articulations*, ed. by Sylviane Agacinski and others (Paris: Flammarion, 1975), pp. 95–163

Konuk, Kader, and Victoria Holbrook, *East West Mimesis: Auerbach in Turkey* (Stanford, CA: Stanford University Press, 2010)

Kornbluh, Anna, *The Order of Forms: Realism, Formalism, and Social Space* (Chicago, IL: Chicago University Press, 2019)

Kortländer, Bernd, and Hans T. Siepe, *Balzac und Deutschland – Deutschland und Balzac* (Tübingen: Narr Verlag, 2012)

Kremer, Detlef (ed.), *E. T. A. Hoffmann: Leben – Werk – Wirkung* (Berlin: De Gruyter, 2009)

—— 'Gebrochene Identität mit Doppelgänger: *Die Elixiere des Teufels* (1815/16)', in *E. T. A. Hoffmann: Erzählungen und Romane* (Berlin: Erich Schmidt, 1999), pp. 40–63

Krieger, Murray, *Ekphrasis: Illusion of the Natural Sign* (Baltimore: Johns Hopkins University Press, 1992)

Kunzle, David, 'Goethe and Caricature: From Hogarth to Töpffer', *Journal of the Warburg and Courtauld Institutes*, 48 (1985), 164–88

Kurbjuhn, Charlotte, 'E. T. A. Hoffmann: Umriss-Bilder und Serapiontisches Erzähl-Prinzip an der Grenze zwischen Kunst und Leben in *Der Artushof*', in *Kontur: Geschichte einer ästhetischen Denkfigur* (Ochsenfurt: De Gruyter, 2014), pp. 655–74

Large, Duncan, 'Derived Lines, Received Opinions: Parodic Plagiarism in Sterne and Hoffmann', *New Comparison: A Journal of Comparative and General Literary Studies* 35/6 (2003), 66–77

Lathers, Marie, 'Modesty and the Artist's Model in *Le Chef-d'œuvre inconnu*', *Symposium*, 46.1 (1992), 49–71

Latifi, Kaltërina, *Perspektivische Ambiguitäten: E. T. A. Hoffmann, poetologisch gelesen* (Baden-Baden: Rombach-Wissenschaft, 2021)

Laubriet, Pierre, *Un catéchisme esthétique: Le Chef d'œuvre inconnu de Balzac* (Paris: Didier, 1961)

—— 'Influences chez Balzac: Swedenborg, Hoffmann', *Les Études balzaciennes*, 5 (1958), 160–80

Lawtoo, Nidesh, 'The Critic as Mime: Wilde's Theatrical Performance', *Symploke*, 26 (2018), 307–28

—— 'The Mimetic Condition: Theories and Concepts', *Countertext*, 6.1 (2022), 1–22

—— *The Phantom of the Ego: Modernism and the Mimetic Unconscious* (East Lansing, MI: Michigan State University Press, 2013)

Lehleiter, Christine, *Romanticism, Origins, and the History of Heredity* (Lewisburg, PA: Bucknell University Press, 2014)

Leonard, Anne (ed.) *Arabesque without End: Across Music and the Arts, from Faust to Shahrazad* (Abingdon-on-Thames: Routledge, 2022)

Levine, George, 'Literary Realism Reconsidered: "The World in its length and breadth"', in *A Concise Companion to Realism*, ed. by Matthew Beaumont (Oxford: Wiley, 2010), pp. 13–19

Lewis, Timothy W., 'The Influence of E. T. A. Hoffmann on Balzac' (unpublished doctoral thesis, University of London, 1991)

Liebrand, Claudia, *Aporie des Kunstmythos: Die Texte E. T. A. Hoffmanns* (Freiburg: Rombach, 1996)

Loève-Veimars, Adolph-François, 'Une représentation de Don Juan, par E. T. A. Hoffmann', *La Revue de Paris*, 6 (1829), 57–69

Lubkoll, Christine, and Harald Neumeyer (ed.), *E. T. A. Hoffmann Handbuch: Leben – Werk – Wirkung* (Stuttgart: Metzler, 2015)

Lucey, Michael, *The Misfit of the Family: Balzac and the Social Forms of Sexuality* (Durham, NC: Duke University Press, 2003)

Lukács, Georg, 'Narrate or Describe? A Preliminary Discussion of Naturalism and Formalism', in *Writer & Critic and other Essays*, ed. and trans. by Arthur D. Kahn (New York, NY: Merlin, 1970), pp. 110–48

—— *Skizze einer Geschichte der neueren deutschen Literatur* (Berlin: Aufbau Verlag, 1953)

Macfarlane, Robert, *Original Copy: Plagiarism and Originality in Nineteenth-Century Literature* (Oxford: Oxford University Press, 2007)

Mandelartz, Michael, '*Berganza* und *Der Artushof*: Poetische (Un-) Gerechtigkeit bei Lope de Vega, Cervantes, und E. T. A. Hoffmann', *Zeitschrift für interkulturelle Germanistik*, 8 (2017), 25–40

Mayer, Hans, 'Die Wirklichkeit E. T. A. Hoffmanns', in *Begriffsbestimmung des literarischen Realismus*, ed. by Richard Brinkmann (Darmstadt: Wissenschaftliche Buchgesellschaft, 1969), pp. 259–300

McGlathery, James, 'The Suicide Motif in E. T. A. Hoffmann's "Der goldne Topf"', *Monatshefte*, 58 (1966), 115–23

Menninghaus, Winfried, 'Hummingbirds, Shells, Picture-Frames: Kant's "Free Beauties" and the Romantic Arabesque', in *Rereading Romanticism*, ed. by Martha B. Helfer (Amsterdam: Rodopi, 2000), pp. 27–46

Merleau-Ponty, Maurice, *Le Visible et l'invisible* (Paris: Gallimard, 1964)

—— *The Visible and the Invisible*, trans. by Alphonso Lingis, ed. by Claude Lefort (Evanston, IL: Northwestern University Press, 1968)

—— 'Eye and Mind', trans. by Carleton Dallery, in Maurice Merleau-Ponty, *The Primacy of Perception*, ed. by James M. Edie (Evanston, IL: Northwestern University Press, 1964), pp. 159–90

—— 'L'Œil et l'esprit' (Paris: Gallimard, 1964)

Meyertholen, Andrea, 'It's Not Easy Being Green: The Failure of Abstract Art in Gottfried Keller's *Der grüne Heinrich*', *German Studies Review*, 39.2 (2016), 241–58

Miller, J. Hillis, *Ariadne's Thread: Story Lines* (New Haven, CT: Yale University Press, 1992)

—— *Reading Narrative* (Norman: University of Oklahoma Press, 1998)

Mitchell, W. J. T., 'Metamorphoses of the Vortex: Hogarth, Turner, and Blake', in *Articulate Images: The Sister Arts from Hogarth to Tennyson*, ed. by Richard Wendorf (Minneapolis, MN: University of Minnesota Press, 1983), pp. 125–69

Momberger, Manfred, *Sonne und Punsch: Die Dissemination des romantischen Kunstbegriffs bei E. T. A. Hoffmann* (Munich: Fink, 1986)

Moritz, Karl Philipp, 'Über die bildende Nachahmung des Schönen', *Werke*, 3 vols, ed. Horst Günther (Frankfurt am Main: Insel, 1981), II, pp. 549–64

Moss, Roger B., 'Sterne's Punctuation', *Eighteenth-Century Studies*, 15.2 (1981–2), 179–200

Müller, Dominik, 'Self-Portraits of the Poet as a Painter: Narratives on Artists and the Bounds between the Arts (Hoffmann-Balzac-Stifter)', in *Text into Image: Image into Text*, ed. by Jeff Morrison and Florian Krobb (Amsterdam: Rodopi, 1997), pp. 169–74

Naumann, Barbara, 'Körperbild und Seelenschrift: Eine Szene in Gottfried Kellers "Der grüne Heinrich"', in *Verkörperungen*, ed. by André Blum and others (Berlin: Oldenbourg Akademieverlag, 2012), pp. 217–22

Negus, Kenneth G., 'The Family Tree in E. T. A. Hoffmann's *Die Elixiere des Teufels*', *PMLA*, 73.5 (1958)

Neilly, Joanna, *E. T. A. Hoffmann's Orient: Romantic Aesthetics and the German Imagination* (Oxford: Legenda, 2016)

Neumann, Gerhard, 'Anamorphose. E. T. A. Hoffmanns Poetik der Defiguration', in *Mimesis und Simulation*, ed. by Andreas Kablitz and Gerhard Neumann (Freiburg im Breisgau: Rombach, 1998), pp. 377–417

Oesterle, Günter, 'Arabeske', in *Ästhetische Grundbegriffe: Historisches Wörterbuch in sieben Bänden*, ed. by Karlheinz Barck and others (Stuttgart: Metzler, 2000), I, pp. 272–86

—— 'Arabeske, Schrift und Poesie in E. T. A. Hoffmanns Kunstmärchen "Der goldne Topf"', *Athenäum*, 1 (1991), 69–107

—— 'Die folgenreiche und strittige Konjuntur des Umrisses in Klassizismus und Romantik', in *Bild und Schrift in der Romantik*, ed. by Günter Oesterle and Gerhard Neumann (Würzburg: Königshausen & Neumann, 1999), pp. 27–58

—— 'Romantische Urbanität? Börse und Kunst in E. T. A. Hoffmanns "Der Artushof"', in *'Hoffmanneske Geschichte': Zu einer Literaturwissenschaft als Kulturwissenschaft*, ed. by Gerhard Neumann (Würzburg: Königshausen & Neumann, 2005), pp. 243–58

—— and Ingrid Oesterle, 'Der Imaginationsreiz der Flecken von Leonardo da Vinci bis Peter Rühmkorf', in *Signaturen der Gegenwartsliteratur: Festschrift für Walter Hinderer*, ed. by Dieter Borchmeyer (Würzburg: Königshausen und Neumann, 1999), pp. 213–38

Pankalla, Gerhard, 'E. T. A. Hoffmann und Frankreich: Beiträge zum Hoffmann-Bild in der französischen Literatur des 19. Jahrhunderts', *Germanisch-Romanische Monatsschrift*, 28 (1939), 308–18

Pankow, Edgar, 'Literatur – Geschichte: Honoré de Balzac und E. T. A. Hoffmann und die Genese von Traditionen im *Élixir de longue vie*', *Arcadia*, 39 (2004), 27–54

Paraschas, Sotirios, '*Illusions Perdues*: Writers, Artists and the Reflexive Novel', in *The Cambridge Companion to Balzac*, ed. by Owen Heathcote and Andrew Watts, pp. 97–110

—— *The Realist Author and the Sympathetic Imagination* (Oxford: Legenda, 2013)

Passage, Charles, 'E. T. A. Hoffmann's "The Devil's Elixirs": A Flawed Masterpiece', Journal of English and Germanic Philology, 75.4 (1976), 531–45

Paulson, William, 'Pour une analyse dynamique de la variation textuelle: *Le Chef-d'œuvre trop connu*', *Nineteenth-Century French Studies*, 19.3 (1991), 404–16

Peters, John G., *Conrad and Impressionism* (Cambridge: Cambridge University Press, 2001)

Petrey, Sandy, *In the Court of the Pear King: French Culture and the Rise of Realism* (Ithaca, NY: Cornell University Press, 2005)

Piketty, Thomas, *Le Capital au XXIe siècle* (Paris: Seuil, 2013)

Pikulik, Lothar, *E. T. A. Hoffmann als Erzähler: ein Kommentar zu den* Serapions-Brüdern (Göttingen: Vandenhoeck & Ruprecht, 1987)

Piper, Andrew, *Dreaming in Books: The Making of the Bibliographic Imagination in the Romantic Age* (Chicago, IL: University of Chicago Press, 2009)

Pirholt, Mattias, *Metamimesis: Imitation in Goethe's* Wilhelm Meisters Lehrjahre *and Early German Romanticism* (Rochester, NY: Camden House, 2012)

Plato, *Republic*, trans. by G. M. A. Grube and C. D. C. Reeve (Indianapolis, IN: Hackett Publishing, 1992)

Ponert, Dietmar, *E. T. A. Hoffmann – Das bildkünstlerische Werk: Ein kritisches Gesamtverzeichnis*, 2 vols (Petersburg: Michael Imhof Verlag, 2012)

Potolsky, Matthew, *Mimesis* (London: Routledge, 2006)

Prendergast, Christopher, *The Order of Mimesis* (Cambridge: Cambridge University Press, 1986)

Pry, Paul, 'L'Élixir de vie', *Le Mercure de France au dix-neuvième siècle*, 31 (1830), 227–9

Rabinbach, Anson, 'Introduction to Walter Benjamin's "Doctrine of the Similar"', *New German Critique*, 17 (1979), 60–4

Reddick, John, 'E. T. A. Hoffmann's "Der goldne Topf" and its "Durch-gehaltene Ironie"', *Modern Language Review*, 71.3 (1976), 577–94

Riem, Adolf, 'Ueber die Arabeske', in *Monatsschrift der Akademie der Künste und Wissenschften zu Berlin*, ed. Karl Philipp Moritz (Berlin: Königl. Preuß akad. Kunst- und Buchhandlung, 1788), pp. 117–37

Robbins, Ruth, and Julian Wolfreys (eds), *Victorian Gothic: Literary and Cultural Manifestations in the Nineteenth Century* (Basingstoke: Palgrave, 2000)

Rogers, Pat, '"How I want thee, humorous Hogart": The Motif of the Absent Artist in Swift, Fielding and Others', *Papers on Language and Literature*, 42.1 (2006), 25–45

Rosen, Charles, and Henri Zerner, *Romanticism and Realism: The Mythology of Nineteenth-Century Art* (New York, NY: Viking Press, 1984)

Rothfield, Lawrence, *Vital Signs: Medical Realism in Nineteenth-Century Fiction* (Princeton, NJ: Princeton University Press, 1992)

Ruprecht, Lucia, *Dances of the Self in Heinrich von Kleist, E. T. A. Hoffmann and Heinrich Heine* (Aldershot: Ashgate, 2006)

Sage, Victor, 'Scott, Hoffmann, and the Persistence of the Gothic', in *Popular Revenants: The German Gothic and its International Reception, 1800–2000*, ed. by Andrew Cusack and Barry Murnane (Rochester, NY: Camden House, 2012), pp. 76–86

Sandeau, Jules, *Vie et malheurs de Horace de Saint-Aubin* (Paris: Pressédition, 1948)

Scher, Steven Paul, 'Hoffmann and Sterne: Unmediated Parallels in Narrative Method', *Comparative Literature*, 28.4 (1976), 309–25

Schlegel, August Wilhelm, 'Über Zeichnungen zu Gedichten und John Flaxman's Umrisse' (1799), *Athenäum* II.2

—— 'Ueber das Verhaeltniss der Schoenen Kunst zur Natur; Ueber Taeuschung und Wahrscheinlichkeit; Ueber Styl und Manier', in *August Wilhelm Schlegel. Kritische Ausgabe der Vorlesungen*, ed. by Ernst Behler and others, 4 vols (Paderborn: Brill/Schöningh, 1989–), vol. II.1, pp. 256–88

Schlegel, Friedrich, 'Rede über die Mythologie', in *Friedrich Schlegel: Kritische Ausgabe seiner Werke*, ed. Ernst Behler and others, 32 vols (Paderborn: Brill/Schöningh, 1966–), II, pp. 312–29

Schmidt, Ricarda, 'Narrative Strukturen romantischer Subjektivität in E. T. A. Hoffmanns *Die Elixiere des Teufels* und *Der Sandmann*', *Germanisch-Romanische Monatsschrift*, 49 (1999), 143–60

—— *Wenn mehrere Künste im Spiel sind: Intermedialität bei E. T. A. Hoffmann* (Göttingen: Vandenhoeck & Ruprecht, 2006)

Schroder, Maurice Z., 'Roman – Romanesque – Romantique – Romantisme', in *'Romantic' and its Cognates: The European History of a Word*, ed. by Hans Eichner (Toronto: University of Toronto Press, 1972), pp. 263–92

Schubert, Caroline, *Defiguration der Schrift: Tintenkleckserei, Makulatur und Schreibfehler bei E. T. A. Hoffmann und Nikolaj Gogol* (Berlin: De Gruyter, 2021)

Scott, Walter, 'Du Merveilleux dans le roman', trans. by Adolphe-François Loève-Veimars, *Revue de Paris*, 1 (1829), 25–33

—— 'On the Supernatural in Fictitious Composition; and Particularly on the Works of Ernest Theodore William Hoffmann', *Foreign Quarterly Review*, 1 (1827), 60–98

Sedgwick, Eve Kosofsky, *Between Men: English Literature and Male Homosocial Desire* (New York, NY: Columbia University Press, 1985)

Sha, Richard C., *The Visual and Verbal Sketch in British Romanticism* (Philadelphia, PA: University of Pennsylvania Press, 1998)

Slusser, George Edgar, 'Rameau's Nephew and his Progeny: The Artist as Performer in E. T. A. Hoffmann and Balzac' (unpublished doctoral thesis, Harvard University, 1974)

Sontag, Susan, 'Notes on "Camp"', in *Camp: Queer Aesthetics and the Performing Subject: A Reader*, ed. by Fabio Cleto (Edinburgh: Edinburgh University Press, 1999), pp. 53–65

—— 'Vautrin's Cigar', *New York Review of Books* (27 October 1977)

Sprenger, Scott, 'Death by Marriage in Balzac's *La Peau de chagrin*', *Dix-Neuf*, 11.1 (2008), 59–75

Stanyon, Miranda, 'Serpentine Sighs: De Quincey's *Suspiria de Profundis* and the Serpentine Line', *Studies in Romanticism*, 53.1 (2014), 31–58

Stephens, Bradley, 'The Novel and the (Il)legibility of History: Victor Hugo, Honoré de Balzac, and Alexandre Dumas', in *The Oxford Handbook of European Romanticism*, ed. by Paul Hamilton (Oxford: Oxford University Press, 2016), pp. 88–104

Sterne, Laurence, *The Letters of Laurence Sterne: Part 1, 1739–1764*, ed. Melvyn New and Peter de Voogd (Gainesville, FL: University Presses of Florida, 2009)

—— *The Life and Opinions of Tristram Shandy, Gentleman: The Text*, ed. by Melvyn New and Joan New, 2 vols (Gainesville, FL: University Presses of Florida, 1978)

Stewart, Elizabeth, *Catastrophe and Survival: Walter Benjamin and Psychoanalysis* (London: Continuum, 2010)

Stewart, Garrett, *The Look of Reading: Book, Painting, Text* (Chicago, IL: University of Chicago Press, 2006)

—— 'Painted Readers, Narrative Regress', *Narrative*, 11.2 (2003), 125–76

Sütterlin, Nicole, 'Transgressions: On the (De-)Figuration of the Vampire in E. T. A. Hoffmann's "Vampyrismus"', trans. by Christopher R. Clason and Alexander Lambrow, in *Transgressive Romanticism*, ed. by Christopher R. Clason (Liverpool: Liverpool University Press, 2018), pp. 114–32

Swahn, Sigbrit, 'Le Chef d'œuvre inconnu, récit hoffmannesque de Balzac', *Studia Neophilologica*, 76.2 (2004), 206–14

Tambling, Jeremy, 'Hoffmann's *Die Elixiere des Teufels*: The Double, the Death Drive, and the Apotropaic', *Forum for Modern Language Studies*, 51.4 (2015), 379–93

Taussig, Michael T., *Mimesis and Alterity: A Particular History of the Senses* (London: Routledge, 1993)

Teichmann, Elizabeth, *La Fortune d'Hoffmann en France* (Geneva: Droz, 1961)

—— 'Une source inconnue de l'*Élixir de longue vie*', *Revue de littérature comparée*, 24 (1955), 536–38

Tilby, Michael, 'Balzac's Convivial Narrations: Intoxication and its Discourse in *La Comédie humaine*', in *Pleasure and Pain in Nineteenth-Century French Literature and Culture*, ed. by David Evans and Kate Griffiths (Amsterdam: Rodopi, 2008), pp. 53–72

Tolley, Bruce, 'The Source of Balzac's *Élixir de longue vie*', *Revue de littérature comparée*, 37 (1963), 91–7

Vachon, S., *Les Travaux et les jours d'Honoré de Balzac: Chronologie de la création balzacienne* (Paris: Presses du CNR and Presses universitaires de Vincennes; Presses de l'Université de Montréal, 1992)

Vialon, Martin, 'Verdichtete Geschichtserfahrung. Erich Auerbachs Brief vom 3.1.1937 an Walter Benjamin', in *Raum der Freiheit. Reflexionen über Idee und Wirklichkeit. Festschrift für Antonia Grunenberg*, ed. by Michale Daxner and others (Bielefeld: Transcript, 2009), pp. 123–50

Vilain, Robert, 'Bringing the Villains to Book: Balzac and Hoffmann as Antecedents of the Modern Detective Story', *Bulletin of the John Rylands Library*, 83.4 (2002), 105–23

Wais, Kurt, 'Le roman d'artiste: E. T. A. Hoffmann et Balzac', in *La Littérature narrative d'imagination, Colloque de Strasbourge* (Paris: PUF, 1961), pp. 137–52

Wannufel, Lucie, 'Balzac, lecteur des Élixirs du Diable', *L'Année balzacienne* (1970), 57–67

—— 'Présence d'Hoffmann dans les œuvres de Balzac (1829–1835), *L'Année balzacienne* (1970), 45–56

Webber, Andrew J., 'About Face: E. T. A. Hoffmann, Weimar Film and the Technological Afterlife of Gothic Physiognomy', in *Popular Revenants: The German Gothic and its International Reception, 1800–2000*, ed. by Andrew Cusack and Barry Murnane (Rochester, NY: Camden House, 2012), pp. 161–80

—— *The Doppelgänger: Double Visions in German Literature* (Oxford: Clarendon Press, 1996)

Wellek, René, *A History of Modern Criticism: 1750–1950*, 8 vols (London: Jonathan Cape, 1955)

Went-Daoust, Yvette Yvonne Marie, 'Le Chef-d'œuvre inconnu de Balzac ou l'écriture picturale', in *Description – Écriture – Peinture*, ed. by Yvette Yvonne Marie Went-Daoust (Groningen: CRIN, 1987), pp. 48–64

Wettlaufer, Alexandra, *Pen vs Paintbrush: Girodet, Balzac, and the Myth of Pygmalion in Post-Revolutionary France* (New York, NY: Palgrave, 2001)

White, Hayden, 'Auerbach's Literary History: Figural Causation and Modernist Historicism', in *Literary History and the Challenge of Philology: The Legacy of Erich Auerbach*, ed. by Seth Lerer (Stanford, CA: Stanford University Press, 1996), pp. 124–39

Wilde, Oscar, *Complete Works of Oscar Wilde* (London: HarperCollins, 2003)

Williams, Seán, 'E. T. A. Hoffmann and the Hairdresser around 1800', *Publications of the English Goethe Society*, 85.1 (2016), 54–66

Willimczik, Kurt, *E. T. A. Hoffmann: Die drei Reiche seiner Gestaltenwelt* (Berlin, 1939)

Winnicott, D. W., 'The Squiggle Game', in *Psycho-Analytic Explorations*, ed. by Claire Winnicott, Ray Shepherd and Madeleine Davis (Cambridge, MA: Harvard University Press, 1989), pp. 299–317

Wirth, Uwe, 'Der goldne Topf', in *E. T. A. Hoffmann: Leben – Werk – Wirkung*, ed. by Detlef Kremer (Berlin: De Gruyter, 2009), pp. 114–24

Zehl Romero, Christiane, 'M. C. Lewis' *The Monk* and E. T. A. Hoffmann's *Die Elixiere des Teufels:* Two Versions of the Gothic', *Neophilologus*, 63 (1979), 574–82

Zenkine, Serge, 'Le Chef-d'œuvre et son modèle. Balzac et ses continuateurs', *Balzac Review/Revue Balzac*, 2 (2019), 167–207

Index

EU representative:
Easy Access System Europe
Mustamäe tee 50, 10621 Tallinn, Estonia
Gpsr.requests@easproject.com

www.ingramcontent.com/pod-product-compliance
Lightning Source LLC
Chambersburg PA
CBHW071713170526
45165CB00005B/1993